SKIES OF FIRE

FOR SIMON

Also by Alfred Price

Air Battle Central Europe
Battle of Britain Day
Blitz on Britain
Focke-Wulf FW 190 in Combat
Great Aircraft of World War II
The Hardest Day
The Last Year of the Luftwaffe
Late Marque Spitfire Aces 1942-45
The Luftwaffe in Camera
The Luftwaffe Data Book
Sky Battles
Sky Warriors
Spitfire: a Complete Fighting History
Spitfire Mark 1/11 Aces 1939-41
Spitfire Mark V Aces 1941-45
The Spitfire Story

SKIES OF FIRE
DRAMATIC AIR COMBAT

Alfred Price

CASSELL&CO

Cassell & Co

Wellington House, 125 Strand, London WC2R 0BB

Copyright © Alfred Price 2002

First published 2002

British Library Cataloguing-in-Publication Data
A catalogue record for this book is available from the British Library
ISBN 0-304-35947-5

Distributed in the United States by
Sterling Publishing Co. Inc., 387 Park Avenue South,
New York NY 10016-8810

Printed and bound in Great Britain by
Creative Print & Design Ltd, Ebbw Vale, Wales

Contents

List of photographs

MAPS AND DIAGRAMS

Acknowledgements

The author and publishers acknowledge permission given by the Association of Old Crows in Washington DC, USA, to use material the author collected while conducting research for the three-volume work *The History of US Electronic Warfare*, written under contract to that organization. The relevant material appears in Chapters 9, 12, 15, 21 and 22.

The author and publishers also acknowledge permission given by Sutton Publishing Ltd to use the account 'No Place for a Beginner', which first appeared in the author's book *The Focke-Wulf Fw 190 in Combat*.

Introduction

Skies of Fire is a companion volume to my earlier books *Sky Battles* and *Sky Warriors*. As in those previous books, it has been my aim to illustrate the evolution of aerial warfare by looking at a series of actions spread over its history. In this case the period covered is almost nine decades, from the Italian–Turkish war in 1911 to the Kosovo conflict in 1999. Twenty-two detailed accounts portray the multi-faceted nature of the air weapon during that period, and show the many different ways aircraft are employed in time of war. They also give an insight on how the various operational roles fit together to give this aspect of military operations such a formidable capability.

Chapter One, 'Warfare Enters the Third Dimension' describes the first combat air operations flown by heavier-than-air machines. These took place in 1911 and 1912, when the Italian air expeditionary force supported that nation's army during its campaign to wrest Libya from Turkish control. Using flimsy planes and even more flimsy dirigibles, the Italian pilots flew almost daily air reconnaissance missions that made a significant contribution to the Italian victory. As Italian ground force commanders soon came to appreciate, their possession of an effective aerial reconnaissance capability prevented the enemy achieving surprise when assembling forces to mount an attack. The Italians faced no such constraint and, moreover, thanks to information provided by aerial reconnaissance, their commanders could select the weak points in the enemy defences and attack there. A further important use of planes and captive balloons during those initial actions was that of correcting the fall of artillery rounds to achieve the destruction of targets. Thus, while the aeroplanes, dirigibles and captive balloons had no direct impact on the enemy, their indirect support had far-reaching effects.

Chapter Two, 'Geoffrey De Havilland's Multi-role Masterpiece', looks in detail at some of the wartime operations carried out by the remarkable British De Havilland 4 aircraft. The type entered operational service in 1917, and its operations show how far the tactics and techniques of air warfare had advanced during the previous six years. Compared with the slow and flimsy Blériot monoplanes flown by the Italian pilots, the D.H.4 was more than twice as fast, it weighed six times as much and carried a bomb load five times heavier. Carrying an observer to assist with navigation and operate the rear gun, D.H.4s delivered numerous bombing attacks. The aircraft was even more successful as a high-altitude photographic reconnaissance aircraft, often reaching altitudes above 23,000ft. Near the end of the war the D.H.4's superb altitude performance was exploited to make it a feared opponent for Zeppelins attacking targets in England.

It was also during the First World War that the Royal Navy devoted considerable effort to experiments aimed at operating landplanes from the decks of ships at sea. Early in 1918 HMS *Furious* re-entered service with flat decks for that purpose mounted forward and aft of her bridge and funnel. Tests showed that, although land planes could take off from the foredeck without difficulty, landing on the rear deck after a mission was impracticable. Nevertheless, despite that imperfection, *Furious* would go into action in her new role.

Chapter Three, 'The First Successful Carrier Air Strike', describes the daring attack launched from *Furious* on the important Zeppelin base at Tondern in northern Germany in the summer of 1918. After delivering their attack the pilots were briefed to alight on the water close to one of the escorting destroyers, which would pick them up. Six Sopwith Camel scouts, each carrying two 50lb bombs, attacked Tondern where they destroyed two Zeppelins on the ground. The Tondern attack was the first successful operation ever conducted by carrier-based aircraft against a land target. In addition, it was one of the very few actions during the First World War where air-dropped bombs inflicted major damage to a military target.

In Chapter Four the account shifts to the Second World War and

1940. The multifarious literature on air warfare contains plenty of accounts of air units that are successful in battle. Yet one side's victory is the other side's defeat. 'Thirteen Days in August' describes the fate of an unfortunate Spitfire squadron during the Battle of Britain. No 266 Squadron suffered a short but devastating run of bad luck, which forced it to withdraw from combat after a few days in combat.

The most obvious way to bring down an attacking bomber is by the use of fighter planes or anti-aircraft guns. Yet another method is to cause the bomber to become lost and run short of fuel, by injecting interference into its electronic navigation systems. During the first two years of the Second World War, bombers engaged in daylight attacks penetrating deep into enemy territory were liable to incur prohibitively heavy losses. That forced them to operate either at night or during spells of poor weather. And that, in turn, meant that crews had to place reliance on electronic systems to find their targets and return to their base after the mission. To exploit that fact the Royal Air Force formed No 80 Wing, a ground organization with the specific role of causing interference to the German electronic navigation aids. Chapter Five, 'One Way to Down a Dornier', provides a glimpse into one successful use of electronic trickery which led a Dornier 217 to become thoroughly lost and crash-land in England.

Chapter Six, 'Spitfires to Malta', describes the dramatic operations to deliver fighters to that beleaguered island during the spring and summer of 1942. The only way to do so was to launch them from the decks of aircraft carriers. The Spitfire had originally been designed as a short-range interceptor. Fitted with a 90-gallon drop tank under the fuselage, these single-seat fighters had to fly a distance equivalent to that from London to Prague in order to reach the island.

Chapter Seven, 'High-altitude Combat', describes the highest aerial engagement of the Second World War and one of the highest engagements of all time. The participants were a specially modified Spitfire IX fighter and a Junkers 86R bomber designed for ultra-high-altitude operations. At one stage in the encounter the contestants climbed above 43,000ft during that combat in September 1942.

Chapter Eight, 'The Twenty-fifth Mission', gives one pilot's recollections of a B-17 Flying Fortress mission over Germany. For US bomber crews operating over Europe during the Second World War the twenty-fifth mission was one everybody aimed at, for it rounded off their combat tour of operations and entitled them to a spell of home leave. As luck would have it, the crew's twenty-fifth mission was against Berlin on 6 March 1944, the day when the US Eighth Air Force fought its hardest air battle. The operation rounded off the pilot's combat tour of operations, but not in the manner he had hoped.

In Chapter Nine, 'The D-Day Spoofs', we return to the theme of electronic trickery. This time the victims were the German radar stations along the north coast of France on the night of 5/6 June 1944, D-Day. As the largest seaborne invasion fleet ever assembled set sail from ports around England, the Allies mounted the largest and most ambitious electronic spoof operation ever attempted. The aim was to produce on the German radar screens the same indications that their operators would expect to see from the approach of a large invasion force, but in areas far removed from the real invasion. That night two 'ghost' invasion armadas headed for France, to divert the attention away from the real troop landing areas in Normandy. The remarkable thing about these 'ghost' invasion fleets was that they employed no full-sized ships, merely a few small motor launches and 14 planes which dropped several tons of radar reflective metal foil in carefully calculated patterns.

Chapter Ten, 'Corking the English Channel', also describes an air operation that formed part of the invasion of Normandy in June 1944. This was the use of aircraft flying interlinked patrol patterns, to prevent German U-boats reaching the Allied lodgement area in France. On the night following the invasion, 49 U-boats set out from their bases in western France. The largest 'wolf pack' ever assembled, it included many of the most experienced and determined crews in the German Navy. If these U-boats could have reached the mass of shipping carrying troops and supplies to the beachhead, they could have throttled the Allied build-up. Such a move was expected, however, and No 19 Group of RAF Coastal Command had prepared an elaborate plan to defeat it.

This chapter describes how the air patrols successfully 'Corked' the western end of the English Channel and prevented the U-boats from reaching their goal.

Chapter Eleven, 'The Flight of the Doodlebug', describes the functioning of the world's first cruise missile to go into action. The V-1 flying bomb, alias the 'Doodlebug', was employed against targets in England from the summer of 1944. This unusual weapon inflicted considerable damage and tied down valuable resources before the defenders learned how to deal with it.

The most advanced bomber type to emerge during the Second World War was the Boeing B-29 Superfortress. With a maximum take-off weight of 67 tons, it was more than twice as heavy as the B-17s and the B-24s that preceded it. It was the first heavy bomber fitted with pressurized cabins for the crew, and it could deliver 6,000lb of bombs to a target 1,700 miles from its base. No other aircraft of the period came close to matching that superb performance. Chapter Twelve, 'The Superfortresses' First Strike on Japan', describes the first B-29 raid on Japan, aimed at the Imperial Iron and Steel Works at Yawata. As remarkable as the aircraft itself was the logistics operation necessary to support each attack. Initially, the only territory held by the Allies within B-29 range of targets in Japan was in a remote part of China. Hundreds of labourers levelled the ground at the airfields and built runways for the big bombers. Since there was no overland supply route to these airfields, every item required for the heavy bombers' attacks had to be flown in. During the period of preparation before each raid, even the B-29s joined in the task of transporting the necessary fuel and supplies to the forward bases.

Earlier, I discussed the difficulties experienced by one unfortunate RAF fighter squadron during the Battle of Britain in 1940. In Chapter Thirteen, 'No Place for a Beginner', we see a similar fate inflicted on a hastily formed *Luftwaffe* Focke-Wulf 190 fighter unit pitchforked into action over France in the summer of 1944.

When a major nation comes face to face with defeat, there is no shortage of brave men willing to sacrifice their lives to save their homeland and their loved ones. Chapter Fourteen, 'Act of Desperation', describes the concept and execution of an operation by German volunteers who had pledged to destroy US heavy bombers by ramming them. In the event, the operation was launched too late and in insufficient strength to have any discernible effect. Yet, had it been undertaken early enough and in the strength originally planned, it might have changed the course of the air war over Germany.

In Chapter Fifteen the arena shifts to the skies over North Vietnam in the mid-1960s. In August 1965, for the first time during that conflict, an SA-2 surface-to-air missile (SAM) battery near Hanoi destroyed a US tactical fighter plane. In the year that followed the missiles caused disconcerting losses to US raiding forces. Yet worse, they forced raiding planes to fly in the lower altitude bands where they were vulnerable to fire from anti-aircraft artillery (AAA). During this period losses to AAA greatly exceeded losses to missiles. Entitled 'Defeating the SAMs', this chapter shows a further example of the successful use of countermeasures trickery to neutralize an enemy electronic system. To jam the radar that controlled the missile system, US attack fighters began carrying external jamming pods and the planes flew in a special formation to enhance the effect of that jamming. These measures reduced the effectiveness of the SA-2 missile system to manageable proportions. Also, by restoring to US raiding forces the free use of the skies at medium and high altitude, the new tactic made US attack fighters far less vulnerable to AAA.

Chapter Sixteen, 'Reconnaissance to Hanoi', also about the air war over North Vietnam, tells the story of an all-too-exciting post-strike reconnaissance photographic mission by a pair of RF-4C Phantoms. As well as facing severe problems from the enemy defences, one aircraft suffered a technical failure that nearly caused it to run out of fuel. Only by dint of some extremely skilful flying did the plane reach the ground safely.

In combat, a military aviator's duties do not end when his plane is shot down. His training has represented a considerable financial investment for his country, and he is expected to do his utmost to return. In the annals of combat flying few people have taken that obligation more seriously than Captain Roger Locher, an F-4 Phantom back-seater whose fighter was shot down over North Vietnam in May 1972. Chapter Seventeen, 'Combat Rescue', describes how he remained at liberty in the enemy homeland for 23 days, avoiding all human contact. Then he was able to call a friendly plane and initiate the deepest penetration helicopter rescue operation ever.

Providing close air support for the ground troops is an important role for attack fighter planes. Yet, in the strictest sense, that type of air operation sees comparatively little use in time of war. Most air support takes the form of battlefield air interdiction missions, attacking targets in enemy territory well back from the battle area. Close air support is defined as an 'air action against hostile targets which are in close proximity to friendly [ground] forces'. The key words are 'in close proximity to friendly forces'. Unless such attacks are very carefully controlled, there is considerable risk of hitting the very troops the attack is intended to assist. That sets the close air support mission apart from other air operations. Ground forces in contact with the enemy often shift position rapidly. It would be courting disaster if pilots hit targets in the battle area, using briefing information on friendly troop positions that might be several hours out of date. For that reason close air support missions need to be guided on to their target by a forward air controller (FAC), usually on the ground, with up-to-date information on both sides' troop dispositions.

A timely close air support mission can have a decisive effect on a land action, however. In Chapter Eighteen, 'Ground Attack Harriers over the Falklands', I look at the crucial close air support mission delivered by RAF Harriers at Goose Green in May 1981. The advancing British paratroops had run into difficulties while engaging a far larger Argentine force. Pinned down by fire from Argentine artillery, the troop commander sent an urgent request for an air strike. The resultant attack, by three Harrier GR3s, was a textbook example of what aircraft can achieve in such a situation. By boosting the paratroops' morale, and collapsing that of their opponents, the air strike played a major part in convincing the Argentine troop commander to surrender.

Chapter Nineteen, 'The Vulcan's Impromptu Visit to Rio', is another of those 'nearly ran out of fuel' stories. In the spring of 1981, the Royal Air Force Vulcan attacks on targets in the Falklands were the longest-range bombing raids ever attempted. For their success they depended on numerous air-to-air refuelling contacts, to pass fuel between the tankers and the bomber. At the critical time, during the final fuel transfer on its way to its base on Ascension Island, a Vulcan broke its refuelling probe. The bomber was forced to divert to Rio de Janeiro in Brazil, but getting it to the ground in one piece required all the skills of one of the RAF's most experienced Vulcan pilots.

Chapter Twenty, 'Desert Storm Warthogs', describes the operations of the A-10 attack fighter, nicknamed the 'Warthog', during the Gulf War against Iraq in 1991. The A-10 had been designed specifically for the close air support role, but during that conflict the plane flew the majority of its sorties as interdiction missions, hitting targets some distance behind the battlefront. Only during the final part of the conflict did A-10s mount close air support operations. This chapter describes one of these missions, once again on enemy artillery that was causing problems for the ground troops advancing into Kuwait.

Chapter Twenty-one, 'Multiple MiG Shoot-down', describes how an American F-15C Eagle engaged and shot down two Yugoslav MiG-29 fighters in rapid succession during the Kosovo conflict in 1999. The action bears comparison with the other two air-to-air engagements described in this book, the 1918 Zeppelin shoot-down in Chapter 2, and the high-altitude combat in 1942 described in Chapter 7.

Chapter Twenty-two, 'The Unmanned Air Vehicle: A Pointer to the Future', provides an insight into the future of combat aviation. In the 1980s a new type of air weapon entered the combat arena, the unmanned air vehicle (UAV). Unlike a guided missile, the UAV is not a one-shot expendable system. At the end of its sortie the UAV is programmed to return to friendly territory, to land and be used again. In this chapter I describe the part played by one type of UAV over Kosovo. The account also shows that, although the UAV itself is unmanned, this is very much a man-controlled system.

Taken as a whole, the series of accounts illustrates the enormous changes made to the capability of military aviation during the final nine decades of the twentieth century. Yet, despite the enormous technical changes, a factor that remains unchanged up to the present is the bravery, the determination and the resourcefulness of those who make the sky their arena for battle.

Author's Note

Unless stated otherwise, in this account all miles are statute miles and all speeds are given in statute miles per hour. Gallons and tons are given in imperial measurements. Times are given in local time for the area where the incident described took place. Weapon calibres are given in the units normal for the weapon being described, e.g. Oerlikon 20mm cannon or Browning .5in machine gun. Where an aircraft's offensive armament load is stated, this is the typical load carried by that type of aircraft during actual operations – somewhat less than the maximum figure given in makers' brochures and which appears in most aircraft data books.

Alfred Price

UPPINGHAM, RUTLAND

JANUARY 2002

CHAPTER ONE

Warfare Enters the Third Dimension

As wars go the conflict in Libya in 1911 and 1912 was relatively short and it involved relatively few people. But the work of a few imaginative and tenacious Italian aviators pointed the way ahead for the development of heavier-than-air and lighter-than-air machines as weapons of war.

ON 17 DECEMBER 1903 Orville Wright made the first powered, controlled and sustained flight in a heavier-than-air flying machine. That first flight was really no more than a 'hop', for the flimsy biplane covered a distance of only about 120ft – less than the wingspan of a modern Boeing 767 airliner. At no point during that first flight did Orville Wright rise more than a few feet above the ground and the maximum speed he attained was about 30mph.

During the years to follow the techniques of aircraft design and construction moved forward rapidly. By the summer of 1911 the performance boundaries of these vehicles had advanced beyond any previous recognition. France now led the world in all aspects of this fledgling science. A Nieuport aircraft held the world airspeed record at 82mph while a Blériot machine held the altitude record at 12,800ft. Three significant flights at that time demonstrated the potential of the new vehicle for military and commercial use. A Breguet aircraft had taken off carrying 11 passengers and a pilot, a payload weight of about 1,900lb, though it carried them for only 3 miles. A Blériot monoplane had flown non-stop from Hendon, north of London, to Issy-les-Moulineaux near Paris, a distance of about 220 miles, in 3 hours 56 minutes. Another Blériot established the record for flight duration at 5 hours 3 minutes.

During 1911 the armies and navies of France, Britain, the USA, Italy and Germany had all conducted small-scale experiments using both heavier-than-air and lighter-than-air craft during military exercises. These novel machines quickly demonstrated their value in performing reconnaissance under peacetime conditions. Yet there were serious doubts whether these flimsy and unreliable vehicles could perform as well in the harsh environment of war. To get a conclusive answer to that question the world had to wait for the next armed conflict to involve a major industrialized nation. It was not to be long in coming.

BY 1911 THE disintegration of the once-powerful Ottoman-Turkish Empire was well advanced. Power politics abhors a vacuum, and the Italian government was casting covetous eyes on the territory of Libya with the Ottoman provinces of Tripolitania and Cyrenaica. That September Italy declared war on Turkey and prepared an expedition to seize the two provinces by force of arms.

On 4 October Italian troops landed at Tobruk in Cyrenaica. On the following day others landed at Tripoli in Tripolitania and quickly took control of its port. Ten days later, the Italian expeditionary air flotilla arrived at Tripoli aboard the freighters *Enrichetta*, *Santino* and *Plata*. The force was equipped with nine aeroplanes – two Blériot monoplanes, three Nieuport monoplanes, two Etrich Taube monoplanes and two Farman biplanes. The Taube monoplanes were from Austria, the remaining aeroplanes had been built in France. Captain Carlo Piazza commanded the force of 11 pilots and 29 ground personnel.

The air flotilla quickly established itself ashore, on a patch of flat ground just outside the city that had been cleared of obstacles. Each plane had its own hangar tent, and once these were erected the task of reassembling the aircraft began. On 22 October the first two planes, a Blériot and a Nieuport, were test-flown.

Shortly after dawn on the following day, 23 October, Carlo Piazza took off in a Blériot to fly the first-ever war mission by a heavier-than-air craft. Following the road to Azizia to the south of Tripoli, he passed over the front line and observed several enemy military encampments, each of which he estimated to house about 200 troops. After just over an hour in the air he returned to Tripoli to make his report. Shortly after Piazza had got airborne, Captain Riccardo Moizo took off to conduct a reconnaissance in a Nieuport. After 40 minutes in the air, he returned to report that he had seen nothing of significance in his assigned area.

On the next day, the24th, Moizo took his Nieuport some 35 miles into enemy territory to the small town of Azizia. On his return flight he noticed a long column of enemy troops, estimated at 2,000 strong, marching towards Tripoli. During a repeat reconnaissance of the area on the following day Moizo became the first pilot of a heavier-than-air craft to be shot at in anger. The fabric of his Nieuport's wings was torn in three places, but that was the limit of the damage. Forewarned of the approach of the enemy force, on 26 October Italian ground forces beat off a determined attack by Turkish–Arab troops.

During the final week in October two more aircraft were made

BLÉRIOT TYPE XI

ROLE   Single-seat, general-purpose monoplane.

POWER   One Gnome, air-cooled, rotary engine developing 50hp at take-off.

ARMAMENT   During these operations Italian pilots sometimes took up small
   bombs up to a total weight of 20lb.

PERFORMANCE   Maximum speed 68mph at sea level; the maximum operational radius of action was about 40 miles.

NORMAL OPERATIONAL TAKE-OFF WEIGHT   660lb.

DIMENSIONS   Span 28ft ¼in; length 25ft 6in; wing area 248 sq ft.

DATE OF FIRST PRODUCTION AIRCRAFT BLÉRIOT XI   1909.

ready for action and these were pressed into use to stiffen the reconnaissance effort. An important part of that role was the correction of
maps. Italian commanders quickly found that those they had of the
area were often unreliable; the town of Azizia, for example, was shown
as being 50 miles from Tripoli but one of Moizo's early flights indicated
the real distance was only about 35 miles. Indications of topographical
features were similarly untrustworthy. To provide the necessary corrections, pilots had to make notes and line drawings of the territory
over which they flew. The task was done with one hand writing on a
kneepad, while flying the unstable aeroplane with the other hand.

During these early experimental air operations the pilots were per-
mitted considerable freedom of action. Consequently, it was not long
before they sought to carry out offensive air operations. The first bombs
available were spherical weapons of the Cipelli type, little larger than
an orange and weighing about 4½lb. To use the weapon the pilot withdrew the safety pin with his teeth, then dropped the missile over the
side. The first such attack took place on 1 November, when Lieutenant
Giulio Gavotti dropped a Cipelli bomb on Ain Zara and three on the
Tagiura oasis. Other bombing attacks soon followed. Given the diminu-
tive power of the Cipelli bomb and the inaccurate delivery method,
these attacks achieved little destructive effect though they gave the
pilots considerable satisfaction.

On 19 November Riccardo Moizo conducted another innovative
experiment. After dropping four Cipelli bombs on a group of enemy
tents at Ain Zara, he observed that an Italian artillery battery was
engaging the same target. The pilot made four attempts to drop messages to the battery to correct its fire, but each time the wind carried
the paper away. Five days later Moizo achieved more success when he
observed and corrected the fall of shells on a Turkish artillery battery.

Although aeroplanes would occasionally serve in the artillery correction role, for this and other observations of territory close to Italian
troop positions the captive balloon proved rather more effective. During
November a small unit equipped with Draken tethered balloons arrived
at Tripoli. The balloons were quickly offloaded and sent into action.

From the 26th, balloons observed and reported on enemy positions at Sidi Messri. Observers aboard the balloons were able to pick out weak points in the defences, and this intelligence assisted in planning a successful attack by Italian troops a few days later.

Initially, messages containing information on the enemy positions were dropped from the balloon in weighted bags. That worked reasonably well, but a far more successful method was to provide a telephone connection between the balloon observer and the ground. The balloons' military value was further enhanced when these were flown from the naval brig *Caval Marino*; the latter was towed to position off the coast to correct the fire of warships bombarding targets ashore. Later a Draken balloon was flown from a lorry fitted with a winch, and this performed a similar task with gun batteries ashore.

As the winter drew on, the weather became progressively worse. On 16 December a severe storm wrecked a hangar used by the air flotilla, causing severe damage to the two Farman biplanes inside. It also damaged two hangars that had been erected in preparation for the arrival of dirigible airships in the operational theatre. In mid-January 1912 two replacement Farman biplanes arrived. At the end of the month another storm hit the area and a Farman suffered serious damage when its hangar collapsed on top of it. As the Turkish troops became accustomed to seeing aeroplanes flying over their positions, they became adept at engaging them with rifle and machine-gun fire. No longer was it unusual for a plane to return with bullet tears in the fabric.

By now Italian planes were also operating from airstrips in Tobruk, Derna and Benghazi in Cyrenaica. There, too, the Turkish troops reacted to the overflights with vigorous return fire. On 31 January a Farman biplane took off from Tobruk, carrying Captain Carlo Montu as observer, to reconnoitre the enemy camp at Emme Dauer. Montu dropped a bomb on the camp from 2,000ft, but then the plane came under vigorous return fire and four bullets struck the wings and propeller. Shortly afterwards Montu was hit on the thigh, to gain the dubious distinction of being the first man wounded in action while flying aboard a heavier-than-air craft. The wound was not serious and the plane returned to base. After the offending bullet was removed, it was mounted on a commemorative plaque and presented to the officer.

In February 1912, in a further extension of technique, Carlo Piazza attached a Zeiss Baby plate camera to the underside of his aircraft with the lens pointing vertically down. It was not possible for the pilot to change the plates one-handed while airborne, so the installation allowed one picture to be taken on each flight. Militarily, the photographs were of little use, but the flights established a future role for the heavier-than-air craft.

In March 1912 two small dirigibles belonging to the Italian Army airship service, the *P.2* and the *P.3*, began operations over Libya. On the19th the airships left their base at Tripoli and rose above 4,000ft to carry out a reconnaissance of the Turkish–Arab encampment at Suani-Beni-Adem. It had been thought that this altitude would render the airships safe from ground fire, but this proved not to be the case. In the vigorous one-sided action that ensued the *P.2* collected 22 hits from rifle and machine-gun rounds, including one that penetrated the aluminium cylinder wall of the engine, though the latter continued running. The airship lost a large amount of hydrogen and became difficult to control, and on returning to base she suffered further damage when the lower fin struck the ground hard. The *P.3* limped home with 17 hits, though none caused serious damage. The incident underlined the vulnerability of dirigibles to fire from small-calibre weapons.

After repairs the two airships resumed operations, but from now on they gave the enemy encampments a very wide berth. On 12 April they set out on an ambitious operation to support a landing by Italian troops at Sidi Said close to the border with Tunisia. The landings, about 90 miles to the west of Tripoli, took place in an area well beyond the radius of action of the heavier-than-air machines. The initial phase of the operation comprised a reconnaissance of the areas to either side of the landings, which was successfully carried out. The *P.2* carried out a reconnaissance as far west as the Tunisian border, then headed inland to the town of Rigdaline where it dropped five bombs on a group of

Turkish army tents. Meanwhile the *P. 3* conducted a reconnaissance to the east of the landing area and afterwards its commander dropped a message to inform the Italian ground commander:

> To the east, as far as Zuara, there is no sign of the enemy. This area seems completely deserted, as does all the territory to the south and west within a radius of 10 miles.

It is difficult to exaggerate the value of that intelligence for army units as they struggled to establish themselves ashore. It allowed the troops to concentrate on the unloading task, without having to divert effort to prepare to meet a possible enemy attack.

Following the initial reconnaissance the plan called for the two airships to rendezvous with a warship off the coast, where they would take on petrol, hydrogen gas and replenish their stocks of bombs. Rough seas prevented the transfer of hydrogen and bombs, and only small amounts of petrol could be passed. After the attempt the *P. 2* had difficulty in rising, and the crew had to offload the bombs and several items of equipment.

The *P. 3* fared even worse. When the dirigible alighted on the water, a wave broke over the cabin and caused the engine to stop. Only with great difficulty was it restarted. Hindered by a headwind, the two airships regained their base on the last of their fuel. There was no further attempt to replenish dirigibles by alighting close to a ship in open water.

In the months that followed the airships continued their reconnaissance activities, bringing a wealth of intelligence on enemy dispositions. They also provided much useful negative intelligence, pointing out areas where there were no enemy ground forces. In May 1912 a third dirigible, the *P. 1*, arrived in Libya and began a similar pattern of operations in the Benghazi area.

Meanwhile, the heavier-than-air units continued to fly reconnaissance missions and occasionally there were excitements for their pilots. On 26 June, Lieutenant Cesare Sacerdoti suffered an engine failure while over nominally enemy territory. He made a forced landing in the desert and after a two-hour walk he reached the Italian position at Bu-Kemesh. Accompanied by Italian troops and a mechanic he returned to the plane, which was as he had left it. The mechanic repaired the engine, Sacerdoti took off and returned to his base.

Throughout their time in Libya thus far the Italian pilots had led charmed lives, and although there were several close shaves there had been no deaths or cases of serious injury. That period of grace ended on the morning of 25 August. Shortly after Lieutenant Piero Manzini had taken off from Tripoli on a reconnaissance mission, his plane appeared to run into turbulent air and it sideslipped into the sea. Manzini was drowned, to become the first pilot of a heavier-than-air machine to be killed while engaged in a combat mission. He would be the only fatality suffered by the Italian expeditionary air flotilla in Libya.

On 10 September Riccardo Moizo suffered an engine failure while conducting a reconnaissance of the coast road between Tripoli and Zuara. He force-landed in the desert and soon afterwards was captured by Turkish–Arab soldiers. In those days aviators were rare and highly respected individuals, accorded treatment similar to that given today to astronauts who have visited the moon. Moizo was passed up the Turkish chain of command, being well received at each point, until he was taken to meet the Chief of the General Staff in Libya, Fethi Bey. After a friendly meeting, the pilot was allowed to send a telegram to his family in Italy to assure them he was well. Moizo's period of captivity did not last long, for in the following month the Turkish government signed a peace treaty which acceded to the Italian demands. Libya now became the cornerstone of Italy's African empire.

WITH HINDSIGHT we can see that during their air operations in Libya the Italian pilots had explored virtually all the possibilities for using the available flying machines in action. Their main role was visual reconnaissance, but the contribution it made to the ground campaign proved decisive. For a ground commander launching an attack or a counter-attack, surprise is the most important ingredient for success. Thanks to aerial reconnaissance from the aeroplanes, dirigibles and captive balloons, no major Turkish attack ever came as a surprise to the Italian commanders. At the same time, again thanks to aerial reconnaissance, when Italian troops attacked they were able to select weak points in the enemy defences and strike there.

The next most important facility provided by aircraft, another aspect of reconnaissance, was that of locating targets for ground artillery and correcting their fire. Artillery fire corrected from the air was devastatingly effective; once the guns were zeroed in they could pound a target until the required level of destruction was achieved. Captive balloons and aeroplanes proved excellent platforms for this purpose.

The remaining two operational roles performed by aircraft over Libya, bombing and photographic reconnaissance, achieved no military effect. Those early planes and dirigibles carried minuscule bomb loads and had no effective bombsights, so their destructive effect was negligible. Similarly, the few photographs taken of enemy positions provided little additional intelligence to amplify that provided by pilots or observers. As we shall observe in later chapters, however, these aspects of air power would be developed mightily in later decades.

CHAPTER TWO

Geoffrey De Havilland's Multi-role Masterpiece

The De Havilland 4, a 1916 design for a bomber and reconnaissance

aircraft, entered service early the following year. For that time it

demonstrated an impressive performance, and in examining some of the

actions it took part in the reader can gain a rare insight into First World

War air operations.

HAVING FLOWN THE D.H.4 on numerous missions while serving with
No 2 Wing Royal Naval Air Service in the eastern Mediterranean in
1917, Lieutenant (later Air Marshal Sir) Ralph Sorley wrote:

> This two-seater bomber was a classic in its class. It seemed a large
> aeroplane for its time and had a performance as good as a 'scout'. It
> could carry two 230-pound bombs and was a dream of an aeroplane
> to fly. It carried fuel for four or fight hours flying and was as reliable as
> a taxicab. I did very many hours in one of these, No 5976 powered by
> the 275 Rolls Royce Eagle [engine], ranging far from base and was
> never once let down.

The D.H.4 was designed as a medium bomber and reconnaissance
aircraft. The prototype was completed in the summer of 1916 at the
Aircraft Manufacturing Co. Ltd factory at Hendon, close to the site of
the present-day RAF Museum. In August 1916 designer Geoffrey de

Havilland made the maiden flight in the new plane, for in those far-off days it was considered appropriate for a designer to demonstrate faith in his product.

Following initial testing, the prototype went to the Central Flying School for service trials. The performance and handling characteristics of the new aircraft drew enthusiastic comments. With full fuel and a 230lb bomb the aircraft weighed 3,150lb, yet it achieved 108mph at 10,000ft and reached that altitude in 19 minutes. For the time it was a sparkling performance. The CFS report on the aircraft went on to state:

> Stability: lateral very good; longitudinal very good; directional very good. Length of run to unstick 150 yds; to pull up (engine stopped) 120 yds ... Machine is exceptionally comfortable to fly and very easy to land. Exceptionally light on controls. Tail adjusting gear enables pilot to fly or glide at any desired speed without effort.

The D.H.4 was ordered into production, and new machines began emerging from the Hendon factory early in 1917. One of the first service units to go into action with the new aircraft was No 57 Squadron based at Fienvillers near Abbeville in France. Lieutenant Andrew Mac-Gregor described the squadron's tactics during formation bombing attacks on targets behind the battle area:

> Escorts were generally provided by SE 5As and [Sopwith] Dolphins, who engaged the enemy while the D.H.4s were flying to their objective. They usually complained that on the way home they were unable to keep up when the bombers got their noses well down for the lines. The fact was that, having dropped their bombs, the D.H.4s were quite able to look after themselves, and if well led could give quite as good as they received. On the return from a bombing raid, the escort being dismissed, the ten D.H.4s in their two "V" formations usually carried out a medium altitude reconnaissance. If attacked, the leader of the front "V" throttled right down to give the slower aeroplanes a margin of power to work with. The rear formation was usually about 500 feet higher than the leading one and flew slightly

on a flank. Good close formation was maintained in this way and concentrated fire could be brought to bear.

The only serious shortcoming of the D.H.4 was that the main 67-gallon petrol tank was located in the fuselage between the pilot and the observer. That separated the two men by more than 3ft and, since there was no electrical intercom, voice communication between them was impossible. For that reason, the bombsight was fitted in the floor of the pilot's cockpit and he released the bombs. On the Western Front anti-aircraft fire could be dangerous at the lower altitudes, and in that theatre D.H.4s usually delivered attacks from altitudes between 14,000 and 17,000ft at an airspeed of 70mph.

In No 57 Squadron it was usual for the formation leader to carry out the bombing run, while the remaining aircraft held close formation and released their bombs when they saw the leader drop his. The bombsight made no allowance for crosswinds so attacks had to be made either running downwind or into wind – usually the latter. Gyro stabilization for bombsights was still some way in the future, so during the bombing run all turns had to be made 'flat' – i.e. with the wings level and no bank applied.

In other theatres of war, where anti-aircraft fire was less of a hazard, D.H.4s could deliver more accurate attacks from lower altitudes. Lieutenant Ralph Sorley described the improvised system that No 2 Wing Royal Naval Air Service used over the eastern Mediterranean in 1917.

Because in the D.H.4 the pilot and the observer were separated by the petrol tank and had no means of inter-communication, he steered me over the target by reins attached to my arms. Smithy's [his observer's] bombsight consisted of a rear sight of one nail, with a row of other nails as foresights spaced [to allow] for various speeds and heights. These were hammered into the outside of the fuselage, the former at the top and the latter at the bottom edge. Believe it or not, we hit bridges and stations from heights of two to eight thousand feet and took good photographs of the results. It was not scientific but it worked through good co-operation and understanding between us.

We were given a free-lance roving commission to operate against the Berlin–Constantinople railway from Imbros [now Göçeada], an island near Gallipoli. Together with another D.H.4 we became a detached Flight, independent of the other unit based on the island. The railway runs through Bulgaria and Turkey and we selected the stretch from west of Adrianopole to east of Muradli, which gave us an element of surprise. We could appear at very different points at different times, to bomb the many bridges and stations past which the German supplies were being sent to the Turks in support of the Palestine campaign.

These forays took us far afield, involving flights of three or four hours away from base with a twenty mile crossing of water at the beginning and the end of each sortie, but never did that trusty Rolls Royce engined D.H.4 let us down or give us a nasty moment. We carried relatively small bombs of 65, 100 or 112 pounds, which were the standard weights available. By using surprise and evasive tactics and by varying the time and place for attack we were not intercepted, and rather laughed to see how AA guns were moved up and down the railway in a game of hide and seek always seeming to be in the wrong place.

IN FRANCE THE D.H.4 units also flew photographic reconnaissance missions, and the type proved well suited to that role. These aircraft operated at altitudes as high as 23,000ft and in their draughty, open cockpits the crews suffered from the intense cold, with temperatures sometimes falling below minus 30°C. At such altitudes the D.H.4s were virtually invulnerable to attack from ground fire or enemy fighters as Lieutenant Benjamin Silly, a pilot with No 55 Squadron, explained:

Photography in the early days of 55 Squadron's service in France was carried out by formations of aircraft, but it was soon found that the D.H.4s could reach such great heights that single aircraft could carry out reconnaissance of this nature in complete immunity. From memory, only one aircraft on high photography was ever shot up by enemy fighters and only one failed to return, due possibly to inexperience of the pilot, whose first high flight it was. Orders were that the lines were not to be crossed under 19,000 feet; normally the height gained was between 20,000 and 22,000 feet, the maximum being 23,000 feet. At these heights no enemy fighter could approach the D.H.4, and one carried out one's job in complete security and peace, provided one's oxygen apparatus and electrically heated clothing functioned. It was found advisable to use oxygen above 16,000 feet, as this height was normally exceeded for periods of two and a half to three hours . . . High flying led also to considerable inconvenience from frost bite on the cheeks, overcome to a great extent by the copious application of whale oil to the skin and by the wearing of chamois leather masks. Hands, body and nether limbs were kept warm by electrically heated clothing of a very satisfactory type.

AS THE WAR progressed the D.H.4 was fitted with progressively more powerful engines, culminating in the Rolls-Royce Eagle VIII, developing 375hp which gave the aircraft an even better high-altitude perform-

---

DE HAVILLAND D.H.4 (EAGLE VIII ENGINE)

ROLE Two-seat bomber and reconnaissance aircraft.

POWER One Rolls-Royce Eagle VIII, liquid-cooled, in-line engine developing 375hp for take-off.

ARMAMENT Maximum bomb load 460lb, carried on racks under the fuselage and the lower wings; one forward-firing Vickers .303in machine gun, synchronized to fire through the airscrew, and one Lewis .303in machine gun on a flexible mounting in the observer's position.

PERFORMANCE (Without bombs) maximum speed 136mph at 5,000ft, 126mph at 15,000 ft; climb to 15,000ft, 16½ min; absolute ceiling 23,000ft.

NORMAL OPERATIONAL TAKE-OFF WEIGHT 3,472lb.

DIMENSIONS Span 42ft 4in; length 30ft 2in; wing area 434 sq ft.

DATE OF FIRST PRODUCTION D.H.4 Spring 1917.

ance. That made the machine suitable for a quite different role: that of engaging the high-flying Zeppelin raiders attacking targets in England.

On the afternoon of 8 August 1918 the German Naval Airship Service dispatched five Zeppelins to attack targets in England. At 2010 hours, when it was still light, the three Zeppelins at the head of the force came within sight of the Leman Tail Lightship 30 miles off the Norfolk coast. Warning of the approaching raiders was passed to the Navy headquarters at Lowestoft, whence it was relayed to airfields in the area.

When the news reached the Great Yarmouth air station, every available aircraft was ordered into action. Among those taking off were Major Egbert Cadbury, with Robert Leckie as gunner, aboard a Rolls-Royce Eagle VIII-powered D.H.4. Cadbury and Leckie made a formidable pair, for in separate earlier actions they had each taken part in the destruction of a Zeppelin. Their D.H.4 had been loaded for a bombing mission planned for the following day, and carried two 100lb bombs under the fuselage. After take-off, Cadbury began a full throttle climb for the 17,000–19,000ft altitude band where he knew he could expect to find the Zeppelins. Once clear of the coast he pulled the lever to jettison the bombs, as he had no use for them. Then he caught a glimpse of his quarry in the distance, silhouetted against the darkening sky. The three airships were cruising a few miles apart, about 40 miles away to the north-east, waiting for nightfall when the darkness would shield them as they ran in to attack their targets.

To his frustration Cadbury found that the Eagle VIII-engined D.H.4's usual brisk climbing performance was lacking from this particular aircraft. Nevertheless, he succeeded in getting close to the airships' altitude in good time. In his combat report Cadbury noted:

At approximately 2145 the Zeppelins, which were flying in Vee-formation, altered course north. At 2210 Zeppelin abeam, 2,000 feet above us at 17,000 feet. At 2220 we climbed to 16,400 feet and I attacked the Zeppelin head on, slightly to port so as to clear any obstruction [i.e. a wireless aerial] that might be suspended from the

airship. My observer trained his gun on the bow of the airship
and the fire was seen to concentrate on a spot under the Zeppelin,
three-quarters way aft.

From previous experience, Leckie knew it was important to concentrate his fire on one single part of the airship. Contrary to popular
belief, hydrogen in its pure form is not an explosive gas. Like petrol, it
forms a combustible mixture only if combined with oxygen in the correct ratio. Now Leckie aimed to puncture one of the Zeppelin's internal
gas cells, allow the hydrogen to escape and mix with the surrounding
air. Then, if he continued firing at the same point, his explosive rounds
might ignite the charge thus formed. In this Leckie was successful, as
Cadbury witnessed:

> The Pommeroy [explosive ammunition] was seen to blow a great
> hole in the fabric and a fire started which quickly ran along the entire
> length of the Zeppelin. The Zeppelin raised her bows as if in an effort
> to escape, then plunged seaward, a blazing mass. The airship was
> completely consumed in about three-quarters of a minute. A large
> petrol tank was seen to become detached from the framework and
> fall blazing into a heavy layer of clouds about 7,000 feet below.

The pyre marked the end of the Zeppelin *L.70*. *Kapitänleutnant*
Michael von Freudenreich, commanding *L.63* some 20 miles to the
north-east of the stricken airship, watched the demise of his comrades
with horror:

> I was near the coast when we suddenly saw a huge flame on the
> L.70. It looked like a huge sun. Then the whole ship was on fire, one
> could see the flames all over her. Then she stood up erect and went
> down like a burning shaft. The whole thing did not last more than
> 30–45 seconds.

Wreckage from the airship rained down on the sea, where the
lighter items that floated continued to burn. Meanwhile, Cadbury
swung round in an attempt to engage a second Zeppelin. He reached a

firing position, but after a few rounds Leckie's gun jammed and in the intense cold and the darkness he was unable to clear the stoppage. In the rarefied air Cadbury could not bring his forward-firing Vickers machine gun to bear on the airship, and after some unsuccessful attempts the cold and fatigue forced him to break off the action.

For the crew of the D.H.4, the return flight would be the most hazardous part of that night's activities. With a modern instrument panel and modern radio aids, it would have been a simple enough matter to return to the airfield at Yarmouth. But Cadbury's biplane lacked such luxuries. His flight instruments comprised an airspeed indicator, a none-too-sensitive altimeter, an unreliable magnetic compass and a cross-level resembling a curved spirit level which served as a rudimentary turn-and-slip indicator. For daylight operations in clear skies, that combination was adequate. But on this very dark night Cadbury had to descend through several layers of cloud without a horizon he could use as reference. Under such conditions, it was all too easy to become disorientated and lose control of the aircraft. Cadbury later recounted that the next half-hour was the most terrible he ever experienced, as he descended through 12,000ft of cloud in inky blackness and headed west trying to find land.

The D.H.4 eventually made a landfall near Burnham Market in Norfolk, some 50 miles to the north-west of Yarmouth. The crew knew they were over England, but had little idea where. Soon afterwards Cadbury caught sight of flares at an airfield, Sedgeford, in the process of recovering its own planes. As Cadbury was about to land another aircraft, intent on the same thing, 'suddenly loomed up in the darkness' and missed him 'by inches'. Cadbury realigned his approach and landed the D.H.4.

As the cold and tired pair eased themselves from their cockpits and stepped to the ground, they had a further shock: the two 100lb bombs were still on their racks. They had failed to release when Cadbury pulled the lever, and had remained in place under the fuselage throughout the flight. No wonder the D.H.4 had lacked its customary fine climbing performance!

From Yarmouth and other airfields in Norfolk, 33 planes had taken off that evening to engage the Zeppelins. By a combination of luck and exceptional flying skill Cadbury had landed safely, but others who encountered the same conditions were not so fortunate. Two aircraft, a Sopwith Camel and a D.H.9, fell into the sea with the loss of their crews, and the pilot of a Bristol Fighter was killed when he crashed on landing.

The second Zeppelin that Cadbury and Leckie engaged escaped with minor damage, but the two men had inflicted sufficient wounds to the German Naval Airship Service. The Zeppelin they destroyed, the *L.70*, was of the latest type and had entered service less than a month earlier. Yet more serious, *Fregatenkapitän* Peter Strasser was among those who met his death when the airship went down. That brave and resolute officer carried the title 'Leader of Airships' and had been the prime exponent of these machines as strategic bombardment weapons. With his death the German Navy lost the driving force for the Zeppelin raids on England, and never again did it attempt such an enterprise.

During 1917 and 1918 factories in Britain turned out 1,449 production D.H.4s. That output was far exceeded by the licence production in the USA, however, where more than 4,300 were built before the war's end.The first US-built D.H.4s arrived in France in May 1918 and it was the only US-built aircraft type to see combat during that conflict. By the armistice in the following November a total of 1,213 US-built D.H.4s had been delivered to the war zone and the type served with thirteen Army and four combined Navy/Marine squadrons.

Following the armistice, the D.H.4 did not survive long in service with the newly constituted Royal Air Force. In the few surviving combat units, the type was soon replaced by later designs. Several D.H.4s were donated to the fledgling air forces then being formed in Canada, Australia, New Zealand and South Africa. Others were sold to Belgium, Chile, Greece, Iran and Spain.

US production of the D.H.4 ended with the armistice. Afterwards, however, the licence-built D.H.4 was the only aircraft type available in the USA in large numbers, at a time when little money was available to buy anything better. It would serve for several years with the Army Air Corps, the Navy and the Marines, in a variety of roles.

In 1918 the US Post Office secured the loan of several D.H.4s from the Army, to pioneer the airmail routes across the country. For this role the D.H.4s were converted into single-seaters, with the pilot's seat resited slightly to the rear of the position originally occupied by the observer. This left room for a cargo compartment occupying those sections of the fuselage that had originally housed the pilot and the observer, allowing the carriage of up to 500lb of mail. D.H.4s carried the bulk of the US airmails for several years, often operating in atrocious weather conditions, until the service to transport airmail was privatized in 1927.

US-built D.H.4s made a number of record-breaking flights. In September 1922 Lieutenant James Doolittle, who would achieve high rank in the Second World War, became the first pilot to complete a coast-to-coast flight across the USA in a single day. His D.H.4 covered the 2,163 miles from Pablo Beach, Florida to San Diego, California in 22 hours 35 minutes, which included a refuelling stop at Kelly Field, Texas.

The same type also featured in the world's first air-to-air refuelling trials. In August 1923 a D.H.4 refuelled 15 times while flying over a measured course at San Diego, California, and took the world endurance record by remaining airborne for 37 hours 15 minutes, covering a distance of 3,293 miles.

D.H.4s last saw action in 1927, when they supported US Marines operating against bandits in Nicaragua. When the postal service ceased using D.H.4s to carry airmail, it returned these planes to the Army. A few of those soldiered on for sometime longer with Army pilots flying fire patrols for the US Forest Service, before the D.H.4 finally passed out of service with the US Army in 1932.

The advance in aeronautical design represented by the D.H.4 can be seen when its performance is compared with the Blériot monoplane that appeared only six years earlier, described in Chapter One. All told, the D.H.4's flying career lasted 15 years, an almost unprecedented longevity for a combat aircraft of that vintage.

CHAPTER THREE

The First Successful Carrier Air Strike

During the First World War numerous aerial bombing operations were flown.

But due to the poor destructive power and unreliability of the bombs, and

inaccuracies in their sighting, these rarely achieved any serious military effect.

One of the few exceptions was the successful attack on the German airship base

at Tondern in 1918 by half a dozen Sopwith Camels. Even more remarkable,

these planes had taken off from HMS Furious, *the world's first aircraft carrier*

able to launch a landplane striking force.

AT THE BEGINNING of 1918 the 19,000-ton HMS *Furious* rejoined the Grand Fleet after modifications intended to make her suitable to operate landplanes with wheeled undercarriages. She was the world's first aircraft carrier, as the term is now used, though there were still aspects of these operations that needed improvement.

Furious had originally been laid down as a large cruiser, but after a change in requirements she had been completed in 1917 as a seaplane carrier with a flat deck 228ft long extending forward from the bridge. The seaplanes would take off from the deck on small wheeled trolleys, which fell away once the plane was airborne. When the seaplanes returned to their carrier they alighted alongside it and were hoisted aboard by crane.

That method worked reasonably well in calm seas, but in high sea states many aircraft were wrecked. Moreover, the drag of the floats imposed severe penalties on an aircraft's performance. It was a relatively simple matter for a high-performance landplane with a wheeled undercarriage to take off from the foredeck of *Furious*, but landing there was quite another matter. In initial experiments a Sopwith Pup landplane had succeeded in landing on the ship's foredeck by approaching it at an oblique angle. But an attempt to repeat the manoeuvre ended in tragedy when the aircraft ran off the end of the deck and crashed into the sea; the pilot was drowned.

In the winter of 1917, *Furious* underwent a further refit. Her rear gun turret was removed, allowing room for a 300ft-long landing platform aft of the funnel. The ship's bridge and funnel remained in their original positions amidships, however.

The Sopwith Camel scout was the landplane type chosen for the next series of deck landing trials aboard *Furious*. The plane was reasonably small and reasonably fast. It carried an armament of two .303in machine guns and, if required, up to 100lb of bombs. The Navy contracted the Beardmore company in Dumbartonshire to build the initial batches of the Camels modified for the shipborne operations, designated 2F.1 Camels. The 2F.1 did not have folding wings like a modern carrier plane. Instead, this variant had a joint just aft of the cockpit, so the front and rear halves of the fuselage could be detached and separated to ease stowage in the ship's hangar below decks. The rear fuselage of the naval version also housed an air bag, which was inflated before a ditching to keep the plane afloat until the pilot could be rescued.

Lieutenant William Dickson took part in the initial landing trials on the afterdeck of *Furious*, and he later described the arrangement of the arrester system:

> The deck was the design of the naval construction department at the Admiralty, and was a surprise to most of the pilots. It was provided with an arresting gear, consisting of longitudinal wire cables

stretched along the deck and anchored at each end. The wires were lifted nine inches off the deck by small wooden props. Lying across the wires were laid ropes at wide intervals, at the ends of which were attached sandbags. A hook was fitted under the aircraft fuselage, and as it passed down the deck it picked up the ropes and dragged along the sandbags.

The intention was that as the aircraft proceeded up the deck, its hook picked up progressively more ropes, which increased the drag until finally the plane came to a halt. However, in practice, that method proved unworkable, as William Dickson explained:

> Of a total of sixteen landings, thirteen ended in a bad crash and the write-off of the aircraft. In every case the pilot was unable to pull up before reaching the end of the wires, and in some cases the aircraft hit the vertical net [positioned to prevent aircraft running into the funnel] almost at flying speed. The cause of this failure was quite evident. The mass of the funnel and mast created severe air disturbances which, added to those made by the funnel gasses, gave a most unstable approach to the deck. To maintain adequate control a pilot had to bring his aircraft in faster than usual. Moreover, the effect of these obstructions immediately in front of the deck seriously reduced the airflow in the deck centre so that an aeroplane, after passing over the after edge [of the deck], had not the same air resistance to land against. By increasing the air speed the trouble was only aggravated. The only successful landings were made when the air speed was reduced to about 25 mph.

The trials established that it was not practical to land aircraft on *Furious*'s afterdeck as it was currently laid out. Nevertheless, if the planes were treated as expendable items, the carrier could launch an air striking force sufficiently strong to deliver an effective surprise attack on a high-value target in enemy territory. After delivering their attack the Camels would alight on the sea near friendly warships, which would rescue their pilots.

The target selected for the operation was the Zeppelin base at Tondern in Schleswig Holstein, a few miles south of the border with neutral Denmark and within 10 miles of the coast. The base had been a thorn in the side of the Royal Navy for much of the war. Airships launched from there had mounted bombing raids against England, and their scouting missions over the North Sea had thwarted several attempts to bring the German fleet into action.

To assist the Camel to alight on the water cleanly, the pilot could jettison the wheels beforehand by pulling on a wire to withdraw the axle pins. Although the recovery of the pilots would be a risky matter, in a conflict that had already claimed many millions of lives those risks were considered acceptable.

Training for the operation began in June 1918, with pilots practising low-altitude attacks on an area of water in the Firth of Forth with buoys laid out to resemble the supposed dimensions of the German airship hangars. To maintain the element of surprise there would be no pre-strike reconnaissance of Tondern. The attacking pilots were briefed that the Zeppelin base probably lay within 5 miles of the town of the same name, and it was expected that its huge airship

---

SOPWITH 2F.1 CAMEL

ROLE   Single-seat fighting scout, modified as general-purpose naval aircraft.

POWER   One Bentley B.R.1 air-cooled rotary engine developing 150 hp at take-off.

ARMAMENT   One .303in Vickers machine gun mounted above the engine and synchronized to fire through the airscrew disk; one .303in Lewis gun mounted above the upper wing. For the Tondern attack operation two 50lb light-case bombs were carried on racks fitted under the wings.

PERFORMANCE   Maximum speed 124mph at 6,500ft; maximum operational radius of action about 120 miles.

NORMAL OPERATIONAL TAKE-OFF WEIGHT   1,530lb.

DIMENSIONS   Span 26ft 11in; length 18ft 8in; wing area 221 sq ft.

DATE OF FIRST PRODUCTION 2F.1 CAMEL   1917.

sheds would be clearly visible when the force arrived in the area.

The Tondern attack operation, code-named 'F.7', began on the evening of 16 July when *Furious* and her escort of eight destroyers set sail from Rosyth. A battle squadron of heavier warships mounted a covering operation. Just before dawn on the 19th, *Furious* and her escorts arrived at the designated launch point some 10 miles off the coast of Denmark and about 80 miles north-north-west of the Zeppelin base. *Furious* turned into the wind and her seven Camels, each carrying two 50lb light-cased bombs, took off in rapid succession. One plane immediately developed engine trouble, so it alighted beside a destroyer and its pilot was rescued.

The remaining Camels formed up in two flights, each of three aircraft, and climbed to 9,000ft. Keeping well out to sea, they headed south following the line of the Danish coast. A layer of patchy cloud at 5,000ft helped to conceal the force from observers on the ground, but there were sufficient gaps to allow the pilots to fix their position at regular intervals from coastal features.

When they reached the small town of Hoyer, the attack force turned on to an easterly heading. At the briefing it had been agreed that, when they reached the target area, if the Zeppelin hangars were not immediately visible the pilots were to split up and search for them independently. William Dickson, who flew with the leading flight of Camels, later wrote:

> I dived on a long flat shed which I saw by itself to the east of the town. This was a low shed, very solidly built and looked semi-underground. It was about the same size as the large [airship] shed at East Fortune [in Scotland]. No chimneys or out buildings could be observed round it, so I decided to drop one bomb on it, which I did from a height of 700 feet hitting it in the middle. I observed no signs of fire as a result of this hit, but only clouds of smoke. Immediately after this I saw Captain Jackson at about 3,000 feet above me and a good distance to the east of the town, coming down in a dive, with Lieut. Williams about half a mile astern of him. I climbed a little and joined in with

them and then observed two very large sheds, larger by quite a considerable amount to the main shed at East Fortune Air Station, and also a smaller one. These were at least 5 miles to the north of the town and were standing quite apart from anything else on the flat ground.

On the ground there was no sign of life until Jackson began his attack dive, then a gun battery positioned near the sheds opened a ferocious but not particularly accurate fire at the planes. Dickson continued:

Capt. Jackson dived right on to the northernmost shed and dropped two bombs, one a direct hit in the middle and the other slightly to the side of the shed. I then dropped my one remaining bomb and Williams two more. Hits were observed. The shed then burst into flames and an enormous conflagration took place rising up to at least 1,000 feet and the whole of the shed being completely engulfed. After dropping, Jackson went straight on, Williams turned to the left and I to the right. Two or more batteries then opened fire on us while we were returning but their shooting was not good.

Meanwhile the second attack flight was also approaching Tondern. Captain Bernhard Smart, the flight leader, later reported:

I was unable to see the sheds for some minutes, but eventually 3 A.A. batteries close together attracted my attention, and near them I discovered the sheds, two large ones and one smaller, one of the larger having the roof partially destroyed and emitting large volumes of dense black smoke. When in position I gave the signal and dived on the remaining large shed, releasing my bombs at 800 to 1,000 feet. The first fell short but the second hit the centre of the shed, sending up a quantity of smoke or dust. Whether this burst into flames later I am unable to state, as the whole surroundings were thick with mechanics or soldiers armed with rifles and machine guns, which gave so disconcerting a fire that I dived with full engine to 50 feet and skimmed over the ground in a zigzag course to avoid it. By the time I had got clear was unable to see the sheds on account of thick screen of smoke from the first shed.

As the pilots sped away from their targets, low cloud and haze prevented them from rejoining formation. Only Dickson and Smart reached the planned rendezvous point with the warships off the coast and ditched their planes as briefed. Dickson was soon picked up but Smart's experience highlighted the dangers of this method of recovery.

After alighting, the Camel came to rest with its fuselage at an angle of about 45 degrees, with its nose pulled down by the weight of the engine and most of its buoyancy coming from the flotation bag in the rear fuselage. After clambering out of the cockpit Smart had to shin up the length of the rear fuselage and cling on to the tail-bracing wires while he awaited rescue. In a letter to his parents, he described what happened when the destroyer approached:

> She came alongside, by which time I was sitting on the tail with much difficulty owing to the rough sea. They threw a line, which I stretched to catch when a big wave caught me on the chest and into the [water] I went. I had had two belts on but the one which I blew up with a compressed air bottle had caught on the machine and [I] had taken it off – the other was of the type you blow up with your mouth. I regained the tail and held on by one wire at the same time trying to blow up the belt. I was too far gone for this though as [I] had swallowed buckets of seawater and simply hadn't the necessary wind! Could only hang on to the tail wire with both hands.
>
> The waves, which were from 10 to 15 feet, kept first lifting the machine bodily during which time my head and everything was totally under water, then as the wave subsided I was left hanging with my whole weight on the wire. By the time they had lowered a boat and got alongside I was completely done to the wide and don't think could have held on more than another minute or two. I hadn't the strength to make an effort to get into the boat but three sturdy ABs [able seamen] clutched hold of any suitable part of my clothes and hauled me inboard like a sack of flour.

Smart was taken to the destroyer captain's cabin. There his wet clothes were removed and he spent the rest of the day in a cot under a pile of blankets. He emerged none the worst for his ordeal.

For his part in the action, Dickson was awarded the Distinguished Service Order. Smart received a bar to the DSO he had won earlier. Of the remaining Camels, three had force-landed in Denmark after running short of fuel. Their pilots were interned briefly in the neutral country, then they were repatriated and all were back in Britain before the end of the month. Only one pilot was lost, Lieutenant W. Yeulett, who was seen to deliver his attack with the second flight but was not seen again.

The airship hangar attacked by the leading flight, Jackson, Dickson and Williams, contained the Zeppelins *L.54* and *L.60*. Both airships caught fire and burned out. However, the airships had burned relatively slowly and there was no explosion. Consequently, apart from the bomb entry holes, the hangar itself escaped serious damage and could easily be repaired. The same went for the smaller hangar, which the second flight of Camels had attacked. Apart from a small captive balloon, that hangar had been empty at the time.

Tondern's two airship hangars survived the bombing, but that would not matter in the long run. The attack had pointed out in the starkest terms the vulnerability of the base. Thereafter Tondern was little used for the remainder of the war, and Zeppelins used it only as an emergency landing ground.

THE ATTACK ON Tondern is noteworthy for two reasons. First, it was the first successful attack by carrier-based aircraft on a major land target. Second, as mentioned at the preamble to this chapter, it was one of the very few instances in the First World War where airdropped bombs inflicted major damage to a military target. As aircraft weapons go, the 50lb bombs used in the attack were puny, yet they proved effective enough when employed against a large inflammable target like an airship on the ground.

THE POST-WAR years brought further significant innovations to carrier design. In her next incarnation, in 1925, HMS *Furious* appeared with a 576ft-long and 107ft-wide flush deck running for most of her length, with the bridge and funnel moved to one side and below the flight deck. That produced a smooth airflow over the deck, and when the ship ran at speed planes could land on without assistance from an external arresting system. The over-complex arresting system used earlier was removed.

Having a workable method for taking off and landing on the deck of a carrier did not mark the end of the development process, however. Lacking an arrester system, each plane needed the entire length of the deck to land. In addition, the next plane could not land until the one in front had been manhandled on to the lift, taken below and the lift had returned to the deck. Thus the recovery of a dozen-plane strike force might take over half an hour. That meant each plane had to return to the ship with a sizeable reserve of fuel, which caused a corresponding reduction in the effective combat radius of the ship's air striking force. Throughout the landing-on operation the carrier needed to head into the wind at close to her maximum speed. That burned a lot of fuel, caused wear and tear to the ship's engines and – potentially significant in any combat situation – it forced the carrier and her escorts to head in a direction that might have taken them into danger. Indeed, at the beginning of the land-on it was necessary to have at least 20 miles of clear sea room upwind of the ship between it and any obstruction – such as the county of Cornwall.

Meanwhile the US Navy had developed two systems that would have a profound effect on carrier air operations. The first was the now-familiar system of arrester wires stretched athwartships across the deck, with a hydraulic braking system to bring the plane smoothly to a halt after its hook picked up a wire. With this system, unless there was little wind, there was no need for a carrier to run at high speed to recover her planes. The second major innovation was the introduction of the crash barrier positioned midway along the deck, which was raised before each plane landed and lowered to allow the plane to taxi over it. Both systems were retrofitted to Royal Navy carriers during the 1930s.

Used together, the arrester wires and the crash barrier greatly shortened the time taken for a force of planes to recover to their carrier. They also brought about a marked reduction in deck-landing accidents. With the arrester wires that brought planes to a halt in a relatively short distance, they no longer needed to use the entire length of the deck to land. The crash barrier effectively divided the ship's deck into two, with the landing area to the rear and the parking area in front. As each plane landed and an arrester wire brought it to a halt, a sailor released the hook and locked it in the up position. The crash barrier was lowered to allow the plane to taxi over it, then it was raised in readiness to catch the next plane should it fail to pick up a wire.

A further move that helped reduce deck-landing accidents was the introduction of the Deck Landing Control Officer, or 'Batsman'. Standing on the port side of the flight deck, he used standardized arm signals to guide the pilot during the landing approach to help bring him down safely on to the deck.

With the many vicissitudes, it took a couple of decades for aircraft carrier development finally to reach the point where these craft were able to serve as floating bases for sustained and effective air operations. By the mid-1930s the carrier was ready to wrest from the battleship the mantle of ultimate arbiter of sea power, though at the time few naval experts believed it. It would take a few more years, and some hard-fought air-sea battles, to establish that view beyond possible doubt.

CHAPTER FOUR

Thirteen Days in August

The Battle of Britain in the summer of 1940 was the largest and most intensive

air campaign fought up to that time. During the battle some squadrons settled

into the fighting gradually and were successful in action. In contrast, a few

units suffered severe losses in their first hard-fought actions and had to be with-

drawn to re-form. One of the latter was No 266 Squadron, a Spitfire unit.

DURING THE INITIAL stages of the battle No 266 Squadron was part of No 12 Group in the Midlands, where it saw little action. That period of quiet for the unit came to an abrupt end early on the morning of 9 August, when it received orders to move south to Northolt for a short detachment. Led by its commander, Squadron Leader Rodney Wilkinson, the twelve Spitfires took off from their base at Wittering soon after dawn. The weather was poor, however, with banks of low cloud concealing the ground. Unable to find Northolt, the squadron headed north until it came to a break in the overcast. The fighters put down at the first airfield they came to, which was at Hatfield.

Flight Lieutenant Dennis Armitage, one of the flight commanders, now takes up the story:

> Someone had thought of the brilliant idea of stringing quantities of barbed wire up and down the aerodrome. At that time Hatfield was

used for ground training only, except for occasional test-flights by de Havilland's. The idea of the barbed wire was that it would upset any airborne divisions which might arrive from Germany. But in practice it was amazingly ineffective. Even with Spitfires, a machine which was notoriously nose-heavy on the ground, only one of the first section to land up-ended. Even that, I think, was due to a feeling that there was something peculiar about those yards of barbed wire trailing behind which caused the pilot to make a too sudden application of the brakes. After that and a few belated red Very lights, hundreds of small boys appeared – cadets who were doing their ground training and had been hurriedly kicked out of bed. They stood in two great lines to mark out a 'secret' landing run which had been left clear for de Havilland's, and the rest of us plonked down one at a time without further incident.

It was still only 6.30 am but someone rustled up some breakfast for us and over this we had a good healthy argument, which our C.O. won in the end, about whether anyone had thought of sending out warning signals about the barbed wire. By 8 o'clock, the clouds had cleared and we flew on to Northolt, re-fuelled and settled down to wait. We were told we should return home at 3 pm; at 3 we were told to wait till 5; at 5 to wait till 6; and at 6 o'clock we were told to take off for Tangmere.

Less the Spitfire that had stood on its nose at Hatfield, the remaining 11 fighters reached Tangmere without further incident.

The squadron remained at Tangmere for the next two days, during which its ground personnel arrived from Wittering. No sooner had the unit collected itself together than it received orders to prepare to move to Eastchurch on the 12th. Dennis Armitage continued:

The C.O., the Senior Flight Commander and myself were summoned to a most secret meeting. We were informed that we had been given special duties escorting Battles [bombers] across the Channel to bomb concentrations of 'E-boats' [fast patrol boats] which were now assembling along the French and Dutch coasts. It sounded horrid for the lads in the slow and aged Battles although not so bad for us. We

were to operate from Eastchurch, on the Isle of Sheppey in the
Thames Estuary, which would be ready for us the next day.

In the meantime, in view of the greatly increased activity around
Portsmouth, we might be called on to patrol the aerodrome if necessary. But under no circumstances were we to engage the enemy if we
could possibly avoid it – they wanted to be sure there would be a full
squadron to go to Eastchurch next day.

Those orders not to engage the enemy were smartly superseded a
couple of hours later, when a large force of Junkers 88s of *Kampfgeschwader 51* attacked Portsmouth at midday. No 266 Squadron
scrambled all its Spitfires and in the action that followed it claimed 4
enemy aircraft destroyed, 2 probably destroyed and 9 damaged. The
unit lost 2 Spitfires and 1 pilot killed. After refuelling at Tangmere after
the action the squadron, now down to 10 Spitfires, took off for
Eastchurch as planned.

We arrived at Eastchurch to find two squadrons of Battles and
another half squadron of Spitfires [No 19] had arrived earlier that
day, and after dinner Flight Commanders and above were summoned
to a conference of war in the Group Captain's office. We were told
the general scheme and apparently only two things were lacking.
One was a special information service, which was going to tell us
where to find the fruitiest targets, and the other snag was that [the
Battles] had not got any bombs. However, the G/C had reason to hope
that both these things would be added unto us by after lunch the
next day and in the meantime he suggested we might all have a really
good night's rest – breakfast at 9.30 a.m. and another conference
about 10 o'clock. It was actually 7.05 hours when the first bomb
arrived. Not ours!

The attack on Eastchurch was carried out by Dornier 17s of *Kampfgeschwader 2* and caused severe damage to the airfield buildings. No
266 Squadron lost 1 airman killed, and 1 officer and 5 airmen injured.
One of its Spitfires suffered damage.

We held a brief council of war and decided to station six Spitfire pilots permanently in their machines. Until the raid we had every reason to expect we should get warning of the approach of the Luftwaffe – why we did not we never discovered. But there was no radio station at Eastchurch and our own R/T sets were, of course, no use until we were airborne, so with the telephone wires down communications were sticky.

Fortunately the [other Spitfires] were practically undamaged, but unfortunately all of our spare ammunition boxes had gone up with our hanger where they were stored – fully loaded, incidentally, which had all helped to make the fire interesting.

Nobody was sorry when the operation to attack the E-boats was quietly abandoned and on the following day, 14 August, the squadron moved to Hornchurch.

One of the hardest-fought days of the Battle of Britain was 15 August and No 266 Squadron was heavily engaged. Late that afternoon the unit went into action and claimed 3 enemy aircraft destroyed and 1 damaged. However, it lost 2 pilots killed. Dennis Armitage's Spitfire was damaged and he suffered leg injuries:

There had been the usual shemozzle which had eventually sorted itself out into one or two Spits, and three or four 109s buzzing round

---

SUPERMARINE SPITFIRE I

ROLE Single-seat fighter.

POWER One Rolls Royce Merlin III, 12-cylinder, liquid-cooled engine developing 1,030hp at 16,250ft.

ARMAMENT Eight .303in Browning machine guns.

PERFORMANCE Maximum speed 353mph at 20,000ft; climb to 20,000ft, 7min 42sec.

NORMAL OPERATIONAL TAKE-OFF WEIGHT 6,050lb.

DIMENSIONS Span 36ft 10in; length 29ft 11in; wing area 242 sq ft.

DATE OF FIRST PRODUCTION SPITFIRE I May 1938.

in tight circles. I had just had the pleasure of seeing the three that I had been closeted with, diving down towards the sea with one of them smoking nicely. Another 'possible', perhaps even a 'probable', but not a 'confirmed' because I was not silly enough to follow him down in case there was another waiting for me up in the sun – and there was. I have no idea how he slipped under my tail, but suddenly I heard a loud bang, something hit me in the leg, and there was a fearful noise of rushing air. Under these circumstances one's reactions are automatic, even though one has no idea what the Dickens has happened. I whipped into a vertical turn, looking fearfully up towards the blazing sun and then, as confidence returned, I spotted what was probably the cause of the trouble diving away, already some 5,000 ft below. I realised that the noise was simply due to my perspex hood having been blown out and, that apart, my machine seemed quite manageable. My left leg was quite numb from the calf down; I put my hand down gingerly to feel if my foot was still there and, reassured on this point, I headed for home.

On landing I found a cannon shell had exploded inside the fuselage, the spent head of the shell having found its way under the armour plating behind the seat and struck me on the leg. One of the elevator control wires was hanging on by a single thread and another cannon shell had just caught my port wing tip.

The next day, 16 August, brought disaster to the squadron. The action soon after noon began well enough, when the unit's seven Spitfires bounced five Messerschmitt 109s of *Jagdgeschwader 26* on their way home after a bomber escort mission. The *Gruppe* leader, *Hauptmann* Karl Ebbighausen, was shot down and a dogfight developed. Suddenly other German fighters joined the fray and these turned the tables on No 266 Squadron. Its commander, Squadron Leader Rodney Wilkinson, was shot down and killed; so were two other pilots. Flight Lieutenant Sydney Bazley, the senior flight commander, baled out and was rushed to hospital with severe burns. Another pilot suffered minor wounds and his Spitfire was wrecked when he made a forced landing. A further fighter returned with damage that was repairable. Only one of the squadron's Spitfires returned from the action undamaged.

In the course of just two days of bitter fighting the unit had lost its commander, both flight commanders and five other pilots either killed or injured. Of its original complement of 19 pilots, it was now reduced to 11. Seven of the unit's Spitfires had been destroyed and 2 damaged.

Despite the injuries to his leg Dennis Armitage, as the senior surviving officer on the squadron, now took charge. In a grim mood he and his engineering warrant officer surveyed the damaged Spitfires in the hangar, including the one in which he had been injured.

One of the E.O.'s [engineering officer's] pet rules was the one about non-cannibalisation of aircraft. Many a time we had waited and waited with three or four unserviceable machines in the hangar, when all but one could have been put into the air by pinching the necessary parts from the remaining machine. But now things were different; we went to any lengths to get a machine flying again, patching and making-do in a thousand ways. And our straight-backed E.O. did not hesitate to cast aside his life-long principles, though I think it still hurt him to do so. And incidentally, for a whole month, he himself worked from dusk till dawn without a break and most of the daylight hours as well.

The jagged hole in the fuselage was nearly a foot in diameter. The E.O. shook his head and with one accord our eyes strayed towards another machine in the hangar with a badly damaged starboard wing. I nodded and he nodded – no words passed but I knew that the starboard wing, the only undamaged part of my airframe, would be transferred by dawn.

On the evening of 17 August, No 266 Squadron took delivery of seven replacement Spitfires to make up those lost. There were no replacement pilots, however, leaving the unit well under strength.

Despite his injured leg, Dennis Armitage had to lead the squadron in the air as well as on the ground. He continued:

> My leg was very stiff and I had to hobble about with the aid of a stick and be helped into my Spit, but once there I was all right. Fortunately there is no place other than bed where full use of the legs is so unimportant as in an aeroplane.

The restoration of No 266 Squadron's full complement of aircraft brought only temporary relief, for on the next day the unit was again hit hard.

On the afternoon of 18 August the squadron was involved in a skirmish with Messerschmitt 109s near the coast and claimed one enemy aircraft destroyed, one probably destroyed and one damaged. Afterwards Dennis Armitage took his 11 Spitfires to Manston to refuel and rearm. No sooner had the last of the aircraft landed, however, than the airfield was strafed by 16 Bf 109s of *Jagdgeschwader 52*. Armitage watched as Sergeant Don Kingaby had a narrow escape:

> He was the last but one to land and seeing the German fighters diving on him began to run for cover, but tripped and fell. Then for a few breathless seconds he rolled along the ground with the bullets kicking up the earth not a foot away as the German tried to swing his aircraft to get his sights on.

A bullet nicked one of Kingaby's fingers and another of the pilots suffered shock, but those were the only injuries suffered. The squadron's Spitfires were less fortunate. Two were set on fire and burned out, 6 others suffered damage. Of the 11 aircraft that had taken off from Hornchurch that morning, only 3 returned in the afternoon.

On 19 August, the weather broke and for the next few days there were no large-scale air operations over southern England. On the 21st, having seen no further action, No 266 Squadron received orders to return to Wittering to re-form. It saw little further action during the remainder of the Battle of Britain.

During its time in the south of England the No 266 Squadron was in action on only four days. Its pilots claimed 9 enemy aircraft destroyed, 6 probably destroyed and 11 damaged. During these actions, however, the unit lost 6 pilots killed (including its commander) and 5 wounded (including both flight commanders), out of the 19 pilots on strength at the beginning of the period. Twelve of its Spitfires had been destroyed and 8 damaged. For No 266 Squadron it had been a very unlucky thirteen days in August.

CHAPTER FIVE

One Way to Down a Dornier

Some will argue that wars should be fought by brave men using guns or missiles. There are other ways to bring down an enemy aircraft, however, and electronic trickery is as valid as any of them.

ON THE EVENING of 11 October 1941 *Oberleutnant* Guenther Dolenga of *Kampfgeschwader 2* lifted his Dornier Do 217 bomber off the runway at Évreux in northern France. The four-man crew had been briefed to conduct an armed reconnaissance of the sea area to the west of the Scilly Isles and in the Irish Sea, and attack any shipping they found.

The Dornier 217, the newest bomber then in service with the *Luft-waffe*, had entered service just a few months earlier. Powered by two big BMW 801 engines it was fast, manoeuvrable, and able to carry a bomb load of more than 8,000lb. This latest acquisition by the *Luftwaffe* was a formidable machine.

Dolenga and his crew found no ships and the armed reconnaissance went off without incident. Shortly after 0200 hours the following morning, the crew set course for base. Unknown to the airmen, however, that night the wind from the south-east had been rather stronger than forecast. As a result, the north coast of France did not appear at the expected time. Assuming he was over the English Channel, at 0230 hours Dolenga turned north to allow his observer to get a fix off a point on the south coast of England. About half an hour later a line of breakers obligingly appeared. The crew tried to link the features they saw on the coast with those marked on their maps, but in the darkness and the patchy cloud cover it was a fruitless exercise. There could be no doubting the existence of that coastline, however, so Dolenga turned south-east and headed the aircraft for the north coast of France. Or so he thought.

Dolenga and his crew had fallen foul of a geographical feature that had caught out, and would continue to catch, many an airman during the conflict. They had mistaken the entrance to the Bristol Channel for the entrance to the English Channel. The coastline they had followed, which had defied identification, was not the south coast of Cornwall but the south coast of Pembrokeshire. Both are rocky coastlines with few man-made features that give an unambiguous fix.

About 20 minutes later the Dornier reached the north coast of Cornwall, which the crew promptly and reasonably assumed to be the north coast of Brittany. In navigational terms, the error was relatively small and it was unlikely to confuse an experienced airman for long. The observer tuned the plane's radio compass to the radio beacon at Paimpol in Brittany. Its Morse identification letters came though loud and clear and the direction-finder needle gave a firm bearing. In normal circumstances the discrepancy between the radio bearing received, and the one expected, would have indicated to the crew that they were some distance away from where they had thought. But on this occasion, the circumstances were anything but normal.

AT THIS TIME NO 80 Wing of the Royal Air Force was engaged in a long-running campaign to jam and spoof the radio navigational systems used by the *Luftwaffe*. No 80 Wing is best known for its attack on the *Knickebein*, *X-Geraet* and *Y-Geraet* beam systems used to guide German bombers to their targets during the night Blitz of 1940 and 1941. Against these devices, the unit employed high-powered jamming transmitters to blot out the beam signals. That had been the 'brute force' approach.

Throughout the area under German control, the *Luftwaffe* signals service had erected a large number of radio beacons, which operated in the medium frequency band. These beacons radiated a two-letter Morse identifier that changed from day to day, followed by a 50-second continuous tone to allow an aircraft's radio direction finder to determine the bearing of the beacon. It was a useful aid to navigation, and particularly valuable in the skies over Europe where cloud often obscured ground features.

To defeat the German radio beacons it was not necessary to jam every one. A far better strategy was to make the beacons so unreliable that German aircrews would be reluctant to use them. No 80 Wing's weapon of choice against the medium frequency beacons was the Meacon, or masking beacon. The device comprised a receiver and a transmitter located some distance apart. The receiver was linked to a directional aerial aligned on the German beacon it was to counter. The receiver picked up the German beacon's emissions, amplified them and fed them by landline to the Meacon transmitter. The Meacon transmitter radiated an exact replica of the German beacon signal, with its Morse identification letters and 50-second tone, *exactly in step with the German signals*. But the Meacon transmitter was, of course, in a quite different position.

Operating in this way, the Meacon produced some interesting effects. If the German aircraft was nearer to the German beacon than the Meacon, the plane's direction-finder needle showed a bearing on the real beacon. If the plane was equidistant between the German beacon and the Meacon, the bearing needle might waver between the two as it hunted for the stronger signal. But if the aircraft was nearer to the Meacon than to the beacon, the plane's direction finder would give a beautifully steady, but quite misleading, bearing on the Meacon transmitter. *And the crew of a German aircraft had no way of knowing that this was the case.*

ON THIS NIGHT, when the Dornier's observer tuned in his direction finder to the beacon at Paimpol, the latter was being mimicked by the

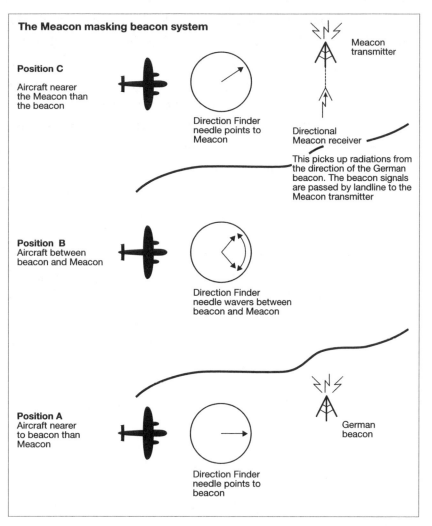

The Meacon masking beacon system

Meacon
transmitter

Position C

Aircraft nearer
the Meacon than
the beacon

Direction Finder
needle points to
Meacon

Directional
Meacon receiver

This picks up radiations from
the direction of the German
beacon. The beacon signals
are passed by landline to the
Meacon transmitter

Position B
Aircraft between
beacon and Meacon

Direction Finder
needle wavers between
beacon and Meacon

Position A
Aircraft nearer
to beacon than
Meacon

German
beacon

Direction Finder
needle points to
beacon

Meacon at Templecombe near Yeovil. Ignorant of what was afoot, the
Dornier crew headed east following the bearing given. They did not
know their exact position, but as they headed east they were confident
that sooner or latter they would pass an identifiable ground feature.
But that never happened

Shortly after 0400 hours, the Dornier arrived over what its crew
assumed to be the beacon at Paimpol. The direction-finder needle
swung round to indicate that the aircraft was directly over the transmitter, yet that did nothing to resolve matters. Paimpol lies on the

coast, but as Dolenga circled the source of the radio signals the expected coastline was nowhere to be seen. (Templecombe in Somerset, the site of the Meacon, is inland.) Obviously something was wrong, so the observer retuned the radio compass to the beacon at the Dornier's base at Évreux. That should solve the problem, he thought.

On that night, however, the No 80 Wing Meacon near Newbury covered the Évreux beacon. As the Dornier flew between the British and the German transmitters, the needle of the direction finder wavered. It seemed the device had gone unserviceable, so Dolenga decided to ignore it. He held a heading of zero-eight-zero degrees, which should have taken the bomber from Paimpol to Évreux. Instead, he unwittingly flew from Templecombe almost to Rochester in Kent.

By 0445 hours dawn was breaking. And, some distance ahead and to port, the German crew made out yet another coastline. It looked plausibly like the north coast of France (actually, it was the Thames Estuary). With the Dornier starting to run short of fuel, Dolenga turned south-east on a heading which he thought would take him to Évreux.

Imagine, then, the consternation in the bomber's cabin about ten

---

DORNIER Do 217E

ROLE Four-seat medium bomber and reconnaissance aircraft.

POWER Two BMW 801, air-cooled, radial engines each developing 1,580hp at take-off.

ARMAMENT Maximum bomb load 8,800lb. One MG 151 15mm machine gun firing forward from a flexible mounting in the nose, one MG 131 13mm machine gun fitted in the dorsal turret and one MG 131 firing rearwards from the ventral gun position.

PERFORMANCE (Without bombs) maximum speed 320mph at 17,000ft; normal cruising speed 258mph at 17,000ft.

NORMAL OPERATIONAL TAKE-OFF WEIGHT 33,070lb.

DIMENSIONS Span: 62ft 4in; length 59ft 8in; wing area 613 sq ft.

DATE OF FIRST PRODUCTION DO 217 Summer 1941.

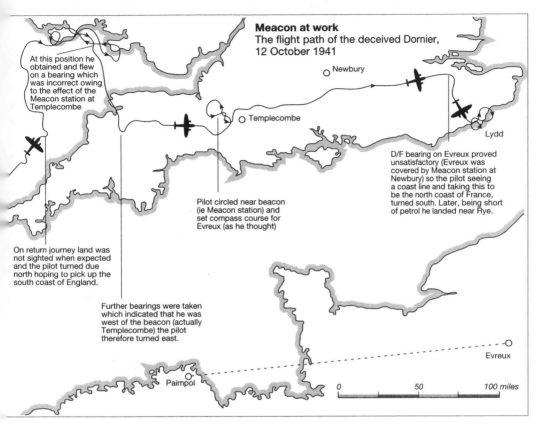

Meacon at work
The flight path of the deceived Dornier,
12 October 1941

At this position he obtained and flew on a bearing which was incorrect owing to the effect of the Meacon station at Templecombe

o Newbury

o Templecombe

Lydd

D/F bearing on Evreux proved unsatisfactory (Evreux was covered by Meacon station at Newbury) so the pilot seeing a coast line and taking this to be the north coast of France, turned south. Later, being short of petrol he landed near Rye.

Pilot circled near beacon (ie Meacon station) and set compass course for Evreux (as he thought)

On return journey land was not sighted when expected and the pilot turned due north hoping to pick up the south coast of England.

Further bearings were taken which indicated that he was west of the beacon (actually Templecombe) the pilot therefore turned east.

Evreux

o Paimpol

0   50   100 miles

minutes later, when yet another coastline appeared in front of the aircraft! Every part of the plane's navigational equipment was now suspect. Almost out of fuel and with no airfield in sight, Dolenga had little alternative but to set down the bomber on a strip of open ground. It came to rest on Romney Marsh near Rye. The once-proud bomber was a sorry sight with her back broken, the blades of both propellers snapped off and one wing under water.

Thinking they were in friendly territory, the crew scrambled out of their wrecked Dornier. Then they saw troops advancing on them, and were amazed to see they wore khaki uniforms. During their next four years, in prisoner-of-war camps, the men would have plenty of time to ruminate on what had gone wrong on that cold October night. For No 80 Wing, the snaring of this example of the newest bomber type in the *Luftwaffe* was another success to be chalked up by that highly secret unit.

CHAPTER SIX

Spitfires to Malta

Lying at the centre of the Mediterranean, Malta possessed huge strategic

importance during the early years of the Second World War. British bombers,

torpedo-bombers and submarines based on the island took a steady toll of ships

carrying supplies and reinforcements for the Axis armies fighting in North

Africa. By the beginning of 1942 these depredations had reached the point

where the Axis powers could no longer shrug them off. Detailed planning began

for an invasion of the island. First, however, it would be necessary to seize control

of the skies over it. To that end, the Luftwaffe *assembled more than 400 combat*

aircraft in Sicily. As the German air attacks became progressively more ferocious,

the defenders' air situation quickly reached a critical stage.

MALTA'S CONTINUED survival would depend to a large extent on the effectiveness of its fighter defences. But as each fighter plane was lost it required considerable effort to replace it. The island lay 1,380 miles from Gibraltar, well beyond the ferry range of any existing British single-engined fighter type. Moreover, the strength of the enemy air forces in Sicily ruled out the delivery of fighters to Malta by freighter: any attempt to do so would result in a full-scale battle, with heavy losses and little prospect of success.

Almost all the Hurricanes sent to the island were transported by aircraft carrier to a launch point off the coast of Algeria, where they took off to fly the rest of the way. The distance flown, 660 miles by the shortest practical route, was about as far as that from London to Prague. For these delivery operations the planes carried a 44-gallon fuel tank mounted under each wing. Each such delivery of fighters required a major operation by the British Mediterranean fleet, involving one or more aircraft carriers with a large force of escorting warships. Several such operations were mounted and by the end of 1941 more than 300 Hurricanes had reached the island in this way.

The new Messerschmitt Bf 109F fighter, recently introduced in the air battle over Malta, completely outclassed the Hurricanes defending the island and losses of the latter increased alarmingly. At that time the RAF had only one fighter type in service that could engage the Bf 109F on equal terms: the Mark V Spitfire. It was decided to send a squadron of these fighters to Malta, to be delivered in the same way as the Hurricanes. To enable Spitfires to cover the distance from the fly-off point to the island, the Supermarine Company developed a new jettisonable fuel tank to fit under the fuselage of the fighter. It would be the first time the Spitfire had carried this modification.

Early in 1942 the process of delivering the first contingent of Spitfires to Malta, code-named Operation Spotter, began. The freighter *Cape Hawk* set sail from Liverpool on 9 February as part of an escorted convoy carrying 16 crated Spitfires, a similar number of pilots and about 100 ground crew. Except for Wing Commander Maclean, the detachment commander, and his senior engineering officer, the members of the Royal Air Force contingent on the ship were ignorant of the intended eventual destination. Their only clue was the issue of tropical kit, which made it clear they were bound for somewhere warm.

Cape Hawk arrived at Gibraltar on 21 February and entered the inner harbour, where she tied up beside the aircraft carrier HMS *Eagle*. By the following day all 16 crates had been offloaded and were lined up on the quay beside the ship. There the boxes remained, however. Secrecy was all-important, and it was known that German agents with high-powered telescopes kept watch on the naval base from the Spanish town of Algeciras on the other side of the bay. Also, several hundred Spanish workmen came to Gibraltar each day, returning each evening before nightfall. It was believed these workers would receive money from the Germans if they reported anything of interest they had seen.

To keep the Spitfires' arrival secret, the crates were not opened until after dark on the 22nd. Corporal Ray Honeybone, an engine fitter, described the start of the operation:

> As the end was unbolted from the first of the large cases, a Spitfire fuselage was revealed. The fuselage with the engine in position lay in the centre, with the wings mounted on the side walls. The propeller was mounted on one side wall. The drill was to drag the fuselage out on its cradle, transfer it to a set of belly jacks, manoeuvre out each wing in turn, fit the main and rear spar bolts, then drop and lock down the undercarriage units. This gave us a mobile structure, to which the propeller was fitted prior to lifting the aircraft on board the carrier ...

Leading Aircraftman George Revell takes up the story, and explains how the need for secrecy dominated every part of the loading operation:

> This activity was taking place at night, but with a generous amount of lighting as Gib wasn't blacked out unless an 'alert' was sounded. However, to reduce the chances of our 'friends' across the bay seeing too much, the lighting on the flight deck was kept to a minimum particularly when the loads reached flight deck level.

In addition, as each Spitfire came on board, a party of sailors at one end of the flight deck would start the engine of one of *Eagle*'s Sea Hurricanes to serve as a diversion. Once on deck, the Spitfire was wheeled across the flight deck to the lift and taken below.

The work went on throughout the hours of darkness, until with the approach of dawn the crates on the quay were restored to make it appear that nothing had happened. The last four Spitfires were hoisted on to *Eagle*'s flight deck during the small hours of the 25th. Now the work of reassembling the fighters went ahead at top speed. The 'erks' were divided into eight gangs, each comprising a corporal and three men, and each gang was allocated two Spitfires. Although these were brand new Spitfires, some of them had parts that needed replacing. There were no spares so Squadron Leader 'Shorty' Hughes, the senior engineering officer, had reluctantly to decree that one fighter was to be cannibalized to provide the necessary spares.

Ray Honeybone described the work of reassembling the Spitfires and getting them ready for flight:

> There were coolant joints to make, hydraulic and air systems to complete, controls to connect and adjust, all the myriad jobs which on a squadron you did occasionally, one at a time as rectification, we now did all at once and in record time.

The 90-gallon drop tank that fitted under the fighter's fuselage was new to everyone, and it gave considerable trouble. The tank had to be securely fixed to the fuselage and a mushroom valve had to make perfect contact, otherwise the feed pipe would not suck fuel up into the carburettor. As the reassembly of each aircraft was completed, it was brought on deck after dark for the engine to be run. Ray Honeybone continued:

> A cock provided selection from Main Fuel to Auxiliary Fuel and it seemed logical to expect that the fluid would flow. But almost as soon as the cock was turned, a small red light indicated lack of fuel pressure. And try as we may, it was a hit and miss affair to arrange the tank and valve position to work with much measure of success.

HMS *Eagle* set out from Gibraltar with her precious cargo during the early morning darkness of 27 February, escorted by a battle group consisting of the aircraft carrier *Argus*, a battleship, a cruiser and nine destroyers. That first attempt to deliver Spitfires to Malta ended in dismal failure. Flight Lieutenant Stanley Grant, who was to lead the fighters to the island, explained why:

The next day when we were well clear of land Hughes brought the aircraft up on deck to run the engines and, above all, to test the functioning of the long-range tanks without which the operation was not on. These first 90-gallon tanks had evidently been produced in a great hurry and were 'a bit of a lash up'. The fuel was drawn up into the main tanks by suction and if there was the slightest air leak in the seal between the tank and the fuselage, there was no transfer.

Hughes soon found that the seals were not satisfactory and although he and his team strove hard all that day and well into the night he could not make them work properly. Accordingly, around midnight, with our take-off due the next morning, Hughes sent a message to the Admiral via Wing Commander Maclean, saying that the aircraft could not be allowed to take off without further extensive tests. And since his men had now been working for over twenty hours without rest they could not continue without some sleep. We heard later that the Admiral nearly exploded, and sent back the message that under no circumstances could his ships hang around in daylight in the middle of the Mediterranean, within easy reach of enemy bombers. The Spitfires had to take off the next morning – at all costs. But Hughes was adamant. The aircraft were not, in his view, serviceable and he could not agree to their take-off until he was certain that the tanks would work. So the Admiral had to give in, and the whole fleet turned around and steamed back to Gibraltar.

Once back at Gibraltar, there was hectic activity to get the Spitfires' new drop tanks to work properly. Ray Honeybone takes up the story:

Our worst enemy was the suction valve in the belly tanks ... In the end a man from Supermarine was flown to Gibraltar to help us get them to work. When I met him I put up a bit of a black. I said the man who designed that system ought to jump off Beachy Head! He said 'Don't say that, Corporal, I designed it ...'

As soon as he saw the drop tanks fitted to the Spitfires, the Supermarine engineer saw why so many had failed to work properly. In the rush and the secrecy of the project, nobody had told the RAF technicians the importance of the small bulbous protrusion at the bottom of each tank that acted as a sump. The fuel transfer pipe reached almost to the bottom of the sump, and if the latter was dented it blocked the end of the pipe and prevented the transfer of fuel.

In the course of crating, uncrating and fitting the tanks to the aircraft, by people unfamiliar with the system, several of the tanks had suffered dented sumps. The remedy was to cut away the dented area and solder a patch over the cut-away area. That cured the problem, and there was a maximum effort to repair the damaged tanks and prove they would transfer fuel satisfactorily.

Early on the morning of 5 March HMS *Eagle* and her covering force again put to sea. Once the ships were clear of land, the Spitfires were brought out on deck. Their engines were started and each of the drop tanks was carefully checked to see that it transferred fuel. They all functioned properly. Each fighter was then pointed in a safe direction so the armourers could fire short bursts to test the guns.

There were to be no test flights of the planes after their reassembly – the flight to Malta would constitute the test flight. If any part of the work had been done incorrectly, a pilot might pay for the error with his

---

SUPERMARINE SPITFIRE V

ROLE   Single-seat interceptor and air superiority fighter.

POWER   One Rolls-Royce Merlin 45 series 12-cylinder, liquid-cooled engine developing 1,470 hp at 9,250ft.

ARMAMENT   (Mark VB) two Hispano 20mm cannon, four .303in Browning machine guns; (Mark VC) two Hispano 20mm cannon, four .303in Browning machine guns, or four Hispano cannon.

PERFORMANCE   Maximum speed 371mph at 20,000ft; climb to 20,000ft, 6min 24sec.

NORMAL OPERATIONAL TAKE-OFF WEIGHT   6,525lb.

DIMENSIONS   Span 36ft 10in; length 29ft 11in; wing area 242 sq ft.

DATE OF FIRST PRODUCTION SPITFIRE V   Summer 1941.

life. Moreover, since the reassembly of the Spitfires had taken place aboard the aircraft carrier, the planes' compasses could not be 'swung' to measure their errors. The compasses might give readings several degrees out and were not be trusted, especially during the long overseas flight the fighters were about to undertake. Because of this, a twin-engined Blenheim bomber was to rendezvous with the carrier at the launch point off the coast of Algeria, and lead the formation of Spitfires to Malta.

Soon after dawn on the morning of 7 March HMS *Eagle* reached the launching position. Sergeant Jack Yarra, of the pilots, described the take-off in his diary:

> When the time came – 7 am on the second day out – everyone was keyed up and expectant and most of us were wondering if the Spitfires would really get off the deck quite OK ... All the aircraft were lined up waiting and everyone was in their cockpits a full half hour before the first Blenheim, which was to lead them there, arrived. The Blenheim was sighted and the ship turned into wind. The first motor started and was run up. Suddenly the naval controller gave 'Chocks Away' and [Flt Lt] Grant opened his throttle and went roaring down the deck. He lifted off the end, sank slightly below the level of the deck, and sailed away, gaining altitude and proving that a Spitfire can take off from an aircraft carrier.

The remaining Spitfires took off in turn, climbed to formate on the Blenheim, then headed east for Malta.

The exaggerated security precautions taken earlier paid off, and German fighters made no attempt to interfere with the operation. All 11 Spitfires reached Malta safely. After landing at Takali the new fighters were assigned to No 249 Squadron and Stanley Grant was appointed commander and promoted to Squadron Leader. He took his Spitfires into action for the first time over the island on 10 March and they claimed 1 enemy aircraft destroyed, 2 probably destroyed and 1 damaged. In return, one Spitfire was destroyed and another suffered damage. On that day and those to follow the Spitfires provided top cover for the slower Hurricanes, allowing the latter to engage the enemy bombers with less risk of being 'bounced' by Messerschmitts.

The bombardment of the island continued without pause, however, and the small force of Spitfires could do little to prevent it. Their number dwindled rapidly as aircraft were destroyed or damaged in the air or on the ground. By 21 March only two Spitfires remained in a state suitable for combat. On that day a further fly-off from HMS *Eagle* yielded nine more Spitfires, a useful reinforcement but insufficient to replace losses.

The ferocious air battles continued unabated, and by the evening of 23 March the island's defenders were down to just five serviceable Spitfires and Hurricanes. Five days later HMS *Eagle* delivered another seven Spitfires. But there could be no further deliveries for about a month, as the warship needed repairs to her steering gear. Since *Eagle* was the only Royal Navy carrier in the Mediterranean suitable for delivering Spitfires, there were doubts whether Malta could survive long enough for the next batch of fighters to be delivered.

During April 1942 the air attacks on the island rose to a crescendo. Some 5,500 tons of bombs fell on Malta, causing extensive damage to her port facilities and airfields. During the first half of the month it was a rare day when the RAF could put up half-a-dozen fighters to challenge the raiders. To escape almost certain destruction all Malta's bombers, torpedo-bombers and submarines had to be evacuated from the island and go to Gibraltar or Egypt.

Salvation was at hand, however. Winston Churchill sent a personal appeal to President Roosevelt asking if a US Navy carrier could be made available to deliver Spitfires to the beleaguered fortress. The President assented, and on 10 April the USS *Wasp* docked at Port Glasgow to pick up a large batch of Spitfires. *Wasp* was a much larger carrier than *Eagle*, and she was able to carry a total of 47 of the British fighters on deck and in her hangar, in addition to a dozen of her own F4F Wildcat fighters for self-protection.

On 13 April the American carrier set sail from the Scottish port for her delivery sortie, Operation Calendar. At first light on the 20th, *Wasp* and a large covering force of Royal Navy ships arrived at the fly-off point. The 12 Spitfires parked on the ship's deck took off first, while the 35 ensconced in her hangar started their engines to warm them up to allow an immediate take-off once they reached the deck. Flight Lieutenant Dennis Barnham of No 601 Squadron described his impressions after he started his engine in the hangar:

> Strapped tight I can't look round. Glancing into the mirror above my windscreen, I observe that the Spitfire behind me, with the CO inside, is being wheeled backwards towards the great lift – a pause – then, with the propeller turning in a transparent arc, the perspective of the plane changes as it disappears bodily, the floor with it, up into the blackness of the girders. Down comes the lift again and monkey-faced Scotty, one of our Australians, gives me a wide grin from the cockpit as his plane is dragged onto it. Down comes the empty floor again, hungry for more machines and their pilots. Up goes Max, it pauses in the roof, makes one gigantic swallow, then comes down again empty, this time for me.
>
> Mechanics grab my wings. I am pulled backwards toward the lift. Last glimpse of the hangar as the floor heaves beneath me ... I'm on the deck in white daylight. Clouds, sea; flight deck in front: the superstructure half way down the right. A white-sweatered American mechanic much too close, wearing goggles – a red skull cap on his head; I must watch him. With his legs apart, he's leaning forward like a rugger player, clenching his hands in the air; I put on the brakes. His hands begin to rotate rapidly: I open the throttle. The engine is roaring, brakes are slipping; a chequered flag falls; release brakes, throttle wide open, gathering speed, tail up, looking over the nose; deck's very short. Going faster. The over-hanging bridge on the superstructure sweeps towards me; pink faces, pink blobs with no features on them – quick, wave goodbye to the Americans! Grab the stick again – end of the deck. Grey waves. Keep her straight – stick back. Out over the sea. Waves nearer. Stick further back – at last she begins to fly. Gaining more speed, I now start climbing. I don't suppose any enemy pilot

could see the battleship, just below on my right, as close as this and survive. Changing on to the long-range tank, I'm circling away to the left, climbing steadily. The engine does not falter, this is fine! With the ships looking like toys, I take position well to the left of the CO while the other three Spitfires which I have to lead clamber into formation behind me.

As we set course toward the east, the sun rises out of the sea filling the whole of space with light.

Of the 47 Spitfires that took off from *Wasp* that morning, all except one reached Malta. The sudden arrival of three Spitfire squadrons injected new life into the island's air defences, but the respite would prove short-lived. The airfields that had received the Spitfires, Luqa and Takali, now came under heavy attack from the air. Within a few hours, several of the new fighters had been destroyed or damaged on the ground. Pilot Officer Mike LeBas, one of the newly arrived pilots, described what happened:

The Germans had watched our arrival on radar and that afternoon all Hell broke loose over the Maltese airfields. In spite of strenuous efforts by the fighters and the anti-aircraft gun defences, the Ju 87 and Ju 88 dive bombers and strafing Messerschmitts managed to damage and destroy several of the newly delivered aircraft on the ground. The blast pens were made of local stone or stacks of petrol tins filled with sand and they provided useful protection against cannon shells and blast from anything but a direct hit. They had no roofs, however, and several aircraft received damage when rocks blown high into the air by exploding bombs fell on them from above.

By the morning of 21 April only 27 of the Spitfires delivered by *Wasp* were still flyable. By that evening, the number had fallen to 17. Meanwhile, in the island's repair workshops, engineers struggled to assemble usable Spitfires and Hurricanes by cannibalizing parts from damaged machines.

As April drew to its close it was clear that despite the euphoria following Operation Calendar, Malta's survival remained in question. Yet again, Churchill asked the US President for *Wasp* to deliver more Spitfires to the island, and again that agreement was forthcoming.

The next resupply operation, Operation Bowery, was the largest of them all. The American carrier returned to Glasgow on 29 April and collected another 47 Spitfires. Meanwhile HMS *Eagle*, lying at Gibraltar with the repairs to her steering gear completed, took on 17 more. As *Wasp* and her covering force passed Gibraltar, *Eagle* set sail from the naval base and the two carriers headed into the Mediterranean. Shortly after dawn on 9 May they began launching the Spitfires, 64 of them.

One Spitfire failed to get airborne and crashed into the sea, killing the pilot. In another Spitfire, Flying Officer Jerry Smith got airborne only to find that the drop tank would not deliver fuel. With no chance of reaching Malta, he orbited *Wasp* until her remaining Spitfires were airborne. Then, rather than abandon his fighter, he decided to attempt a deck landing even though his aircraft lacked an arrester hook. After one baulked attempt he made a reasonable landing on his second try, and with the application of harsh braking he brought the Spitfire to a halt just short of the end of the deck. Smith and his Spitfire remained on the *Wasp* until the carrier was about to leave the Mediterranean, then he took off from the carrier once more for the short flight to Gibraltar.

Of the 62 other Spitfires that took off from *Wasp* and *Eagle*, 60 reached Malta. At Luqa airfield Mike LeBas was one of the pilots anxiously awaiting the arrival of the incoming fighters:

> One of the problems when I had arrived [during Operation Calendar] was that the operation had been kept so secret that too few people had been told we were coming; the Spitfires had not been refuelled and rearmed quickly enough, with the result that they could not take off to meet the attacks and several were knocked out on the ground. This time we were much better organised. As each Spitfire came in it was picked up at the end of the runway by a resident

Malta pilot, who sat on the wing and guided the aircraft to its blast pen. At each pen there were waiting an RAF ground crew and some soldiers to help with the refuelling. I guided one Spitfire in and, even before the pilot had shut down, men were clambering on the wings to load the cannon with their full complement of ammunition and the soldiers had started a human chain to pass up the petrol tins. The pilot pulled off his helmet and shouted to me 'That's jolly good. Where's the war?' I told him 'The war hasn't started for you yet, mate. Get out and be quick about it!'

Within 15 minutes the Spitfire's drop tank had been removed and the plane was refuelled and rearmed. LeBas climbed in the cockpit and shortly afterwards he was scrambled to meet an incoming raid.

In the days that followed there were several ferocious air actions, but the arrival of that large batch of fighters from *Wasp* and *Eagle* meant that at last Malta had the critical mass of modern fighters she needed to defend herself. Instead of the token fighter force available at the beginning of May, she now had five Spitfire squadrons at full strength.

With that increase in strength it became clear to the Axis high command that any invasion of Malta would be fraught with danger, and shortly afterwards they abandoned their plan to seize the island. Within a couple of weeks the *Luftwaffe* strength on Sicily had dropped sharply, as *Gruppen* moved to the Eastern Front or to Libya to support the major offensives in progress there. Meanwhile, deliveries of Spitfires to Malta continued unabated. Between 18 May and 9 June HMS *Eagle* made three further delivery runs, bringing a further 76 of these fighters to the island. From now on Malta had sufficient Spitfires to deal harshly with attacks mounted by the German and Italian Air Forces. Never again would the islanders face as great a peril as they did during that first week in May 1942.

The establishment of air superiority over Malta had important implications for the Allied strategy for the war in the Mediterranean. Following the withdrawal of Malta's anti-shipping forces and submarines in April, the Axis supply convoys had plied between Italy and North Africa almost without hindrance. That had allowed a rapid build-up of supplies in Libya in preparation for the new German offensive there. Now that situation had changed. With an adequate air defence restored to Malta, the anti-shipping units and submarines were able to return. Early in June they resumed their debilitating attacks on Axis supply convoys.

Meanwhile, HMS *Eagle* continued making regular 'top up' runs to supply the island with Spitfires to replace losses in action. During Operation Style, on 3 June, the *Luftwaffe* made its only successful bid to hit a formation of incoming Spitfires. A dozen Messerschmitt Bf 109s from *Jagdgeschwader 53* took off from the island of Pantelleria and intercepted one of the formations, shooting down four Spitfires in rapid succession.

SPITFIRE DELIVERY OPERATIONS TO MALTA, 1942

Date	Operation	Carrier	Took Off	Arrived
7 March	Spotter	HMS *Eagle*	15	15
21 March	Picket I	HMS *Eagle*	9	9
29 March	Picket II	HMS *Eagle*	7	7
20 April	Calendar	USS *Wasp*	47	46
9 May	Bowery	USS *Wasp*	64	60
		HMS *Eagle*		
18 May	L.B.	HMS *Eagle*	17	17
3 June	Style	HMS *Eagle*	31	27
9 June	Salient	HMS *Eagle*	32	32
15 July	Pinpoint	HMS *Eagle*	32	31
21 July	Insect	HMS *Eagle*	30	28
11 August	Bellows	HMS *Furious*	38	37
17 August	Baritone	HMS *Furious*	32	29
24 October	Train	HMS *Furious*	31	29
25 October to end November, flights direct from Gibraltar			16	15

The delivery flights to Malta from the aircraft carriers had been remarkable enough demonstrations of the Spitfire's long-range ferry capability, but even that was eclipsed in the autumn of 1942. Supermarine engineers developed an even larger ferry tank, with a capacity of 170 gallons, which would fit under the Spitfire's fuselage. Together with an auxiliary tank in the plane's rear fuselage holding 29 gallons, the fighter could carry a total fuel load of 284 gallons. That was sufficient for a Spitfire to fly the 1,100 miles from Gibraltar to Malta in a single hop, and with a reasonable fuel reserve. That flight equated to the distance from London to St Petersburg in Russia.

Now Spitfires could be delivered to the island as and when required, without the need to mount a major naval operation involving an aircraft carrier and a large force of escorting warships. The first direct flight of a Spitfire from Gibraltar to Malta was on 25 October 1942 and took 5¼ hours. Between then and the end of November 15 more Spitfires set out from Gibraltar; all except one reached Malta.

Had Malta required more Spitfires, they too would have been flown to the island direct. Yet during the autumn of 1942 the Allied strategic position in the Mediterranean area changed beyond all previous recognition. Following the victory at El Alamein in October, Allied ground forces had advanced rapidly through Libya. The siege of Malta was lifted, never to resume.

CHAPTER SEVEN

High-altitude Combat

The highest air combat during the Second World War took place on

12 September 1942, when in a unique action both contestants reached

altitudes above 43,000ft.

IN AUGUST 1942 a newly formed *Luftwaffe* bomber unit moved to Beauvais in northern France to commence a new phase in the air attack on Britain: the *Höhenkampfkommando* (High-altitude Bomber Detachment). With German cities suffering increasingly heavy attacks from the Royal Air Force that nation's leaders judged it vitally important to retaliate, if only in limited force, for propaganda purposes. Attacks by conventional German bombers, nuisance raids by day or heavier raids by night, took heavy losses from the steadily improving defences. Now the *Luftwaffe* was to try a new ploy, that of operating planes at ultra-high altitude to give them immunity from the defences.

The *Höhenkampfkommando* was a small unit, having been formed with only two planes. Technically, however, the detachment was rich in interest. Its Junkers Ju 86R bombers had been specially designed for operations above 40,000ft and were powered by two Jumo 207 compression-ignition diesel engines fitted with turbo-superchargers. This engine was fitted with a nitrous oxide boosting system, which provided additional oxygen to assist combustion and gave significantly increased power for short periods at high altitude.

The two-man crew of the Ju 86R sat in a fully pressurized cabin, which enabled them to perform effectively for long periods at the ultra-high altitude. With a long wing spanning 105ft, the Ju 86R easily exceeded 45,000ft during test flights when unladen. That altitude performance was to be the key to its survival, and it normally cruised at 155mph at over 40,000ft. Given the technical brilliance of the Ju 86R's design, it might seem carping to mention that the plane could carry only one 550lb bomb during its high-altitude missions. As mentioned earlier, however, the main consideration in mounting these attacks was to derive propaganda value from mounting daylight attacks over Britain which the defenders had no means of countering.

The new bombers delivered the first in the new series of attacks on 24 August 1942. Two Ju 86Rs took part; one bombed Camberley and the other bombed Southampton. To meet the incursions Fighter Command scrambled 15 Spitfires, but none could get anywhere near the high-altitude raiders. That evening the German propaganda ministry jubilantly announced the success of the revenge attack mounted by the *Höhenkampfkommando*, though without mentioning that only two aircraft had been involved or that they had each carried only a single bomb.

On the following day one Ju 86R flew over Britain. Confident of

---

JUNKERS Ju 86R

ROLE Two-seat, ultra-high-altitude bomber; some of them were modified as reconnaissance aircraft.

POWER Two Junkers Jumo 207B six-cylinder, vertically opposed, two-stroke diesel engines with turbo-supercharging, rated at 1,000hp at take-off and 750hp at 40,000ft when using nitrous oxide injection.

ARMAMENT One 550lb bomb carried during operations against Britain; no defensive armament carried.

PERFORMANCE Maximum speed 261mph at 19,500ft; normal cruising speed 155mph at 44,000ft.

NORMAL OPERATIONAL TAKE-OFF WEIGHT 25,400lb.

DIMENSIONS Span 105ft; length 55ft; wing area 1,049 sq ft.

DATE OF ENTRY INTO SERVICE Spring 1942.

their immunity to interception, the German crew flew a meandering course that took them over Southampton and to north of London. The aim was to cause as many air raid sirens as possible to sound, thereby causing maximum disruption to production. The plane dropped its bomb on Stanstead, then flew down the east side of London and left the coast at Shoreham. Nine Spitfires were scrambled to engage the intruder but again they failed to get anywhere near it. During the next two and a half weeks the Ju 86Rs flew nine further sorties over England. On each incursion RAF fighters took off and climbed as high as they could in attempts to intercept the Ju 86Rs, but yet again none reached a firing position.

Meanwhile, as the nature of the new threat became clear, Fighter Command developed a more effective response. At Northolt a new unit, the Special Service Flight, was formed to operate a small number of Spitfire Mark IX fighters specially modified for the high-altitude interception role. Early in September the first of the modified Spitfire IXs arrived at Northolt. Pilot Officer Emanuel Galitzine was one of the pilots who volunteered for service with the Special Service Flight. He described the modified Spitfire IX and the effect of the changes made to it:

> The aircraft had been lightened in almost every way possible. A lighter wooden propeller had been substituted for the normal metal one; all of the armour had been removed as had the four machine guns, leaving an armament of only the two 20-mm Hispano cannons. The aircraft was painted in a special lightweight finish, which gave it a colour rather like Cambridge blue, and all equipment not strictly necessary for high-altitude fighting was removed. Of course, a pressure cabin would have been very nice; but the Spitfire VII, which was in effect a Mark IX with a pressure cabin, was not yet ready for operations.
>
> On September 10th I made my first flight in the modified Spitfire IX and found it absolutely delightful to handle; during the war I flew 11 different versions of the Spitfire and this was far and away the best. The 450-pound reduction in weight was immediately

noticeable once one was airborne, and she had plenty of power and was very lively. I made a second flight that day to test the cannons, during which I took her up to 43,400 feet.

Two days later Galitzine was again airborne in the modified Mark IX, and this time he was in earnest. At 0927 hours he was scrambled to intercept an aircraft detected on radar climbing to high altitude over northern France. By now the British fighter controllers were familiar with the Ju 86R's mode of attack, which always began with the plane making a spiral climb to high altitude over France before it turned on to a heading for the south coast of England.

Galitzine climbed to 15,000ft over Northolt, then his ground controller informed him that the intruder was running in at high altitude towards the Isle of Wight. The Spitfire turned on to a south-westerly heading and continued its climb. As he approached the Solent at 40,000 feet Galitzine caught sight of the enemy plane slightly higher than he was and out to starboard.

> I continued my climb and headed after him, closing in until I could make out the outline of a Junkers 86; by then I was about half a mile

---

SUPERMARINE SPITFIRE IX

(*Figures for production aircraft, Galitzine's aircraft in parentheses*)

ROLE Single-seat interceptor and air superiority fighter.

POWER One Rolls-Royce Merlin 45 series, 12-cylinder, liquid-cooled engine developing 1,470hp at 9,250ft.

ARMAMENT Two Hispano 20mm cannon, four Browning .303in machine guns (two 20mm cannon).

PERFORMANCE Maximum speed 371mph at 20,000ft; climb to 20,000ft, 6min 24sec (Galitzine's lightened aircraft had a substantially better rate of climb).

NORMAL OPERATIONAL TAKE-OFF WEIGHT 6,525lb (about 6,075lb).

DIMENSIONS Span 36ft 10in; length 30ft; wing area 242 sq ft.

DATE OF FIRST PRODUCTION SPITFIRE IX Spring 1942.

away from him and we were both at 42,000 feet to the north of Southampton. The German crew had obviously seen me, because I saw the Junkers jettison its bomb, put up its nose to gain altitude and turn round for home. My Spitfire had plenty of performance in hand, however. I jettisoned my 30-gallon slipper tank which was now empty, and had little difficulty in following him in the climb and getting about 200 feet above the bomber.

Oberfeldwebel Horst Goetz, the highly experienced pilot at the controls of the Junkers, now takes up the story:

Suddenly Erich [Leutnant Erich Sommer, the navigator], sitting on my right, said that there was a fighter closing in from his side. I thought there was nothing remarkable about that – almost every time we had been over England in the Ju 86R, fighters had tried to intercept us. Then he said the fighter was climbing very fast and was nearly at our altitude. The next thing, it was above us. I thought Erich's eyes must have been playing him tricks, so I leaned over to his side of the cabin to see for myself. To my horror I saw the Spitfire, a little above us and still climbing.

Goetz jettisoned the bomb, switched in full nitrous oxide injection and partially depressurized the cabin to reduce the risk of an explosive decompression if it was hit and punctured. He then pushed open the throttles to try to out-climb his would-be assailant.

To the Spitfire pilot, the German bomber seemed enormous and the long curling condensation trail behind it looked like the wake from a large liner ploughing through a calm sea at speed. Galitzine continued:

I positioned myself for an attack and dived to about 200 yards astern of him, where I opened up with a three second burst. At the end of the burst my port cannon jammed and the Spitfire slewed round to starboard. Then, as I passed through the bomber's slipstream, my canopy misted over. The canopy took about a minute to clear completely, during which time I climbed back into position for the next attack. When I next saw the Junkers, it was heading southwards, trying to escape out to sea. I knew I had to get right in close behind him if I was to stand any change of scoring hits, because it would be difficult to hold the Spitfire straight when the starboard cannon fired and she went into a yaw. Again I dived to attack but when I was about a hundred yards away, the bomber went into a surprisingly tight turn to starboard. I opened fire but the Spitfire went into a yaw and fell out of the sky; I broke off the attack, turned outside him and climbed to 44,000 feet.

Goetz successfully avoided the next two attacks, then he made good his escape by descending into a patch of mist. Galitzine broke off the action and, by now short of fuel, landed at Tangmere.

Goetz knew the Junkers 86R had suffered damage so he landed at the first available airfield, near Caen. There he and Erich Sommer climbed out of their bomber and walked round it making a careful examination. They found it had suffered just one hit, but that one had nearly been lethal. A 20mm round had entered the top surface of the port wing and exited through the leading edge, passing clean though the main spar on the way. The two Germans had indeed had a lucky escape, and it was clear that the high-flying bombers' brief period of immunity from fighter attack was at an end. Less than three weeks after they started, the operations of the *Höhenkampfkommando* were halted, never to resume.

While attending a reunion of bomber crews in Germany I met Horst Goetz, and was able to put him in contact with Emanuel Galitzine. Later, Erich Sommer, then living in Australia, also came to England to meet his one-time assailant. After his first meeting with Galitzine, Goetz commented, tongue firmly in cheek:

Emanuel and I have talked about our battle in great detail and now we understand each other's problems. The next time we fly against each other, we shall be able to do things better!

CHAPTER EIGHT

The Twenty-fifth Mission

For the crews of US heavy bombers flying missions over Europe, the standard tour of duty comprised 25 missions. Once they had completed that number, crews were entitled to a spell of well-earned home leave before being reassigned to new posts. As crews approached that magic number of missions they became progressively more nervous that they might fail to reach it. This chapter tells the story of the pilot of one such crew.

LIEUTENANT LOWELL Watts, a B-17 pilot, joined the 388th Bomb Group based at Knettishall in Norfolk in November 1943. By the morning of 6 March 1944, he and his crew had flown twenty-four combat missions. As the briefing opened for his twenty-fifth mission, Watts was disconcerted to learn that this would not be the 'milk run' he had hoped for: the target was Berlin.

Until now distance, the strength of fighter defences and, latterly, bad weather, had shielded the German capital from full-scale attack by the Eighth Air Force. Earlier that week US bombers had taken off to attack targets close to the city, but on each occasion thick banks of cloud had defeated these attempts. Now the 'Mighty Eighth' girded itself for another try. With the rest of the 3rd Bomb Division, the 388th Bomb Group was to attack the Robert Bosch plant at Klein Machnow on the south-western side of Berlin, which was mass-producing electrical systems for motor vehicles and aircraft.

For this maximum-effort mission the 388th Bomb Group put up 33 B-17 Flying Fortresses. Lowell Watts's and his crew, flying in B-17 'Blitzin Betty', were briefed to lead the Low Squadron. He recalled:

> Our take-off was perfect. We slid into our formation position without trouble, the rest of the squadron was with us a few minutes later. Everything was working perfectly, engines, guns, interphone. We were well set for this final and greatest combat test. We crossed the English coastline and the gunners tested their .50 calibre guns. Then Dutch coast passed under us followed by the Zuider Zee.

When the leading bombers crossed the border between Holland and Germany, the bomber stream was 94 miles long. The 1st Bomb Division, with B-17 Flying Fortresses, was in the lead. The 3rd Bomb Division, also with B-17s and including Watts's unit, was in the middle. The 2nd Bomb Division, with B-24 Liberators, brought up the rear.

At noon, shortly after the 3rd Bomb Division crossed the border, German fighters struck that part of the formation. Lowell Watts had a ringside seat as the Combat Wing ahead took a fearful beating:

> About two or three miles ahead of us was the 13th Combat Wing. Their formation had tightened up since I last looked at it. Little dots that were German fighters were diving into those formations, circling, and attacking again. Out of one high squadron a B-17 slowly climbed away from its formation, the entire right wing a mass of flames. I looked again a second later. There was a flash – then nothing but little specks drifting, tumbling down. Seconds later another bomber tipped up on a wing, rolled over and dived straight for the ground. Little white puffs of parachutes began to float beneath us, then fell behind as we flew toward our target.
>
> Our interphone came suddenly to life. 'Enemy fighters, 3 o'clock level!' 'Enemy fighters, 1 o'clock high!' Then they were on us. One could feel the tenseness, the electrifying impulse that swept through

each individual crewmember when the Focke-Wulf 190s sailed through our formation. Now we were fighting for our lives, for the plane and the crew and for the formation. Should that formation be badly chewed up now, we'd catch a great deal of Hell during the next six hours.

Roy Island, flying on my left wing, peeled off and headed west. His place was taken by another ship. Another of our planes feathered an engine and began dropping behind, the target for several fighters.

Two silvery streaks flashed past us – P-47s. Our fighter escort had caught up with us. As the 47s came in, the Jerries dropped away and made only sporadic passes. Once again we could breathe a little easier.

For the rest of the way to Berlin, the German fighters concentrated their attentions against other parts of the force and Watts and his squadron were left alone. Their next big test came as the formation made its final turn before the target and commenced its bombing run. A bank of cloud prevented the bombers attacking their primary target at Klein Machnow, so the formation leader picked out a target of opportunity that was visible, in the Oranienburg district. As the bombers commenced their bomb runs on the new target the flak defences opened fire:

They didn't start out with wild shots and work in closer. The first salvo they sent up was right on us. We could hear the metal of our plane rend and tear as each volley exploded. The hits weren't direct. They were just far enough away so they didn't take off a wing, the tail or blow the plane up; they would just tear a ship half apart without completely knocking it out. Big ragged holes appeared in the wings and the fuselage. Kennedy, the co-pilot, was watching nothing but the instruments, waiting for the tell-tale indication of a damaged or ruined engine. But they kept up their steady roar, even as the ship rocked from the nearness of the flak bursts.

One shell burst close to 'Blitzin Betty' and sent shell splinters tearing into the bomber. One severed the pipe carrying oxygen to the men in the rear part of the aircraft. Hastily the crewmen grabbed for the plane's 'walk-around' portable oxygen bottles, and connected their masks to those. Still the pounding continued:

> The flak was coming up as close as ever, increasing in intensity. Above and to the right of us a string of bombs trailed out from our lead ship. Simultaneously our ship jumped upwards, relieved of its explosive load as the call 'Bombs away!' came over the interphone. Our left-wing ship, one engine feathered, dropped behind the formation. That left only four of us in the low squadron. A few minutes later the flak stopped. We had come through it and all four engines were still purring away.

Having survived that ordeal intact, it seemed that now nothing could stop 'Blitzin Betty'. Lowell Watts continued:

> As we settled down into the routine of the trip home I began to feel a glow of happiness. We had come through Hell without injury to the crew. Shot up as we were, the plane was still flying smoothly. Now we were heading for home. There was an immeasurable relief in knowing that a target had been crossed for the last time, at least in our present combat tour. No longer would we have to worry about the alerts that meant fitful sleep before another mission.
>
> The interphone came to life: 'Fighters at 10 o'clock high ... Hey! They're 47s!' Oh what a beautiful and welcome sight they made as they swooped over us, dipped their wings and wheeled away. With our first sight of them, a terrific sense of relief swept away the horrible feeling of alone-ness and danger that had ridden the skies with us all the way from Berlin. We were now protected and would soon be over the English Channel. I began to think about the buzz job I was going to give at base for my crew chief and also to wonder how I'd word the cable home to my wife Betty when we landed. With only 15 to 20 minutes flying to the channel, we felt that we could fight our way through anything. We hadn't seen a Focke-Wulf for almost an hour.

Within a few minutes, however, that aura of security was wrenched away. The P-47s that had swooped past the bombers had been near the limit of their fuel, and after the briefest of appearances they had pointed their noses to England and soon were out of sight. The next gaggle of fighters to swing into view had altogether different intentions.

> The interphone snapped to life: 'Focke-Wulfs at 3 o'clock level!' Yes, there they were. What seemed at a hurried count to be about 30 fighters flying along just out of range beside us. They pulled ahead of us, turned across our flight path and attacked from ahead and slightly below us. Turrets swung forward throughout the formation and began spitting out their .50 calibre challenge. Some Focke-Wulfs pulled above us and hit us from behind while most dived in from the front, coming in from 11 to 1 o'clock level, so close that only every second or third plane could be sighted on by the gunners. Still they came, rolling, firing and diving away, then attacking again.

In rapid succession two B-17s fell out of the formation and went down. Then 'Blitzin Betty' was hit.

> Brassfield called from the tail position 'I've got one, I've got one!' Then, almost with the same breath, 'I've been hit!' No sooner had the interphone cleared from that message when an even more ominous one cracked into the headsets: 'We're on fire!' Looking forwards, I saw a Focke-Wulf coming at us from dead level at 12 o'clock. The fire from our top and chin turrets shook the B-17. At the same instant his wings lit up with fire from his guns. The 20-mm rounds crashed through our nose and exploded beneath my feet amongst the oxygen tanks. At the same time they slashed through some of the gasoline cross-feed lines. The flames which started here, fed by the pure oxygen and the gasoline, almost exploded through the front of the ship. The companionway to the nose, the cockpit and the bomb bays was a solid mass of flame.

Watts ordered his crew to bail out, and struggled to hold the bomber under control as they scrambled for the escape hatches. Because of the flames he was unable to see anything in front of the bomber, and he had no way of knowing that his aircraft was edging dangerously close to another plane in the formation. His B-17 smashed into the other bomber then, shedding pieces, the two broke apart and started to fall out of the sky.

At the time Lowell Watts was unaware that there had been a collision, though its effects were obvious enough. Seemingly for no reason, almost the whole of the cabin roof above his head suddenly vanished.

It was a wild ride from that point. I could tell we had rolled upside down. My safety belt had been unbuckled. I fell away from the seat, but held myself in with the grasp I had on the control wheel. After a few weird sensations I was pinned to the seat, unable to move or even raise my hand to pull off the throttles or try to cut the gas to the inboard engines. My left foot had fallen off the rudder bars while we were on our back. I couldn't even slide it across the floor to get it back on the pedal. Flames now swept past my face, between my legs and past my arms as though sucked by a giant vacuum. Unable to see, I

BOEING B-17G FLYING FORTRESS

ROLE Heavy bomber.

POWER Four Wright R-1820 turbo-supercharged, 14-cylinder, air-cooled, radial engines each developing 1,200hp at take-off.

ARMAMENT The bomb load carried depended upon the distance to be flown. During the attack on Berlin, these aircraft carried ten 500lb high-explosive bombs. The defensive armament comprised two Browning .5in machine guns in turrets in the nose, above and below the fuselage and in the tail; in addition, there were single weapons on hand-held mountings in each waist gun position and above the radio operator's position.

PERFORMANCE Maximum speed 300mph at 30,000ft; formation cruising speed 180mph at 22,000ft.

NORMAL OPERATIONAL TAKE-OFF WEIGHT 55,000lb.

DIMENSIONS Span 103ft 9½ in; length 74ft 4in; wing area 1,420 sq ft.

DATE OF FIRST PRODUCTION B-17G September 1943.

could tell only that we were spinning and diving at a terrific rate. That wild eerie ride down the corridors of the sky in a flaming bomber still haunts my memory. But it wasn't just the terror of death, it was the unending confusion and pain of a hopeless fight and the worry for the nine other men that were my responsibility. Contrary to the usual stories, my past life failed to flash in review through my mind. I was too busy fighting to keep that life.

The next thing Watts knew, he was hurtling through space. The violent G forces induced by the spinning bomber had catapulted him through the open top of the cabin. His body was rotating so fast for several seconds he had no control over his flailing arms and legs.

Something jerked heavily past my face. That was my flak jacket. Then my oxygen mask flew off, followed by my goggles and helmet. I automatically reached for my chest. Yes, there was the ripcord, right where it should have been. Until then I hadn't once thought about my chute. I jerked the ripcord and waited. Nothing happened and I thought 'Oh Hell, the whole day is screwed up!' I jerked it harder. There was a soft swish, then a hard sharp jerk and I was suspended in space, hanging in the most complete silence I have ever known. I anxiously looked up at the billowy white nylon of my chute, fully expecting it to be on fire. I knew great relief when I saw it intact. Above me the formation roared on into the west, the battle still raging. I looked for our plane. An engine went by, still burning. A few pieces of metal wrinkled on down, and further away I caught sight of the bright yellow of the dinghy radio falling through space. What a screwy time to notice that radio, but ever since the sight of it has stayed in my mind more clearly than anything else.

Watts looked around to see if other members of his crew were descending by parachute. He saw only three, though in fact five others had jumped clear of the plane and would reach the ground safely. Then he saw a Focke Wulf 190 curving towards him and for a few moments he thought its pilot might be about to open fire at him.

I tried to swing the chute, feeling very helpless. Then I noticed that
he was still turning, going on by me. A few seconds later he crashed
about half a mile from where I landed – I could see that the pilot had
been shot. I saw three other planes burning on the ground as I came
down.

Watts landed on wet, snow-covered ground. He bundled his parachute under his arm and ran from the scene. Finding a shallow ditch,
he dropped into it to hide while he collected his thoughts. When he left
the blazing bomber his escape kit, map and money had torn away from
his flying suit. As a result, he had little idea where he had come down.
Later in the afternoon a man and woman came walking past and saw
him. They indicated that he was about 2½ miles inside Holland, but
were too afraid to assist him further. The American pilot remained
hidden until it was dark, then he set out heading south-west trying to
link up with the Dutch resistance. Although he was not seriously
injured, the burns to his skin were painful. He continued walking
throughout the night, passing through open country, and at first light
he hid under some bushes. At around midday, cold and hungry, he
resumed his trek to the south-east. Soon afterwards he was seen by
armed German civilians and after a brief chase he was caught.

What I didn't know was that I had landed in a spot just north of the
jog in the German border where it extends westwards into Holland.
So all of my walking simply took me back into Germany! It was a
year before I figured that one out!

For Lowell Watts the war was over.

CHAPTER NINE

The D-Day Spoofs

During the Second World War, all the major combatants employed radar to

detect enemy ships and aircraft at long ranges and at night. Those who placed

too much trust in this equipment might do so at their peril, however, for a

clever enemy could manipulate the radar returns to give a completely

misleading picture of what was happening.

DETAILED PLANNING for the invasion of France, code-named Operation Overlord, began late in 1943. Whatever the fate of the landings, they were certain to define the future course of the Second World War. If they succeeded, the German army would be forced to commit forces to fight major battles in the west as well as on the eastern front. Should the landings fail, Allied losses in men and material would be so high as to preclude any repeat for at least a year. In the interval the German high command could switch the bulk of its troops to the eastern front and might possibly secure a decisive victory.

For so important an operation, it was vital to conceal the passage and arrival of the invasion fleet for as long as possible. Also, spoof airborne and seaborne landings could serve as diversions, to confuse the defenders and tie down their forces in positions remote from the landings for as long as possible.

Adolf Hitler's so-called 'West Wall' included no fewer than 92 radar

sites along the north coasts of France and Belgium, positioned to warn
of an approaching Allied seaborne landing force. If the multiplicity of
these radar 'eyes' made jamming more difficult than anything else previously attempted, the deception problem promised to be even more
formidable. Using electronic deception methods to keep the defenders
guessing for half an hour regarding the target of a bomber stream
moving at 225mph was one thing; producing a 'ghost' invasion fleet
moving at 8 knots, for several hours, was quite another.

Dr Robert Cockburn, head of the countermeasures section at the
Telecommunications Research Establishment at Malvern, was brought
into the operation early on. He later told me:

> In December 1943 I was visited by a chap who cautiously mentioned
> the invasion and asked if I could help with the countermeasures.
> Could I produce any sort of spoof to deceive the enemy on where the
> landings were to take place? I said I thought I could. The next thing I
> knew I was 'Bigoted', the code name given to those cleared to see the
> invasion plan. In February 1944 I was summoned to Northwick
> House near London and taken into the war room, and there plotted
> out on a map on the wall was the invasion plan. I was horrified! I
> couldn't sleep for nights afterwards, having the terrible responsibility
> of knowing where the invasion was going to fall.

Dr Cockburn and his team, together with the ABL-15 American countermeasures organization co-located at Malvern, began working on
the countermeasures plan to support the invasion. The plane was
drawn up under the tightest security, with nobody allowed to know
any more of the overall plan than was strictly necessary for their
assigned task.

Cockburn's countermeasures plan to support 'Overlord' fell into
four main parts. First, the enemy coastal radar stations had to be
located accurately. Then, secondly, the majority would be 'taken out' by
air attacks. Thirdly, on the night of the invasion, feint invasion forces
were to draw the defenders' attention away from the airborne and
seaborne landing areas. At the same time, and fourthly, any radars

that remained operational in the main invasion area were to be rendered useless by jamming.

Attacking radar stations from the air was no easy task. These were small pinpoint targets, usually well protected by 20mm and 37mm anti-aircraft guns. The specialized task of destroying the stations was assigned to the Mosquito, Spitfire and Typhoon squadrons of the 2nd Tactical Air Force. It was important that these attacks did not produce a recognizable pattern that would betray where the real landings would take place. Thus, for every target attacked in the area of the intended invasion, at least three were attacked in areas outside it.

To assist the plotting of radar stations, Dr Cockburn's staff produced a special ground direction-finding system that could measure the bearing of an enemy radar transmitter to within a quarter of one degree. Three such sets, code-named 'Ping-Pongs', were set up along the southern coast of England where they provided fixes on several enemy radar stations. Once a radar station's position had been triangulated, its exact location was confirmed by photographic reconnaissance.

The 2nd Tactical Air Force began the task of knocking out the more prominent radar stations on 16 March 1944. Twelve Typhoon fighter-bombers of No 198 Squadron set about the big *Wassermann* early-warning station on the Belgian coast near Ostend. The planes crossed the coast in formation shortly after midday, flying at 8,000ft as though heading for an inland target. Once they were inland, however, the four leading aircraft dived to treetop height and streaked towards the towering aerial, while the other Typhoons ran in to strafe the flak emplacements surrounding the radar. The four leading aircraft each launched eight rockets, which scored several hits on the aerial structure. However, as the planes thundered into the distance, the 130ft radar aerial tower remained upright. So, later that afternoon, the squadron delivered a second attack on the tower and scored several more hits. Yet still the battered structure remained standing.

Although it seemed that the radar was invulnerable to this type of attack, that was not the case. The Achilles' heel of the *Wassermann* lay in its turning mechanism. The aerial tower was mounted on a rotating sleeve that turned in a fixed vertical cylinder. The blast from the exploding rockets had distorted the sleeve, jamming it in position. Moreover, the tower could not be lowered to the ground for repair unless it faced in a certain direction. The entire aerial structure had to be dismantled before repairs could begin. In fact, the Ostend *Wassermann* would still be off the air when the invasion was launched.

As the systematic destruction of the coastal radar network in France and Belgium proceeded apace, Dr Cockburn and his team put the finishing touches to a remarkable piece of electronic spoofery. Their aim was to simulate on enemy radar the approach of two huge ghost 'fleets', to divert attention away from the main Allied landings. The simplest method of producing such a feint would have been to use a large number of full-sized ships. But the invasion was stretching Allied shipping resources to the utmost and no full-sized ships could be spared for that purpose. So Cockburn worked out a method of producing the huge radar echo similar to that from a large assembly of ships, without using any real ships at all. Under his scheme, aircraft flying carefully arranged tracks and dropping large quantities of 'Rope' – long lengths of 'Window' radar-reflective metal foil descending on small parachutes — would erect an enormous radar reflector covering an area

---

SEETAKT SURFACE VESSEL REPORTING AND GUN-RANGING RADAR

INSTALLATION At land sites and aboard warships.

PERFORMANCE Maximum range against ships, depending on site, up to 28 miles; maximum range against aircraft 100 miles.

RADAR PARAMETERS

Frequency: spot frequencies between 368 and 390MHz.

Peak power: 8kW.

Pulse length: 3 microseconds.

Pulse repetition frequency: 500.

FIRST *SEETAKT* RADAR BUILT 1938.

measuring 14 miles wide and 16 miles deep, an area of 224 sq miles.

The most numerous type of coast-watching radar deployed along the coast of Europe was the *Seetakt*, so Cockburn planned his ghost 'fleet' spoof to work against that system. The aim was to plant one bundle of 'Rope' (see Glossary) into each radar resolution cell (see Glossary) of *Seetakt*. The radar's beam width was 15 degrees, so at 10 miles from the radar that beam was just over 2 miles wide. The radar's pulse

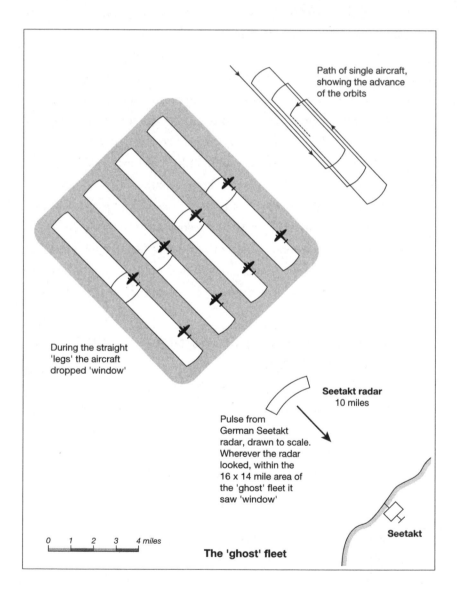

Path of single aircraft, showing the advance of the orbits

During the straight 'legs' the aircraft dropped 'window'

Seetakt radar
10 miles

Pulse from German Seetakt radar, drawn to scale. Wherever the radar looked, within the 16 x 14 mile area of the 'ghost' fleet it saw 'window'

0 1 2 3 4 miles

Seetakt

The 'ghost' fleet

width did not permit it to discriminate between two or more objects less than 520yd apart in range. So, if one bundle of 'Rope' was dropped in each *Seetakt* resolution cell measuring 2 miles by 520yd, it would produce a huge continuous 'blip' measuring 14 miles by 16 miles without any gaps.

So much for the theory behind the spoof operation. The mechanics of laying out the required field of 'Rope' would require precision flying of a high order, however. The full ghost 'fleet' operation required eight aircraft, split into two waves of four. The planes in each wave were to fly in line abreast but out of sight of each other, with 4 miles between adjacent aircraft. Eight miles behind the first wave of four planes came the second wave, which was similarly arranged. Maintaining their formation, the two waves of aircraft were to fly a series of oblong 'race-track' patterns, with each oblong measuring 8 miles by 2 miles. The 2-mile distance between the sides of the pattern, and the similar 2-mile distance between one plane's orbit pattern and that of its neighbour, would produce a continuous 'blip' on the radar in azimuth.

Holding such a formation accurately at night, without visual contact between planes or any visual reference points, would be no easy matter. To assist with navigation each plane would carry a Gee or a GH radar navigational system. The planes releasing the 'Rope' were to fly at 180mph, or 3 miles per minute. So dropping one bundle of 'Rope' every five seconds placed one bundle every 440yd. That was sufficient to produce a continuous 'blip' on *Seetakt* in range.

Having erected that huge radar reflector, the next trick was to get it to appear to move plausibly towards the coast. Each orbit took 7 minutes, and at the end of each orbit the entire formation moved forward 1 mile. That gave the ghost 'fleet' a rate of advance equivalent to 8 knots, making it look realistically like an assembly of ships advancing towards the shore.

During the preceding months the long-running Allied strategic deception plan had sought to convince the German High Command that the main landings would take place either near Le Havre or near Boulogne. Those two points were therefore the objectives for the ghost 'fleet' operations; Operation Taxable was the spoof invasion aimed at Le Havre, while Operation Glimmer was the spoof invasion aimed at the Dunkirk–Boulogne area.

Dr Cockburn's ghost 'fleet' plan looked fine on paper, but would it work in practice? It was May 1944 before he gained control of the two bomber units that would fly the operations, No 218 Squadron with Stirlings and No 617 Squadron – the 'Dam Busters' – with Lancasters. He visited each squadron in turn and told them what he wanted, then had the crews rehearse the complicated flight patterns. The planes ran a ghost 'fleet' towards a bevy of captured German radars set up on cliffs overlooking the Firth of Forth in Scotland. The spoof looked effective, but those watching it had known they were looking at a simulated invasion fleet. The acid test of the method came a few days later, when Cockburn had some bombers fly the spoof against the British coastal radar site at Flamborough Head whose operators had not been told what was happening. There the operators agreed that the returns on their screen appeared to have come from a very large convoy indeed – a convoy larger than any they had seen before. Cockburn could now be confident that his spoof was likely to deceive enemy radar operators.

Shortly before the invasion, Cockburn obtained some additional units to add to the realism of his spoofs. Four high-speed air-sea rescue launches were fitted with the 'Moonshine' electronic repeater. This device picked up the signals from the *Hohentwiel* ship-search radar carried in *Luftwaffe* planes. It amplified and multiplied the signals, then retransmitted them. On the plane's radar screen this would give the impression of a huge force of ships running close together. The rescue launches, and 14 small launches also assigned to the operation, were each to tow a float flying a 'Filbert': a 29-ft-long naval barrage balloon with a 9ft-diameter radar reflector fitted inside the envelope; this would give a radar echo similar to that from a large ship. In addition to towing the floats, the naval launches each flew one 'Filbert' from their hulls. These craft were to cruise underneath the falling 'Rope' to give substance to the hoaxes.

Despite the elaborate planning Cockburn and his team had devoted to the radar spoof operation, it had one major weakness that critics of the scheme were quick to point out. They asked what would happen if the *Luftwaffe* sent reconnaissance planes into the area, and their crews reported that no invasion fleet was present. Cockburn told me his usual reply to such a question:

> Imagine the scene: a frightened undertrained young conscript radar operator sees the ghost 'fleet' on his screen and reports it to his headquarters as the long-expected enemy invasion force; so do his colleagues at other radar stations along the coast. Soon there appears a nice broad arrow on the situation map at the headquarters: the 'ghost' fleet is now a military fact. If aircraft were then to fly into the area and report it clear of ships, would their reports be believed? Probably not. The operation was to take place at night and the aircraft might be far off their intended tracks. Once a broad arrow representing an enemy attack appears on the situation map at a military headquarters, it's a military fact and it takes a lot to remove it.

Those with military backgrounds agreed that Cockburn's analysis was probably correct, but it remained to be seen if he would be proved right 'on the night'.

ON 5 JUNE 1944, as the invasion fleet prepared to set out from England, all but 16 of the original 92 radar sites along the northern coasts of France and Belgium were off the air. No radar site in the invasion area was working fully. With the 'softening-up' phase of 'Overlord' complete, the jamming and spoofing phases could go ahead.

As the myriad collection of invasion craft streamed out of port, the two 'ghost' invasion armadas also 'set sail'. Operation Taxable, with eight Lancasters from No 617 Squadron, made for Le Havre. Operation Glimmer, a smaller spoof using six Stirlings of No 218 Squadron, made for the Dunkirk–Boulogne area. Orbiting over the English Channel were four B-17 Flying Fortresses of the US 803rd Bombardment Squadron and 16 Stirlings of the RAF No 199 Squadron, transmitting

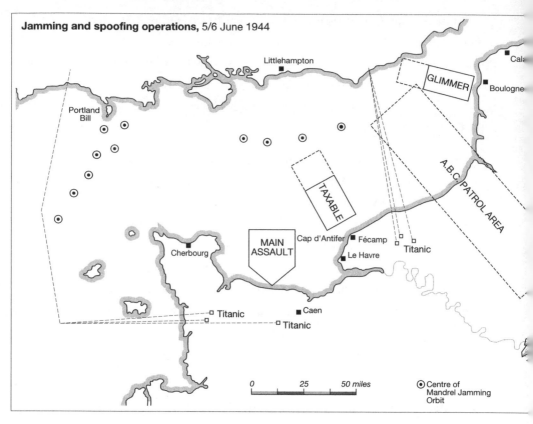

Jamming and spoofing operations, 5/6 June 1944

jamming to screen the various operations that night. The planes' orbit positions had been carefully calculated to ensure that the jamming would conceal the real invasion force, but would be sufficiently thin in the 'Taxable' and 'Glimmer' areas to allow enemy radar operators to observe the approach of the spoof fleets.

Beneath the falling clouds of 'Rope', the small flotilla of launches headed south into the choppy sea trailing their ungainly 'Filbert' balloons downwind. Just after midnight the Moonshine operator in rescue launch No 1249 operating with the 'Glimmer' spoof picked up signals from an enemy airborne radar. He returned them 'with interest'. During the next two hours he logged signals from eight separate aircraft and 'Moonshined' nearly all of them. Fifty miles to the west the Moonshine operators with the 'Taxable' force also picked up enemy aircraft radar transmissions and replied to them in the same way.

The operation to drop the large quantities of 'Rope' from the bombers went off without a hitch, though it was a disconcerting business for the crews concerned. One of those who flew with No 617 Squadron that night later recalled:

At the time I was rather concerned about what the Germans would do when they saw Taxable. We knew that we were bait and expected just about every night-fighter in creation to roll up at any moment. Our Lancaster was packed full [of 'Rope'] from nose to tail. If we were forced down in the sea, there would be little chance of our getting out before the aircraft sank. We finished [dropping 'Rope'] at 4 a.m. by which time it was just beginning to get light. The sky seemed to be full of transport aircraft and gliders: the 'Red Berets' were going in. We hoped we had made things a little easier for them.

In the event the bombers engaged in the ghost 'fleet' operations suffered no interference from enemy night fighters.

About 10 miles off the coast of France the two ghost 'fleets' arrived at their stop lines. The launches anchored the floats flying the 'Filbert' balloons, then laid smokescreens and broadcast on loudspeakers the squeals, rattles and splashes heard when several ships dropped anchor. Having completed their deception task, the boats withdrew at top speed.

While the planes assigned to the Taxable and Glimmer operations moved their laborious ways towards the coast of France, other mischief was afoot. Twenty-nine Stirling and Halifax bombers of Nos 90, 138, 149 and 161 Squadrons staged a mock airborne invasion in the Caen and Cap d'Antifer areas under the code name Titanic. En route to the spoof 'dropping zones', the bombers released large quantities of 'Window' to increase the size of the force when seen on radar. In the dummy landing areas they unloaded special fireworks which fell to the ground and produced an uneven pattern of bangs to sound like a ground battle in progress. A few men from the Special Air Service were also dropped in the area, with orders to 'make a lot of noise'.

Meanwhile, the real armada of aircraft laden with airborne troops droned towards their dropping zones in Normandy. The planes presented a perfect target for *Luftwaffe* night fighters: 1,069 heavy-laden transport planes, the majority of them unarmed and some towing gliders. On either flank of the transports' routes, scores of Mosquito night fighters thirsted for the chance to do battle. But even they could give no guarantee that determined enemy fighter crews would not penetrate their escort lines to inflict savage destruction. To serve as a distraction for *Luftwaffe* night fighters, 24 Lancaster bombers of No 101 Squadron and five Flying Fortresses from No 214 Squadron flew a ghost 'bomber stream' along the line of the River Somme. On board each aircraft the 'Window' man tossed out bundles of tinfoil at regular intervals. While he did so, the special equipment operator aboard each plane transmitted jamming on the *Luftwaffe* fighter control channels. Other jamming transmitters, situated in southern England, added to the cacophony of noise. The aim was to ensure that any *Luftwaffe* night fighter that ventured over north-west France would get no help to find targets from its ground controllers.

As planned, the *Luftwaffe* controllers vectored their night fighters into the area occupied by the ghost 'bomber stream'. But once the fighters had entered the morass of jamming, they could not be contacted again. One Lancaster was shot down but its crew was saved. Meanwhile the transport planes unloaded their human cargoes over Normandy and withdrew, unchallenged by enemy fighters.

In the invasion area, a powerhouse of jamming shimmered across the screens of the few partially working coastal radars which had survived the bombing and strafing attacks of the previous weeks. More than 200 ships in the armada carried jamming transmitters and all were switched on. There was nothing subtle about this, the final trick in the Allies' radio countermeasures repertoire. It blinded the defenders as cruelly and effectively as pepper thrown into their eyes. Only one radar glimpsed the approaching armada, but such was the level of confusion that its warning went unheeded.

The first positive indication that the invasion fleet was moving towards Normandy reached the German army headquarters at 0200 hours on 6 June. The report came from observers on the eastern side of the Cherbourg peninsula, who had heard with naked ears the rumble of many hundreds of the ships' engines. No conceivable radar-jamming effort could have achieved more, for the invaders' approach had passed undetected until then. Off the landing areas, jamming of the *Seetakt* fire control radars greatly reduced the accuracy of fire from the coastal gun batteries. Only one Allied warship, a destroyer, was lost to this cause though others suffered damage.

There is clear evidence that radar operators observed and reported the approach of the Glimmer 'fleet', and a full-scale invasion alert was issued for the Calais–Dunkirk area. Dr Cockburn had predicted, 'Once a broad arrow representing an enemy attack appears on the situation map at a military headquarters, it's a military fact and it takes a lot to remove it.' His forecast is borne out to a remarkable degree by a German record of that morning's events. A telephone message logged at 1015 hours on D-Day at the forward echelon of the *Luftwaffe* High Command outlined what was known about the main landings to the west of Le Havre. It went on to state:

'The reports of ships assembling off Calais and Dunkirk at 0400 hours have not, so far, been confirmed.'

More than six hours after the spoof operation had ended, reconnaissance aircraft and patrol boats were still scouring the coast between Dunkirk and Boulogne looking for the reported invasion force. Even more important, several German divisions that might have begun moving west to engage Allied forces ashore were forced to remain in place waiting to repel invaders that would never come.

Operation Taxable appeared to draw only slight attention, perhaps because it was too close to the main invasion area for its effects to be observed with certainty. It is also possible that the fighter-bomber attacks of the previous weeks had left no working radars in the area to see the approaching 'fleet'. While it had been expected that replacement sets would be moved in to replace key equipments that had been destroyed, in some areas this failed to happen.

The rest of the story is history. With the Allied troops established ashore in Normandy, no power at Adolf Hitler's command could dislodge them. There can be no doubt that the radar jamming and spoofing operations materially assisted the landings and reduced casualties. In terms of what they achieved, the resources committed to those operations had been minimal. Operation Overlord provides an object lesson on what can be accomplished, if a carefully planned programme of electronic countermeasures is used to support a one-of-a-kind operation of the highest importance.

CHAPTER TEN

Corking the English Channel

In a speech in August 1942, commander of German U-boats Admiral

Karl Doenitz had commented, 'The aeroplane can no more eliminate

the submarine than the crow can fight a mole.' In the days immediately

following the Allied invasion of France in June 1944 that statement

would be put to the acid test of combat.

DURING THE EARLY spring of 1944 the Atlantic convoy routes went quiet, as *Admiral* Doenitz husbanded his forces in readiness to meet the long-predicted Allied invasion of western Europe. Wherever that blow fell one thing was clear: the vast majority of the troops, equipment and supplies for the invasion would have to be transported by sea. The huge armada of transport ships carrying the Allied force would present the U-boat force with hundreds of fat targets. As mentioned in the previous chapter, the future course of the war depended on the outcome of the invasion. With that in mind *Admiral* Doenitz was prepared to risk a substantial part of his force, provided his boats were able to sink a reasonable number of the transports carrying troops, equipment and supplies to the beachheads.

The Type VII U-boat, the mainstay of the German submarine service, had a maximum speed of 17 knots and a maximum range of

6,500 miles running on the surface at 12 knots. Submerged, running on the limited battery power, its maximum speed was reduced to 8 knots and even that could not be maintained for long. Its maximum range submerged was 80 miles running at 4 knots, but at the end of such a run the batteries would be exhausted. The boat then needed to spend several hours on the surface to recharge its batteries and during that time, being unable to dive, it would be vulnerable to air attack. Because of their limited speed and range when running underwater, the U-boats spent most of their time on the surface and they submerged only when they needed to avoid being seen or to avoid enemy attack. In this context the term 'submarine' was a misnomer; 'submersible boat' describes their capabilities more accurately.

During 1943, in a bid to make U-boats less vulnerable to detection from the air, the German Navy developed the *Schnorkel* (nose) device. This consisted of an air pipe that could be raised above the surface of the sea while the boat ran at periscope depth; a simple ballcock mechanism closed off the top of the pipe whenever a wave washed over it. By drawing the necessary air through the *Schnorkel*, a U-boat could run on its diesel engines indefinitely. It could cruise at a maximum of 6 knots

---

U-373(TYPE VIIC U-BOAT)

SURFACE DISPLACEMENT 769 tons.

ARMAMENT (Offensive) Four bow and one stern torpedo tubes with fourteen 533mm torpedoes (770lb warheads). (Defensive anti-aircraft armament, 1944) Four 20mm cannon in two paired installations and one 37mm cannon, all mounted on a platform aft of the conning tower.

PERFORMANCE Maximum speed (on the surface, using diesel engines) 17 knots; submerged (using electric motors driven from batteries) 7 knots. Endurance (surface) 7,480 miles at 12 knots, (submerged) 70 miles at 4 knots; minimum time to submerge 50sec; maximum safe diving depth 650ft.

DIMENSIONS Length 220ft 3in; bcam 20ft 4in.

DATE OF LAUNCH OF FIRST TYPE VIIC U-BOAT Early 1941.

without depleting the charge in its batteries or exposing its hull to radar detection. From the early months of 1944 the *Schnorkel* was being fitted to all new U-boats, and a crash programme was instituted to retrofit the device to existing boats.

Despite strenuous efforts by dockyard personnel, the *Schnorkel* retrofit programme at the operational bases in France ran into difficulties. Hindered by the systematic disruption of the French rail system in the run-up to the Allied landings, the modification work took far longer than expected. At the beginning of June 1944 the counter-invasion force numbered 49 U-boats of which only nine had the *Schnorkel*. The assembled force, designated Group *Landwirt*, awaited its decisive battle in the massive bombproof concrete pens at the five operational bases on the west coast of France.

On 6 June 1944 the longest day dawned and the invasion began. At dusk that evening the entire Group *Landwirt* put to sea. The largest U-boat 'wolf pack' ever assembled was on its way to do battle, crewed by the bravest and most determined in the German Navy. The boats from the nearest bases had to cover only a couple of hundred miles to reach the main sea artery leading to the invasion area. At the end of that run there lay an unprecedented array of targets, and the boats had the potential to throttle the Allied build-up of reinforcements and supplies in the beachhead. If the U-boats could reach the shipping lanes, the only factor limiting the mayhem and destruction they could inflict was the number of torpedoes that each boat carried.

ON THE ALLIED side, those charged with formulating a plan to prevent a massed attack by U-boats on the invasion fleet faced a difficult challenge. From Brest, the most northerly of the bases in France, a U-boat making a high-speed dash on the surface could cover most of the 200 miles to the invasion area in a single night.

No 19 Group of Royal Air Force Coastal Command, commanded by Air Vice Marshal Brian Baker, would provide the first line of defence against the U-boats' charge. For that purpose, the Group was reinforced to 23 squadrons of anti-submarine aircraft. There were 320

Sunderlands, Wellingtons, Liberators, Halifaxes and Swordfish flown by British, American, Canadian, Australian, Czech and Polish crews.

It fell to Group Captain Dick Richardson and his navigation staff at Coastal Command headquarters to devise a method of systematically overseeing every part of an area of 20,000 sq miles of sea, stretching from Brittany to the south coast of Ireland, once every 30 minutes. After much discussion, one of Richardson's staff officers, Flight Lieutenant James Perry, produced a workable solution. It was a clever plan and, like most clever plans, it was essentially a simple one. On a map of the area to be 'plugged' he drew 12 oblong boxes, each one tailored to the capabilities of one type of patrol aircraft and its radar. The circumference of each box equalled the distance the aircraft would cover in either 30 or 60 minutes; if the latter, two aircraft were to follow each other round the circumference of the box at 30-minute intervals. The width of each oblong, and the distance between it and its neighbour, was twice the range at which the aircraft's radar could detect a U-boat. In this way the plan overcame the problem of coordinating the patrols of several different types of aircraft, with differing cruising speeds and radars of varying performance.

The 20,000-square-mile area of water under scrutiny was to be like an enormous cork stopping one end of the English Channel, and Perry's system of oblongs accordingly became known as 'Cork Patrols'. With the requisite number of planes in position to 'man' each of the oblong patrol lines, the plane's radar operators would examine every part of the 'Cork' area once every 30 minutes. As each aircraft reached the end of its allotted time on patrol, the plan provided for another plane of the same type to relieve it. When darkness fell, anti-submarine aircraft equipped for night attack with searchlights or flares would take over the patrol orbits. Any U-boat commander who chose to submerge each time he detected enemy radar signals would soon end up with flat batteries and insufficient compressed air to regain the surface. The only alternative was to remain on the surface, but then his boat would be vulnerable to attack.

The 'Cork Patrols' would need to be mounted round the clock for an

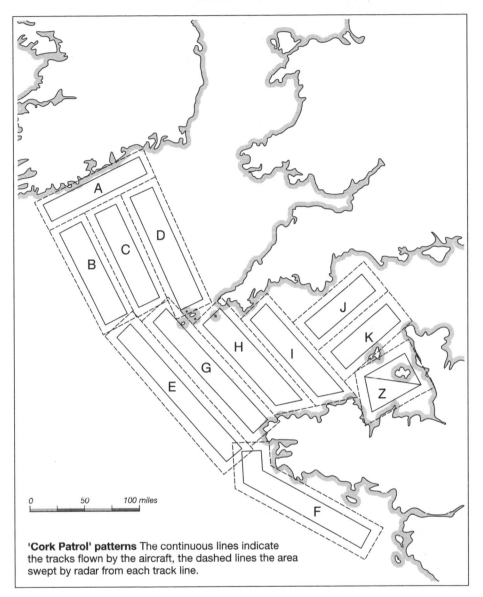

'Cork Patrol' patterns The continuous lines indicate the tracks flown by the aircraft, the dashed lines the area swept by radar from each track line.

undefined period that might run into several weeks, as long as the U-boat threat to the invasion existed. The normal establishment for each squadron was 15 aircraft, which meant it had between 8 and 12 planes serviceable at any one time. Each squadron was expected to maintain two aircraft continuously airborne, either in the patrol area or flying to or from it. In addition, each squadron would need to hold a reserve aircraft and crew at readiness on the ground, ready to replace any plane that became unserviceable or was shot down. Some patrol lines would require aircraft to patrol within a few miles of German-held France, and the planners had to expect that German fighters would attempt to interfere with the lumbering patrol planes. To guard against this, during the daylight hours Allied fighters were programmed to fly standing patrols in those areas.

Even the best-laid air plan would fail if the planes' crews lacked sufficient training to carry out their tasks. During the lull in the U-boat war in the spring of 1944, relays of squadrons were released from their front-line duties to undergo extra training to bring them to peak performance.

In the spring of 1944 No 19 Group ran a realistic full-scale trial in the Irish Sea to test the likely effectiveness of the 'Cork Patrols', the quarry being the British submarine *Viking*. The boat's commander was told to take his craft as fast as possible, either surfaced or submerged, over a 90-mile course patrolled to the same intensity as the planned 'Corked' area. He was to do all he could to complete the course with his boat in a condition fit for action. On the other hand he had to do his utmost to avoid the 'air attacks', and dive each time an aircraft appeared in a threatening position.

The trial began on 6 April 1944, but initially fog at the airfields kept the aircraft on the ground. *Viking* was allowed to cruise on the surface undisturbed for an hour and a half before the first aircraft reached her area. This forced the boat to dive, and for the next 28 hours she was able to spend barely two hours on the surface. Those two hours were made up of nine periods on the surface, each one averaging about 13 minutes. None of those periods was long enough to add any significant charge to her batteries, nor to top up her rapidly dwindling supply of compressed air. Finally, with 5 miles still to go, *Viking*'s commander threw in the towel; his batteries were depleted to the point where the boat could do no more than 3 knots underwater, so she would stand little chance of escaping if she launched a torpedo attack on enemy shipping. Moreover, she had only sufficient compressed air left to bring the boat to the surface once more. The submarine was no longer fit for action.

When the next aircraft arrived in the area of *Viking*, however, the submarine commander was able to avoid detection by keeping the stern pointing towards the hunter. This manoeuvre, coupled with a poor radar and visual watch by the plane's crew, saved the boat from detection. Because of this unexpected piece of luck the submarine was able to complete the course without being 'sunk', though she was in no condition to press home an attack on an escorted enemy convoy.

All the more remarkable, then, was the fact that of the 19 aircraft that took part in the trial, only two of their crews had actually detected *Viking*. And on neither occasion would they have been able to deliver an attack on the boat before she dived to safety. For *Viking*'s crew the exercise had been a game, with no personal danger to themselves if one of the hunters had 'caught' them. For a U-boat trying to cover the far greater distance to the invasion area, the Royal Navy skipper judged that such a passage would have been both exhausting and highly demoralizing for the crew.

In any case, No 19 Group's 'Cork Patrols' would constitute only the first of two strong lines of defence. Any U-boats that penetrated the 200-mile-deep thicket of air patrols still had to run the gauntlet of some 300 destroyers, frigates, sloops, corvettes and anti-submarine trawlers guarding the flanks of the sea lanes leading to the beachhead.

AT DUSK ON 6 June 1944 Group *Landwirt*, the largest 'wolf pack' ever assembled, set sail for the invasion area. The 40 U-boats lacking *Schnorkel* ran on the surface at their maximum speed of 17 knots, intending to maintain their batteries at full charge ready for the expected underwater run when dawn came. The nine *Schnorkel*-fitted boats, running at periscope depth at 6 knots, were soon left behind.

The non-*Schnorkel* boats soon reached the 'Corked' area and began to experience the stifling effect of the air patrols. The log of *U-415* conveys a vivid picture of the difficulties the boats' crews experienced:

0140. Bright moonlight, good visibility. Left the escort off Brest. Course 270 degrees, full speed.

0145. The boat astern, U-256, is attacked by aircraft. We also open fire. U-256 shoots down a plane. There are radar impulses coming from all round us, strength 3–4.

0220. Radar impulses increasing in strength, from the starboard. A Sunderland appears and attacks from 40° to starboard. I open fire. He drops four bombs ahead of me . . .

The boat's commander, *Oberleutnant* Herbert Werner, continued the story in an account he later wrote:

An instant later, four detonations amidships. Four savage eruptions heaved U-415 out of the water and threw our men flat on the deck plates. Then she fell back, and four collapsing geysers showered us with tons of water and sent cascades through the hatch. This was the end. Both diesels stopped, the rudder jammed hard a starboard. U-415 swerved in an arc, gradually losing speed ... a target to be finished off at ease.

Before the expected deathblow arrived, however, Werner's engineers succeeded in restarting the boat's engines and freeing her rudder. *U-415* limped back to Brest in company with the similarly shaken *U-256*.

A few hours later a Sunderland of No 201 Squadron on its patrol line picked up a radar contact on an object on the surface 11 miles away. The radar operator, Flight Sergeant D. Currie, guided the flying boat in for a perfect homing and, at a range of half a mile, the crew released a salvo of high-intensity flares that illuminated the boat for attack. At that point the U-boat opened up with inaccurate fire from its 20mm deck guns, but this ceased when the plane's front gunner replied. The pilot of the flying boat, Flight Lieutenant L. Bavystock, held his course at a height of 75ft and released a stick of six depth charges. As the weapons exploded, in the light of the flares the plane's rear gunner saw the U-boat's silhouette disappear under a wall of water. That commotion marked the end of *U-955*.

On that first night the 'Cork Patrols' reported 22 contacts with U-boats, leading to seven attacks. Two U-boats had been sunk and five damaged. At dawn, as the surviving U-boats dived to continue their passage under water, the action petered out. Although the night had gone well for No 19 Group, the battle was far from over. Five-sixths of the Group *Landwirt*'s boats, 42 in total, remained in battleworthy condition and continued heading towards the invasion area. As darkness fell on 7 June the action resumed, as the 36 U-boats without *Schnorkel* rose to the surface to resume their full-speed runs for the invasion area.

As the leading boats entered the western end of the English Channel, the 'Cork Patrols' were ready to receive them. Shortly after midnight Flying Officer Kenneth Moore was 'pacing his beat' in a Liberator of No 224 Squadron when his radar operator reported a contact 12 miles ahead. The Canadian pilot skilfully side-stepped his aircraft to place the contact between himself and the bright moon, then turned

---

SHORT SUNDERLAND MARK II

ROLE Maritime patrol flying boat.

POWER Four Bristol Pegasus XVIII nine-cylinder, air-cooled, radial engines each developing 1,050hp at take-off.

ARMAMENT A typical offensive armament was eight 250lb depth charges. The defensive armament comprised two Browning .303in machine guns in a turret in the nose, and a four-gun turret in the tail; in addition, there were single Vickers .303in weapons on hand-held mountings in each waist gun position.

PERFORMANCE Maximum speed 205mph at 5,000ft; cruising speed 170mph at 5,000ft. A typical patrol mission was two hours on patrol at 600 miles from base.

NORMAL OPERATIONAL TAKE-OFF WEIGHT 56,000lb.

DIMENSIONS Span 112ft 9½in; length 85ft 4in; wing area 1,687 sq ft.

DATE OF FIRST PRODUCTION SUNDERLAND II April 1942.

towards it and accelerated to attack speed. A few minutes later his navigator sighted a U-boat against the shimmering line of the moon on the water: 'It was a perfect silhouette, as if it were painted on white paper', Moore later remarked. With the target in sight, he told his radar operator to cease transmitting so as not to alert the boat's crew. The Liberator delivered an accurate attack and straddled the boat with six depth charges, three on either side of her hull. *U-629*, her back broken, sank leaving a growing patch of oil on the surface.

In the Liberator, the elated crew resumed their patrol. Their bomb bay still held six depth charges and a homing torpedo, sufficient for another attack. Jokingly, Moore commented: 'Now let's get another one.' And they did. A few minutes later the radar operator reported a contact at a range of 6 miles. The second attack was almost a carbon copy of the first. Again there was the adroit positioning of the U-boat 'up-moon', again the imposition of radar silence and again the accurate straddle with six depth charges. *Oberleutnant* von Lehsten and 43 of his crew were able to take to their life rafts before *U-373* sank. Kenneth Moore's achievement – sinking two U-boats in less than half an hour – was a unique performance and for it he was later awarded the Distinguished Service Order.

The nightly contests between the U-boats and the 'Cork Patrols' continued in similar vein over the next few days. By dawn on 10 June the aircraft had sunk six U-boats and inflicted serious damage on six more: almost a quarter of Group *Landwirt*'s boats had now been sunk or put out of action. Even more important, the planes had prevented any U-boats getting to the shipping lanes leading to the invasion area.

On 12 June the German Naval High Command conceded defeat. Its war diarist grimly noted that day:

> All U-boats operating without Schnorkel in the Bay of Biscay have been ordered to return to their bases, as the enemy air attacks are causing too many losses and too much damage. Only if an enemy landing seems imminent on the Biscay coast are the boats to operate. They will remain under shelter in a state of readiness.

As the surviving U-boats without *Schnorkel* headed west trying to extricate themselves from the air patrols, one boat was sunk and five more suffered damage. The unlucky craft was *U-441*, which had managed to avoid air attack so far and was on the final leg of the return journey to her base at Brest. About 50 miles separated the boat from the safety of the protective concrete pens, and by rights she should have made it. The Wellington assigned to patrol that area had suffered a radar failure but its pilot, Flight Lieutenant Antoniewicz of No 304 (Polish) Squadron, decided to continue his patrol without the device. Suddenly, in the moonlight, he caught sight of a U-boat in the act of surfacing just to starboard. Antoniewicz swung the aircraft round and attacked the boat, releasing six 250lb depth charges in long stick. The weapons splashed into the sea on either side of *U-441*'s conning tower and she disappeared in a wall of foaming water.

This left the boats with *Schnorkel*, and six of the original nine were still trying to pick their way past the air and sea patrols to reach the transport ships. Able to run indefinitely on their diesel engines, they kept their batteries fully charged. All they exposed above the surface was the top 3 or 4ft of the air pipe, capped by the float valve assembly 3ft long and 1ft wide. These craft were far less vulnerable to air attack than their counterparts without the breathing device.

Even under ideal conditions, the best radar sets then available could not detect the head at distances greater than 4 miles. Moreover, even if a skilful operator recognized the small radar return from a *Schnorkel* head, as the aircraft closed in the head usually disappeared in sea clutter before it could be seen visually. If the sea was rough, a radar search for *Schnorkel* heads was a futile business.

Sometimes, if the conditions were exactly right, a visual search might be more successful. If the sea was flat calm and the U-boat was moving at speed at *Schnorkel* depth, the wake from the breathing tube could be seen at distances up to 5 miles. And sometimes the exhaust fumes from the boat condensed when they met the cold outside air, producing a smoke trail that might be seen at distances up to 7 miles.

On 15 June, nine days after the landings had begun, the first

Schnorkel-fitted U-boat reached the main shipping route to Normandy. *U-621* sank a tank-landing ship and made two unsuccessful attacks on battleships before the Allied surface hunting teams hounded her out of the area. A fortnight elapsed before the next U-boat reached those rich if hazardous hunting grounds, but by then the critical period for the landings had passed and Allied troops were firmly established ashore.

The first air attack on a *Schnorkel*-fitted U-boat took place on 18 June, after an observant crewman aboard a Liberator of US Navy Patrol Squadron 110 sighted the head protruding above the surface. The subsequent depth charge attack inflicted damage on *U-275*.

More than three weeks elapsed before the next sighting of a *Schnorkel*. On 11 July, a crewman aboard a Sunderland flying boat of No 201 Squadron sighted the *Schnorkel* head of *U-1222*. The flying boat was also seen, however, and in the scramble to dive to a safe depth the boat went down at too steep an angle. Her stern rose out of the water, thereby presenting the Sunderland crew with an unexpectedly large and almost stationary target. Their stick of depth charges was both accurate and destructive.

JAMES PERRY'S carefully worked-out pattern of 'Cork Patrols' to seal the mouth of the English Channel against the marauding U-boats proved even more successful than expected. Not a single U-boat without *Schnorkel* reached the invasion area. Only half the *Schnorkel*-fitted boats got through to the invasion area, but once there they were hounded by the powerful surface patrols and achieved little. The 'crow' had shown itself remarkably adept at attacking the 'mole'.

CHAPTER ELEVEN

The Flight of the Doodlebug

The V-1 flying bomb, nicknamed the 'Doodlebug', was launched in large numbers against London and other targets during the late spring and summer of 1944. This chapter describes the flight of one of the first to be launched. Although the German records of the launching of that particular flying bomb did not survive, it has been possible to reconstruct an accurate picture of what took place from the laid-down firing procedure and from British records of the night's events.

AUCHY-LES-HESDINS, northern France, 0350 hours on 13 June 1944. After much hard work during the previous six days, the firing crew from *II. Abteilung, Flak Regiment 155 W* were ready to conduct their initial firing. At a camouflaged launching ramp outside the village, the V-1 flying bomb sat on its wheeled cradle at the base of the launching ramp. The missile was fully fuelled, its electrical system had been checked out and the weapon was ready to go.

After seeing that all his men were well clear of the ramp or else under cover, the *Oberleutnant* commanding the firing troop joined his firing NCO and radio operator in the concrete command post near the base of the launching ramp. He then ordered the firing NCO to commence the launch sequence. With a hiss of compressed air, 75-octane petrol from the missile's fuel tank was forced upwards to the Argus pulse-jet engine mounted above the fuselage. A spark plug crackled and the fuel ignited. The engine roared into life, belching flames from the rear end.

At the same time, below the base of the launching ramp, separate supplies of compressed air forced hydrogen peroxide and calcium permanganate from their respective tanks into a combustion chamber. As the two liquids came into contact, they set up a violent chemical reaction that produced superheated steam and oxygen at rapidly increasing pressure.

Within about seven seconds of engine start, the Argus pulse jet was developing its full 770lb of thrust. Meanwhile, in the combustion chamber at the base of the ramp, the combined pressure of steam and oxygen built up rapidly.

When the combination of engine thrust and the chemical reaction produced sufficient force, it sheered the ¼in-diameter steel pin holding the firing piston in place. With nothing to restrain it, the piston accelerated rapidly up the launching ramp taking with it the flying bomb on its cradle. By the time the V-1 and cradle reached the end of the 156ft ramp they were moving at about 250mph, comfortably above the minimum flying speed of the missile. As the V-1 left the ramp, the firing piston and launching cradle fell away and thudded to the ground in front of the ramp.

Trailing flames, the V-1 flew straight ahead after launch and climbed at a shallow angle as its speed slowly built up. When the missile reached its pre-set cruising altitude of 3,300ft it levelled off. Shortly afterwards the compass began feeding course corrections to the servo system driving the rudder in order to turn the nose of the V-1 on to the previously set course for its target: Tower Bridge in London.

At 0357 hours the missile crossed the coast near Étaples and rumbled out to sea. Shortly afterwards the distance counter mechanism, driven by a small propeller on the nose, made the warhead live. (Whether the Hesdins missile was the first to be launched that night is not known – four out of the initial salvo of ten flying bombs crashed shortly after they came off the ramp. But there is no doubt that the weapon fired from Hesdins was the first to come within view of Britain's defences.)

Four minutes after it left the French coast, at 0401 hours, operators at the radar station at Swingate near Dover unknowingly caught a glimpse of the V-1. For a few sweeps of the scanner, the radar plotted an approaching 'aircraft'. Then the plot ended. Four minutes afterwards came the first reported visual sighting from the British side. A Royal Navy motor torpedo boat in mid-channel reported a 'bright horizontal flame' coming from the direction of the French coast and moving rapidly on a north-westerly heading.

At 0407 hours an Observer Corps post near Dymchurch sighted the incoming 'aircraft' approaching from the south-east. The sighting was immediately linked to intelligence warnings circulated previously on the long-expected attack by a new type of German 'pilotless aircraft'. The new weapon had been code-named 'Diver', and from then on the

---

FIESELER Fi 103, ALIAS V-1, ALIAS 'DOODLEBUG'

(*Main production version*)

ROLE Medium-range bombardment missile.

POWER One Argus 014 pulse-jet engine developing 770lb thrust at sea level.

WARHEAD This contained 1,870lb of high explosive.

PERFORMANCE Note that the V-1 was not built to normal aircraft manufacturing tolerances and as a result there were considerable variations in performance from missile to missile. Its maximum speed was around 400mph, but many missiles flew somewhat slower than that. Its typical cruising altitude was 3,300ft, though some crossed the coast at treetop height, which soon led to their demise. The highest altitude recorded for a V-1 was 8,000ft; its maximum range was 150 miles.

WEIGHT AT LAUNCH 4,800lb.

DIMENSIONS Span 17ft 4³/₄in; length 22ft 7³/₄in; wing area 50.5 sq ft.

DATE OF FIRST PRODUCTION FIESELER 103 Summer 1943.

'Diver' was reported by a succession of observer posts as it passed across Kent at about 270mph. The deep-throated rumble of the missile's pulse jet sounded quite different from any aircraft propulsion system previously heard, and was likened to 'a two-stroke motorcycle without a silencer', 'a motor boat' or 'a Model T Ford going up a hill'.

As the missile continued its undeviating path towards London, the counter mechanism measured off the distance flown. At 0420 hours, the counter reached the previously set figure at which the flight was to end. A pair of electrical contacts closed so as to fire two detonators which locked the missile's elevator and rudder in the neutral position. At the same time spoilers under the tailplane sprang out, to thrust the tail upwards and force the missile into a steep dive so it would make a clean impact with the ground. That bunting manoeuvre imposed severe negative G on the vehicle, however, and the remaining petrol sloshed to the top of the almost empty fuel tank. With the feed pipe uncovered, the supply of fuel to the engine ceased and the pulse jet flamed out. The engine roar suddenly ceased and, whistling quietly, the weapon dived on to a patch of open land at Stone near Dartford. The multiple fuses set off the 1,870lb of high explosive in the warhead, to carve a shallow crater and cause blast damage over a large area. There were no casualties. The V-1 was no precision weapon; the first to arrive had impacted about 15 miles east of the intended target, Tower Bridge in London.

During the next hour, three more flying bombs crossed the coast of England. One crashed on Bethnal Green – within 2 miles of the aiming point – where it killed six people and injured nine. The remaining two missiles crashed on open land well short of the target, one near Cuckfield in Sussex and one near Sevenoaks in Kent; neither weapon caused casualties.

Of the ten flying bombs launched against London during the early morning darkness on 13 July, only four impacted on English soil. As recounted earlier, four of those missiles had crashed shortly after leaving their ramps in France. Two more suffered mechanical failures and crashed into the sea before they reached the English coast.

So began the V-1 bombardment of London, long predicted by the British Intelligence services. The War Cabinet had expected the initial onslaught to be far heavier. Indeed, the German intention was that this should have been the case.

A WEEK EARLIER, on 6 June, Allied troops had landed in Normandy. The German high command had assessed this as a diversionary operation, with the intention of drawing forces away from the Pas de Calais area where the main invasion was expected. If that was the case, the area from which the V-1s were to be launched at London might be threatened or even lost before the weapon went into action. By that time the preparations for the bombardment of the British capital were well advanced, though they were still some way from completion. *Oberst* (Colonel) Max Wachtel, commander of *Flak Regiment 155 W* responsible for the ground launching operation, received orders to commence the bombardment of London late on the afternoon of 12 June.

Wachtel and his men did their best, but it was a hopelessly tight schedule. The hefty steel prefabricated launching ramp sections had to be brought by rail from depots in Germany, offloaded on to trucks and then manhandled into the position of the previously laid concrete plinths. The same went for the firing equipment and the missiles themselves. With the Allied air forces conducting a systematic attack on the French rail network to isolate the invasion area, Wachtel's movement schedule did not go smoothly. Toiling round the clock, his men installed the necessary equipment at 55 of the regiment's 64 firing sites. It was a highly creditable achievement, but when the deadline was reached many sites lacked essential items. Of the regiment's four firing *Abteilungen* (battalions), each responsible for 16 missile launchers, one had no fuel for its diesel generators and another lacked the chemical fuels to power its launching ramps; neither *Abteilung* was able to take part in the initial firings. The other two *Abteilungen* did little better and, as we have seen, only ten missiles were launched in the initial salvo.

After those first problems, Wachtel was given a three-day respite in which to bring all firing units to full readiness. The bombardment reopened on the evening of 15 June, and then the results were more gratifying from the German viewpoint. Between then and midnight on the following day 244 flying bombs were launched. Of those, 45 (18 per cent) failed to launch properly. A few missiles impacted close to their ramps, in some cases causing them damage. It seems that a further 40 or so missiles fell into the sea, for only 153 (62 per cent of those fired) crossed the coast of England or were otherwise seen by British observers.

During the lull following the initial attack, the fighters and anti-aircraft guns had been deployed to the south of England to counter the new threat. The fighters and guns shot down 22 bombs, and about 50 fell on open ground clear of the capital. However, 73 bombs (30 per cent of those fired) reached the Greater London built-up area where they caused widespread damage and casualties.

In the 16 days between the resumption of firings and the end of June, 2,442 flying bombs were launched. Approximately one-third crashed or were shot down before they reached the English coast, and one-third crashed or were shot down over southern England before they reached the target area. The remaining one-third, about 800 missiles, reached the Greater London conurbation where they caused 2,441 deaths and 7,107 cases of serious injury. On average, 153 missiles were launched each day, and on average each V-1 launched caused one death and three cases of serious injury in England.

People living in the areas overflown by V-1s (including this writer, who at the time was a nine-year-old living in Ewell, to the south of London) quickly developed an ear for the distinctive rumble of the V-1's pulse jet. They knew they were safe so long as that engine rumble continued. When it stopped abruptly, they had about 10 seconds to get to cover. Undoubtedly that unintended final warning saved many lives.

Given the indiscriminate nature of the V-1 bombardment, it is remarkable that the most serious single incident in June occurred at a military target. A flying bomb crashed into the Guards' Chapel at Wellington Barracks on the 18th, while a service was in progress. Of the 121 people killed, 63 were soldiers.

Allied reconnaissance aircraft flew saturation coverage of the launch areas, searching for the launching ramps. When these were found they came under repeated air attack. But the elaborate camouflage discipline practised by Wachtel's men stood them in good stead. The regiment's War Diary records reveal that between the start of the bombardment and 1 July, only 2 of the 64 launching sites were completely destroyed. Twenty-two suffered heavy damage, 8 had moderate damage and 10 sites suffered slight damage. Casualties to firing crews totalled 28 killed and 80 wounded.

The most serious effect of the Allied air attacks was the hindrance to the rail system used to deliver missiles to the launching sites. Once a site had fired its stock of missiles, it sometimes had to wait a day or more for the next batch to arrive. The ability of the supply organization to deliver missiles fell far short of the ramps' capacity to fire them. As a result the average time interval between shots was 60 to 90 minutes, compared with a minimum firing interval of 26 minutes for launching sites that had a full complement of missiles.

The bombardment of London continued throughout July and into August. On 2 August the regiment launched what was to be its heaviest attack during a 24-hour period, when it fired 316 missiles from 38 serviceable launchers; about 107 of those missiles impacted in the Greater London area. Throughout the bombardment the aiming point had been Tower Bridge and on that day, for the first time, a flying bomb scored a direct hit on the famous landmark and caused damage to the roadway.

At the end of the first week in August, the German Army began to pull back from western France. *Flak Regiment 155 W* then ordered that construction of new launching sites was to cease south of the River Somme, and there was to be only minimum repair work on damaged sites there. New launch sites were to be surveyed and constructed as far east as possible, allowing for the limited range of the V-1. In the third week in August, the front collapsed and German forces began a head-long retreat out of France. One by one, the flying bomb launching sites were abandoned. At 0400 hours on 1 September, the last of 8,617 flying bombs was dispatched from a launching site in northern France. That marked the end of the first, and most destructive, phase of the V-1 bombardment.

The great majority of flying bombs launched against England had come from launching sites in the Pas de Calais area. There was another source, however. Since 9 July, IIIrd *Gruppe* of *Kampfgeschwader 3*, with a nominal strength of 39 Heinkel He 111 bombers specially modified to air-launch V-1s, had joined in the bombardment. The 2½-ton weight, and the drag of the flying bomb mounted externally under the starboard wing root, imposed severe penalties on the bomber's performance. As they headed for their designated launch points, these bombers cruised over the sea at 170mph, keeping below 300ft to remain unobserved by British coastal radars.

The Heinkels operated at night or in bad weather from Gilze Rijen and Venlo in Holland and sometimes from Beauvais in France. As a bomber neared the launching point, it turned on to the attack heading and began a slow climb to the missile's minimum safe launching altitude of 1,700ft. Once there, the Heinkel levelled out and accelerated to 200mph, the minimum flying speed for the V-1. Ten seconds before release the flying bomb's pulse jet was started. With its flame lighting up the sky for miles around, the bomber crew felt very vulnerable indeed. Once the missile was released, it fell about 300ft before the autopilot took control and established the weapon on a climb to its pre-set cruising altitude. While that was happening the Heinkel entered a descending turn at full throttle, as its crew sought to put as much distance as possible between themselves and the highly visible missile they had unleashed.

Up to the first week of September *III./KG 3* launched about 300 bombs at London, 90 at Southampton and a score at Gloucester. Its final attack during this phase was during the early morning darkness on 5 September, with a nine-bomb salvo aimed at London. The air-launched flying bombs were far less accurate than their ground-launched counterparts. The attacks on Gloucester and Southampton were complete failures. No flying bomb fell on the former, while the spread of craters south of Southampton covered so large an area that British Intelligence thought the intended target was Portsmouth!

The Allied advance forced *III./KG 3* to pull back the airfields at Aalhorn, Varelbusch, Zwischenahn and Handorf-bei-Munster in northern Germany. Then the bombardment of London resumed. The attack using air-launched V-1s failed to achieve any degree of intensity, however. Following their release, more than a third of the flying bombs failed to function correctly and crashed soon afterwards. Many of the remainder were shot down by fighters or guns. Moreover, as mentioned earlier, the accuracy of air-launched missiles was even worse than that of their ground-launched counterparts.

To observe a typical air-launched missile attack, let us look at the one that took place on 16 September 1944. Over the North Sea the weather conditions were perfect from the Heinkel crews' viewpoint: thick overcast, with the cloud base between 700 to 1,200ft and light drizzle rain. Soon after dark 15 Heinkels took off at five-minute intervals from bases in northern Germany and headed for their missile-launching area in the Thames Estuary. Nine V-1s got under way satisfactorily, of which three were destroyed by British ships and aircraft before they reached the coast. Over land, two more of the flying bombs were shot down by fighters. Two of the remaining four missiles came down in open countryside in Essex. Only two V-1s reached the Greater London area; one fell on Woolwich and the other on Barking. No Heinkel was lost.

As might be expected, the Royal Air Force spared no effort to engage the missile-launching bombers. Each night when operations were considered likely, Mosquito intruders flew standing patrols over the bombers' bases. At the same time, Mosquito night fighters flew standing patrols in the areas from which the Heinkels launched their missiles.

In the autumn of 1944 the V-1 launching force was expanded from a *Gruppe* to a full *Geschwader*, *Kampfgeschwader 53*, with a nominal strength of 90 Heinkels; *III./KG 3* was redesignated *I./KG 53*, and two *Gruppen* of *KG 53* converted to the stand-off role and became operational in November.

Remarkably, from the beginning of September almost to the end of the year there had been no attempt to exploit the flexibility conferred by air launching. Had the missiles been launched against targets other than London, the fighter and gun defences would have had to be spread more thinly.

Not until the early morning darkness of 24 December was there an attempt to strike in strength at another target. Then some 50 Heinkels flew to a spread of launch points over the North Sea and launched their missiles at Manchester. Thirty flying bombs crossed the coast between Skegness and Bridlington and rumbled westwards. Eleven bombs fell within 15 miles of the centre of Manchester but only one impacted within the city limits. Thirty-seven people were killed and 67 seriously injured. One Heinkel was shot down by a night fighter.

On 10 January 1945 *KG 53* reported 79 serviceable He 111s on strength. Four days later the unit ceased operations, due to the severe fuel shortage that now afflicted every part of the *Luftwaffe*. From first to last, the stand-off bombing force lost 77 Heinkels. Sixteen were claimed shot down by British night fighters, but most of the remainder were lost in accidents resulting from the hazards of flying at low altitude at night in bad weather.

In March 1945 the bombardment of London was resumed, using an extended-range version of the V-1 fitted with a larger fuel tank but carrying a smaller warhead. With a maximum range of 200 miles, these modified missiles could reach the capital from launching sites in German-held areas in Holland. The new attack opened on 3 March and closed at the end of the month, after 275 bombs had been launched. The longer flights meant that more bombs crashed into the sea or were shot down by fighters, and by this time the British fighter and gun defences had reached a peak of efficiency. Only 13 bombs – less than one-in-five of those from Holland – reached the London area.

Just over 10,000 Fieseler V-1 flying bombs were launched against England. The great majority, about 85 per cent, came from ground launchers. Of the total, 7,488 crossed the British coast or were otherwise observed by the defences, and 3,957 were shot down short of their targets. Of the 3,531 flying bombs that eluded the defences, 2,419 reached the London conurbation, about 30 reached Southampton and Portsmouth and one hit Manchester. Thus only about a quarter of the ground-launched bombs reached the area of their intended targets; of the air-launched bombs, the figure was about one in ten. In England the flying bombs caused 6,184 deaths – an average of three deaths for every five bombs fired – with a further 17,981 people injured.

CHAPTER TWELVE

The Superfortresses' First Strike on Japan

In June 1943 an important new bomber type entered service with the

US Army Air Forces: the Boeing B-29 Superfortress. With a maximum

all-up weight of 67 tons, the B-29 was more than twice as heavy

as the B-17s and the B-24s that had preceded it.

THE B-29 SUPERFORTRESS represented the zenith of heavy bomber design during the Second World War. It was the first heavy bomber to feature pressurized cabins for its crew. The plane's defensive armament, comprising ten .5in machine guns in four remotely controlled barbettes, plus one 20mm cannon and two machine guns in the tail position, was the most powerful yet seen. The B-29 could deliver 6,000lb of bombs to a target 1,700 miles from its base and return, carrying normal operational fuel reserves. No other aircraft of that period came close to matching this superb performance.

As remarkable as anything else about the B-29 programme was the speed with which the revolutionary new bomber was brought into service. The initial contract to develop the bomber was signed in June 1940 and the prototype made its maiden flight in September 1942. In June 1943 the first Superfortress unit, the 58th Bombardment Wing (Very Heavy), took delivery of production aircraft from the initial batch. In November 1943 the XXth Bomber Command was formed

Officers of the Italian Air Expeditionary Force in Libya in 1911, from *left to right*: Lieutenant Constantino Quaglia, Captain Riccardo Moizo, Captain Agostoni, Captain Carlo Piazza and Lieutenant Savoia (see Chapter 1). (Aeronautica Militare)

The Blériot monoplane in which Carlo Piazza flew the world's first combat aviation sortie on 23 October 1911. (Aeronautica Militare)

Carlo Piazza pictured in 1911 flying kit, with a leather jacket and early type 'bone dome'. (Aeronautica Militare)

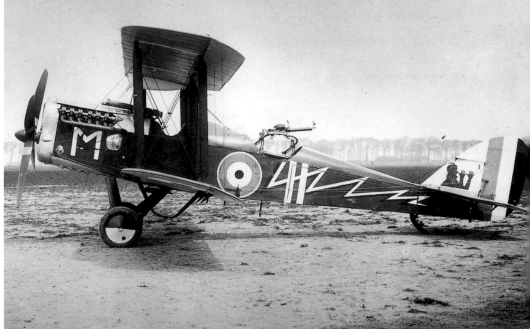

Sopwith Camel scouts ranged on the foredeck of the aircraft carrier HMS *Furious* in July 1918, as the ship headed to the launch point for the attack on the Zeppelin base at Tondern in Schleswig Holstein (see Chapter 3). (IWM)

OPPOSITE PAGE
Major Egburt Cadbury and Captain Robert Leckie photographed at the Great Yarmouth air station a few hours after they had shot down the Zeppelin *L.70* over the North Sea (see Chapter 2).

A de Havilland 4 biplane belonging to No 202 Squadron, which operated the type over France from May 1917 until the end of the war.

A Spitfire from No 266 Squadron, a unit that suffered heavy losses during the Battle of Britain (see Chapter 4).

Oberleutnant Guenther Dolenga's Dornier Do 217 lying on Romney Marsh, after RAF Meacon transmitters had fed false bearings into the plane's radio compass system and caused it to become lost (see Chapter 5). (IWM)

OPPOSITE PAGE
Loading a Spitfire by crane on to the aircraft carrier USS *Wasp* at Port Glasgow in April 1942, at the start of Operation Calendar (see Chapter 6). (USN)

A Spitfire about to start its take-off run on *Wasp*. The aircraft that had taken off ahead of it is visible above its starboard wing tip. Already the lift is on its way down to the hangar to pick up the next fighter. (USN)

A Junkers 86R ultra-high-altitude bomber that took part in the highest air combat of the Second World War, at 43,500ft over Southampton (see Chapter 7).

BELOW LEFT Horst Goetz, an *Oberfeldwebel* at the time of the incident, piloted the Ju 86R during the high-altitude action over Southampton. (Goetz)

BELOW RIGHT Pilot Officer Emanuel Galitzine, who piloted the modified Spitfire IX during the same high-altitude action. (Galitzine)

Emanuel Galitzine (*left*), pictured with Horst Goetz in 1975, after they were introduced by the author. (Galitzine)

Boeing B-17 bombers being heavily engaged by flak, as happened during the attack on Berlin on 6 March 1944 (see Chapter 8). (USAF)

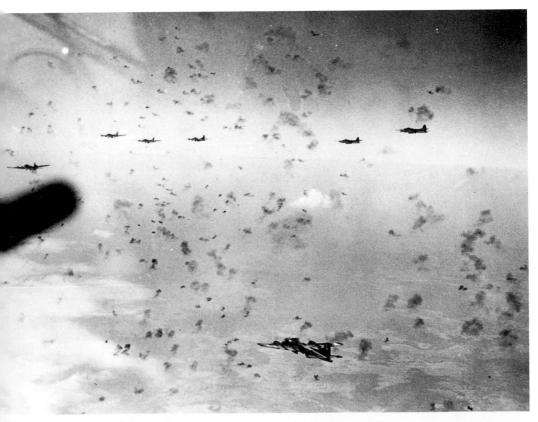

A German radar station on the
north coast of France under
attack from RAF fighter-bombers
in the spring of 1944, as part of
the softening-up operations that
preceded the D-Day landings (see
Chapter 9). (IWM)

German *Seetakt* coast-watching
radar, used for surface search
and gunnery control. The Taxable
and Glimmer ghost 'fleet' operations were primarily designed to
deceive this type of radar.

A Consolidated Liberator maritime
patrol plane, one of the types
that took part in the operation to
prevent U-boats entering the
English Channel to strike at the
invasion fleet (see Chapter 10).
(IWM)

RIGHT Flying Officer Kenneth Moore, a Liberator pilot of No 224 Squadron, sank
two U-boats in the space of half an hour during the 'Corking' operation. (IWM)

A Short Sunderland flying boat, another of the aircraft types employed during the
'Corking' operation. (Short Bros.)

A V-1 flying bomb in flight (see Chapter 11).

Boeing B-29 Superfortress bombers pictured during a training mission (see Chapter 12).

Feldwebel Fritz Buchholz, a Focke-Wulf 190 pilot who was pitchforked into the Battle of France in August 1944 with little training (see Chapter 13). (Buchholz)

Oberst Hans-Joachim Herrmann (*facing camera*) with *Reichsmarschall* Hermann Goering, inspecting *Luftwaffe* pilots. Herrmann was the originator of the plan for German fighters to ram US heavy bombers (see Chapter 14). (Herrmann)

A late model Messerschmitt 109G fighter, one of the types used in the ramming operation.

Republic F-105D attack fighters bore the brunt of the US losses over North Vietnam, following the introduction of the SA-2 surface-to-air missile system (see Chapter 15). (USAF)

A General Electric QRC-160 radar-jamming pod mounted on an F-105. When carried by planes flying the special four-plane jamming pod formation, this jammer successfully neutralized the SA-2 missile system. (USAF)

ABOVE LEFT An SA-2 Guideline two-stage surface-to-air missile on its launcher.

ABOVE RIGHT Captain Don Pickard, who piloted one of the RF-4C Phantoms conducting a post-strike reconnaissance mission to Hanoi on 10 May 1972. After suffering technical problems, Pickard was fortunate to regain his base (see Chapter 16). (Pickard)

Captain Roger Locher pictured immediately after his rescue from North Vietnam. To his left is General John Vogt, the Seventh Air Force commander, who ordered the daring rescue operation (see Chapter 17). (Locher)

A Vulcan bomber modified to carry a Shrike anti-radar missile under each wing. Squadron Leader Neil McDougall flew this same plane, modified to carry two Shrikes under each wing, when he was forced to divert to Rio de Janeiro on 3 June 1982 (see Chapter 19).

The Fairchild Republic A-10 ground attack fighter, nicknamed the 'Warthog', was flown over Iraq and Kuwait by Captain Todd Sheehy of the 511th Tactical Fighter Squadron (see Chapter 20). (USAF)

OPPOSITE PAGE
A trio of Royal Air Force Harrier GR 3s on the deck of HMS *Hermes*, about to take off for an air strike on a target in the Falklands during the spring of 1982. (British Aerospace)

Pilots of No 1 Squadron Royal Air Force, during the Falklands conflict. From *left to right*: Squadron Leader 'Bomber' Harris, Flight Lieutenant Jeff Glover, Flight Lieutenant Mark Hare, Flight Lieutenant John Rochfort, Squadron Leader Jerry Pook, Wing Commander Peter Squire (commander), Squadron Leader Bob Iveson and (*seated*) Flight Lieutenant Tony Harper.

F-15C Eagle air superiority fighters of the 48th Tactical Fighter Wing on the flight line at Aviano in Italy during the Kosovo conflict in 1999 (see Chapter 21).

BELOW LEFT A Hunter unmanned air vehicle (UAV) pictured during a training launch with rocket assistance at Fort Huachuca, Arizona (see Chapter 22). (TRW)

The interior of the control cabin for the Hunter UAV. On the left, in the internal pilot's position, is Sergeant Antonio Mitchell, controlling the UAV's flight by data link. He describes the operation in Chapter 22. To Mitchell's right sits the mission payload operator, responsible for training the UAV's sensors on targets and adjusting the zoom lens to get the required imagery. (TRW)

to train crews and form Superfortress units at airfields in Kansas.

The bomber's hasty introduction into service meant that many of its initial teething troubles remained to be resolved, however. The Wright R-3350 engine, a newly developed 18-cylinder radial rated at 2,200hp, gave particular trouble. B-29s returned so often with one engine shut down that crews dubbed the B-29 'by far the best three-engined bomber in the world'.

In April 1944 the 58th Wing, comprising the 40th, the 444th, the 462nd and the 468th Bomb Groups, flew its B-29s via Newfoundland, Morocco and Egypt to its rear operational airfields situated around Kharagpur in north-east India. From there, the force was to commence a bombardment of targets in Japan itself. In readiness for these attacks, four forward operating bases for the B-29s had been prepared in the area around Chengtu in China. The Allies possessed no secure land route to that part of China, so every item of equipment required for the operations had to be carried there by air. The distance from Kharagpur to Chengtu was 1,200 miles by the most direct route, and the aircraft had to cross the Himalayan mountain range with some of the highest peaks in the world. The forward airfields at Chengtu had been constructed using local labour. They were primitive in the extreme, with poor facilities for both men and machines.

For the air transportation task, 54 Curtiss C-46 transport planes were assigned to airlift supplies into Chengtu. But these transports' carrying capacity was insufficient, alone, to support a sustained bombardment by the B-29s. A large proportion of the fuel and other supplies required at the forward airfields had to be carried by the B-29 units themselves. Twenty B-29s were converted into flying tankers, with their armament and bomb racks stripped out, allowing them to carry 9 tons of aviation fuel to China on each sortie. Other fuel and supplies were flown to the forward bases aboard B-29s fully equipped for the bomber role. During May 1944, bomber and tanker B-29s flew 238 transport sorties into China. It required *twelve* cargo flights from India to Chengtu to support a single B-29 sortie against Japan.

While the build-up of supplies at Chengtu continued, the

Superfortresses mounted their first shakedown attack on Thailand from bases in India. On 5 June, 98 B-29s took off for a daylight attack on the Makasan railway workshops near Bangkok. Several B-29s encountered technical problems and of the five aircraft lost, none fell to enemy action. One B-29 crashed shortly after take-off, two ditched in the Bay of Bengal following mechanical failures, one ran out of fuel and the reason for the loss of the fifth bomber was never ascertained. Twenty bombers were forced to abort the mission due to technical failures.

The 58th Wing's second operation was much more ambitious than the first. This time the target was the huge Imperial Iron and Steel Works at Yawata on the southern Japanese island of Kyushu, thought to produce almost one quarter of the nation's steel. The round trip from Chengtu would cover a distance of 2,400 miles, making this the longest-range aerial bombing operation yet attempted.

On 13 June, the B-29s began to deploy to their forward bases. Two

---

BOEING B-29 SUPERFORTRESS

ROLE Very heavy bomber.

POWER Four Wright Cyclone R-3350-23 turbo-supercharged, 18-cylinder, air-cooled, radial engines each developing 2,200hp at take-off.

ARMAMENT The bomb load carried depended upon the distance to be flown. During the attacks on Japan from forward bases in China, these aircraft carried eight 500lb high-explosive bombs. The plane's defensive armament comprised ten Browning .5in machine guns in four remotely controlled barbettes above and below the fuselage, and two of these weapons plus a 20mm cannon in the tail turret.

PERFORMANCE Over target, attack speed 260mph at 20,000ft; cruising speed for maximum range 205mph at 5,000ft.

NORMAL OPERATIONAL TAKE-OFF WEIGHT 135,000lb.

DIMENSIONS Span: 141ft 3in; length 99ft; wing area 1,736 sq ft.

DATE OF FIRST PRODUCTION B-29 September 1943.

days later, on the 15th, sixty-eight Superfortresses took off to attack Yawata. Burdened by a huge weight of fuel, each B-29 was able to carry only eight 500lb bombs.

In mid-1944 the Allies had little hard information on the capabilities of the air defence system covering the Japanese home islands. To discover more, one B-29 in four carried a radio countermeasures officer and a set of Elint receivers to monitor the Japanese radar frequencies. Lieutenant Tom Friedman, a radio countermeasures officer with the 40th Bomb Group, recalled:

> We were scheduled to reach the target around midnight and attack singly, so there was no attempt to assemble in formation. During the long approach flight, I moved into the waist gunner's position to gaze out at the panorama of ancient China spread out below me in the late afternoon.
>
> As dusk fell I crawled back to the windowless, crowded radar compartment, to my position in the aircraft. The countermeasures equipment had been a late addition to the B-29's inventory and, in spite of its great size, there was little spare space inside the pressurized compartments. The racks for my equipment had been squeezed in between the bulkhead and the chemical toilet. As the twelfth man in the aircraft, my 'seat' was the lid of the toilet itself – a subject for numerous wisecracks on the appropriateness of my position!

As the B-29 neared enemy territory, Friedman's special receivers picked up signals from a Japanese early warning radar.

> So our approach had been detected well before we reached the coast of China and several hours before our target. It remained to be seen what use if any the enemy would make of this information. As we neared the coast of China further signals came in from other early warning radars ... The strengths of the signals slowly increased until at times I thought we passed directly over the sites. A glance at the scope of the bombing radar behind me showed the mainland of China receding to the southwest. Over the sea we passed through

some rough weather and our big plane was tossed violently. With no safety belt for my improvised 'seat', I had to brace myself between the countermeasures equipment and the back of the bombing radar.

Gradually the turbulence died away as the B-29 headed over the Strait of Tsushima and began its bomb run:

> By this time the enemy radar activity had risen to a crescendo. It was an eerie feeling to know that far below us our every move was being carefully watched on the enemy scopes and noted on their plotting boards. The $64,000 question was what could, or would, they do about it? Busily I logged the characteristics of each set of radar signals in turn, carefully noting the time of each so that after the flight the positions where the signals had been received could be plotted.

Friedman identified several early warning radars, but other signals were new to him.

> Nearly a score of enemy radars were following us during our bomb run. From time to time I switched my earphones from the search receiver to the regular interphone, and could hear the chatter of the gunners and the bombardier as they noted the searchlights' beams around us and the flashes of the bursting [anti aircraft] shells.
>
> For the attack we were all fully accoutred for combat. Over my coveralls I had on so much equipment I could hardly move: Mae West, parachute, emergency kit, pistol, canteen, flak suit and flak helmet. I glanced around and saw our radar man toggle the bombs at our aiming point, the anchorage beside the Yawata steel works, then I returned to my receiver as I felt the bomber swing on to the opposite heading for home.

At the target, the B-29 crews found the steelworks covered by five-tenths cloud on top of a layer of industrial haze. Fifteen crews delivered visual attacks on the plant, while 32 others bombed the plant using radar. Post strike reconnaissance revealed little damage to the steel works, though several bombs fell on nearby industrial and business areas. Two aircraft attacked the secondary target at Laoyao and five bombed targets of opportunity,

Over the target, six B-29s suffered minor damage from flak. Crews noted that the anti-aircraft fire was moderate in intensity and generally inaccurate. It appeared that gunners waited until a plane was illuminated by searchlights before they opened fire. On numerous occasions planes were 'coned' by searchlights, but only after one light had first found it. That pointed to a lack of gunlaying or searchlight control radars in that area. There were 16 reports of sightings of enemy night fighters. Only five sightings culminated in firing passes, however, and no bomber suffered hits from that cause.

On the way back to Chengtu, Friedman logged Japanese radar signals similar to those he had found on the way to the target. As the last of the signals faded out, the B-29 crossed into friendly territory.

At 4 am we had a meal of K rations to celebrate the success of the mission, then I stretched out for a short nap on one of the canvas bunks in the rear compartment. Soon after dawn, I woke up to find that we were almost at our base. I climbed through the long tunnel over the bomb bays to the nose compartment and watched our pilot, Captain Jack Ledford, bring the bomber in for a perfect landing. We had been airborne for more than 14 hours.

Of the 68 Superfortresses that had taken off for Yawata, seven failed to return due to accidents or mechanical failures. Enemy action played a contributory part to only one of these losses. The bomber in question had suffered an engine fire and made a forced landing in Chinese-held territory, but was then destroyed on the ground during a strafing attack by Japanese planes. Six aircraft suffered mechanical failures that forced their crews to abandon the mission.

The Superfortress was still too new and it suffered from too many teething troubles for it to achieve much during its initial attacks. Moreover, the primitive forward bases in China, totally reliant on air supply, were unsuitable to support a sustained bombardment by the big bombers. In fact, the B-29s would go on to mount only nine attacks on Japan from bases in China, before they ceased operations from that area in January 1945.

In the meantime US forces had captured several islands in the Mariana group, and construction teams quickly built airfields there to accommodate B-29s. These bases could easily be supplied by sea, allowing the B-29s to confine their activities to the bomber role. And also by that time, the crash programmes to cure the new bomber's various teething troubles had taken effect. B-29s began attacks on Japan from the Marianas in November 1944, and the raids from that quarter rapidly built up in both strength and ferocity. In the nine months that followed the heavy bombers laid waste much of Japanese industry, before the two atomic bomb attacks forced the Japanese government to surrender. So ended the train of events set in motion by that first, largely ineffectual, probing attack on Yawata in June 1944.

CHAPTER THIRTEEN

No Place for a Beginner

Air warfare could be a brutal business for those who entered the fray

with insufficient training, especially if the opposing air force possessed

overwhelming strength. Many of the German pilots sent to fight over

France in the late spring and summer of 1944 faced both these

misfortunes.

DURING THE EARLY part of 1944, *Feldwebel* [Sergeant] Fritz Buchholz flew the twin-engined Messerschmitt Me 410 bomber-destroyer against the US bomber formations. The powerfully armed Me 410s had been very effective against the heavy bombers, but they fell as easy prey to the US long-range escort fighters which now ranged to almost every part of German-occupied Europe.

No longer able to survive in this type of action, the Me 410 bomber-destroyer units were disbanded in July 1944. Buchholz and other pilots from his unit were sent to the newly formed IInd *Gruppe* of *Jagdgeschwader* 6 operating Focke-Wulf Fw 190 single-engined fighters. The pilots received only the sketchiest training in flying their new mounts before they were ordered into action. Fritz Buchholz recalled:

Flying against the heavy bombers in the Me 410 had been rather like driving one truck against another; fighter-versus-fighter combat in an

Fw 190 was something quite different. This might not have been so
bad, had there been sufficient time for us to assimilate our new role.
But this was not the case. The battle round the Allied bridgeheads in
Normandy was entering its most critical phase and we were to go into
action as soon as possible.

On 18 August, just over two weeks later and when he had less than
eleven hours flying time in the Fw 190, Buchholz's unit received orders
to prepare to move to France.

It took four days to move the *Gruppe* with its forty or so Fw 190s
from Koenigsberg to its operational base at Herpy near Reims. The
Allied air forces possessed almost complete air supremacy and permanent *Luftwaffe* bases in France were being bombed regularly. Most operational units had been forced to use improvised airstrips in the
surrounding countryside, and Buchholz described his impressions of
the one at Herpy.

> Our airstrip at Herpy was nothing more than a piece of flat cow
> pasture surrounded by trees in which our aircraft could be hidden;
> nearby was our tented accommodation. The Allied fighter-bombers
> seemed to be everywhere and our survival depended on the strictest
> attention to camouflage. As part of this we even had a herd of cows
> which were moved on to the airfield when no flying was in progress.
> As well as giving the place a rustic look, these performed the valuable
> task of obliterating the tracks made on the grass by the aircraft. Such
> attention to detail paid off and there were no attacks on Herpy while I
> was there.

On the two days following his arrival at Herpy, 23 and 24 August,
Fritz Buchholz and other pilots flew on familiarization flights. Given the
careful camouflage of their base, it was important to know the land-
marks in the local area so they could find their base. During these
flights Buchholz did not make contact with the enemy aircraft, though
some pilots did.

For pilots accustomed to operating from permanent airfields in

Germany, flying from the ill-equipped forward airfield in France was a disconcerting experience. While the small pasture was easily concealed, the confined space made it difficult if it was necessary for the unit to get airborne rapidly. During the first day at the new airfield two aircraft collided on take-off, probably because one of them had run into the turbulent slipstream from the pair that had taken off immediately ahead.

By the time the *Gruppe* was ready to go into action from Herpy, the Battle of France had already been lost. The German Army was retreating from Normandy, with troops streaming eastward across the Seine. The hard-pressed *Luftwaffe* fighter force in the area was ordered to do whatever it could to cover the retreat. On 25 August the *Gruppe* took off for its first full-scale operation: an offensive sweep as far as the River Seine, or as directed by their ground controller as soon as the force was airborne.

> Led by our commander, Hauptmann Elstermann, the forty-odd
> Fw 190s took off shortly after noon. So sketchy had our training
> been that this was the first occasion on which *II./JG 6* had
> flown together as a *Gruppe*. My *Staffel*, the 7th, was to fly as
> top-cover and so took off first; we orbited the field while the
> others got airborne, then the large formation climbed away to
> the west with our *Staffel* about 6,000 feet above the other two.

Soon after leaving Herpy, the *Gruppe* received new orders. There was a report that enemy fighter-bombers were attacking the nearby airfield at Chastres near St Quentin, and the Focke-Wulfs were to engage these. The *Gruppe* turned on to a northerly heading and shortly afterwards Buchholz caught sight of unidentified aircraft a few miles away to the north, below the level of his *Staffel* but above the main part of the formation. Buchholz reported the sighting to the *Gruppe* commander:

> He acknowledged my call and identified the aircraft as American
> P-38 Lightnings. With the sun on our backs we went after them
> and as we got closer I counted about twelve. Elstermann gave the

order 'Zusatzbehaelter weg!' and the drop tanks tumbled away from the aircraft.

My *Staffel* commander, Oberleutnant Paffrath, took us down to attack. I took my *Schwarm* [four-plane flight] to follow him in a tight turn, but suddenly my Focke-Wulf gave a shudder. The wing dropped and I found myself spinning helplessly into the mêlée below. I had to take the standard spin recovery action, pushing the stick forwards and applying opposite rudder, with the dogfight going on all around me. It was utter chaos, with Focke-Wulfs chasing Lightnings chasing Focke-Wulfs. I recovered from my spin and fired a burst at one Lightning, only to have to break away when another Lightning curved round and opened fire at me.

As Buchholz pulled away, he discovered why his fighter had entered the spin: his drop tank was still in place and now resisted all his efforts to jettison it. It was almost full of fuel and weighed about 550lb. No wonder his Focke-Wulf could not turn as tightly as the others that had released their tanks!

The twelve P-38s the *Gruppe* was engaging belonged to the 394th Squadron of the 367th Fighter Group. Heavily outnumbered, the American unit began to take losses. Following frantic radio calls for

---

FOCKE-WULF Fw 190A-8

ROLE Single-seat interceptor and air superiority fighter.

POWER One BMW 801D 14-cylinder, air-cooled, radial engine developing 1,700hp at take-off.

ARMAMENT Two MG 131 13mm machine guns mounted above the engine and two MG 151 20mm cannon mounted in the wing routes, all four weapons being synchronized to fire through the airscrew; two MG 151 in the outer wing panels.

PERFORMANCE Maximum speed 408mph at 20,700ft.

NORMAL OPERATIONAL TAKE-OFF WEIGHT 9,660lb.

DIMENSIONS Span 34ft 5½in; length 29ft 4¾in; wing area 197 sq ft.

DATE OF FIRST PRODUCTION FW 190A-8 1944.

assistance, the other two squadrons in the US Group sped to the scene. Buchholz continued:

> Our initial attack hit the Americans hard and I saw some Lightnings go down. We might have been new to the business of dog fighting, but with the advantage of the sun and numbers we held the initiative. The surviving American fighters twisted and turned, trying to avoid our repeated attacks.

Then, suddenly, other Lightnings dived into the fight from above. Now the Focke-Wulfs were the hunted. The American pilots, far the more experienced in fighter-versus-fighter combat, cruised overhead selecting their victims. Then a pair would dive down to pick off a German fighter, before zooming back to altitude.

> We were being chopped up by experts, and I watched Focke-Wulf after Focke-Wulf go down. I climbed and tried to re-join the fight, moving in to cover the tail of a Focke-Wulf without any protection. But as I got there a pair of Lightnings came down after us; he went into a tight turn and as I tried to follow him I found myself spinning out of control again.

Buchholz repeated this unnerving experience twice more, then he decided to give up. His meagre experience in the Fw 190 was insufficient to cope with the situation, and the middle of a dogfight was no place to learn. He continued:

> I was doing nothing to help my comrades and if I stayed around much longer, I would almost certainly make an easy victim for one of the Lightnings. I broke away and dived to low altitude, making good my escape. I landed back at Herpy, taxied to my dispersal point, shut down the engine and clambered out; my flying suit was wringing wet with sweat.

In ones and twos the surviving Focke-Wulfs returned, some bearing the scars of battle. As the afternoon wore on it became clear that the *Gruppe* had suffered disastrous losses. Sixteen of its aircraft had been destroyed, fourteen pilots were killed or missing and three more were wounded. Buchholz's *Staffel* commander, *Oberleutnant* Paffrath, was wounded. During that engagement the American 367th Fighter Group lost seven Lightnings, six of them from the 394th Squadron that the Focke-Wulfs had attacked initially.

The scale of the losses on 25 August came as a great shock to Buchholz and his comrades. The fighting strength of the *Gruppe* had been reduced by almost half during its first day in combat. The German pilots were having to learn the harsh realities of air fighting in the most brutal school of all.

There was no time to mourn for the lost pilots, however. The battle in Normandy was continuing with the retreating German ground troops taking a terrible beating from the Allied aircraft. On the following day, 26 August, the surviving Focke-Wulfs of *II./JG 6* were again ordered to mount an offensive sweep to the River Seine to cover the German withdrawal. Buchholz led his *Schwarm* to their briefed patrol area near Rouen, and shortly after their arrival they were 'bounced' from out of the sun by Mustangs. Buchholz's fighter was one of the first to go down:

> I never even saw the aircraft that hit me. All I heard was a loud bang
> and the next thing I knew my aircraft was tumbling out of the sky
> with part of the tail shot away. I blew off the canopy and struggled to

---

LOCKHEED P-38L LIGHTNING

ROLE Single-seat, long-range fighter and fighter-bomber.

POWER Two Allison V-1750, 12-cylinder, liquid-cooled engines developing 1,425hp at take-off.

ARMAMENT One Hispano 20mm cannon and four Browning .5in machine guns mounted in the nose.

PERFORMANCE Maximum speed 390mph at 15,000ft.

NORMAL OPERATIONAL TAKE-OFF WEIGHT 17,500lb.

DIMENSIONS Span 52ft; length 37ft 10in; wing area 328 sq ft.

DATE OF FIRST PRODUCTION P-38L 1944.

get clear of the spinning aircraft, but my right foot became wedged under the instrument panel. After what seemed an age I managed to wrench it away, though I left my flying boot behind and my foot collided with the tailplane as I was falling clear. My parachute opened normally and I landed on the west bank of the Seine near Duclair. A rearguard unit of the SS picked me up and took me to their field dressing station, where one of their doctors removed a metal splinter from my left foot and bound it up. During the night I was taken across the river on board an army ferry.

The retreating army unit carried Buchholz 140 miles, to the *Luftwaffe* airfield at Juvincourt near Paris. Allied spearhead units were nearing the area and everyone was getting ready to leave.

Every serviceable aircraft had already left, and army engineers had placed demolition charges ready to blow up the runway and taxi tracks. Somebody suggested that I might like to fly out a partially serviceable Fw 190, which would otherwise have to be blown up. I jumped at the chance, I thought that no flight in an aircraft could possibly be worse than the journey I had just made by road.

There were a few small problems, however. At Juvincourt the stores had either been moved out or destroyed. Buchholz had no flying helmet, no parachute and no map. The Focke-Wulf's guns had no ammunition and its tanks held fuel for only about 40-minutes flying. A folded blanket in the seat well filled the space normally occupied by the parachute. With his foot bandaged, the German pilot was lifted into the cockpit.

Few flights have begun less auspiciously, a point that was drummed home to Buchholz as he was strapping in. As he was about to start the engine, an engineering officer appeared and said that the aircraft was not in a fit state to fly. He could accept no responsibility for the fighter in its present condition; it had several uncleared faults. Moreover, it had recently been involved in a heavy landing which had put strain on the fuselage, the tail and possibly the undercarriage as well. Buchholz replied that he noted the objections, but as pilot he was willing to accept the aircraft as it stood. That freed the officer of possible future recriminations for allowing a non-airworthy plane to take off, and he agreed to let the Focke-Wulf go.

Buchholz took off, aiming to get to the *Luftwaffe* airfield at Florennes near Namur in Belgium. That was about 80 miles away as the crow flies, but lacking a map he could not take the most direct route. He decided to follow the line of the Aisne River and canal to Sedan, then the Meuse River which flowed close to Florennes. However, soon after take-off, the first problem manifested itself: the undercarriage refused to retract. Buchholz continued:

> With the gear down the limiting speed of the Fw 190 was 160 mph;
> if I was spotted by enemy fighters, I would be easy meat. Even so, I
> reasoned, I was far better off in an aircraft going at 160 mph than a
> car moving at 30 mph. There could be no thought to returning to
> Juvincourt, having got this far. I kept low to avoid trouble.

Twenty minutes into the flight, things began to go really wrong as the German pilot noticed the needle of the oil temperature gauge was slowly rising past the danger mark.

> This was bad news: the rear cylinders of the BMW 801 always ran hot
> and if there was any failure in their lubrication, the engine was liable
> to seize. Now I really was in a fix. I had no parachute so I could not
> bale out, and if I crash-landed with the undercarriage extended, and
> the ground was not hard enough, the aircraft was liable to nose over
> on to its back. As the oil temperature rose still higher it became clear
> that I had better choose a field soon, and get the Focke-Wulf down
> while the motor still had some life in it. If the engine failed suddenly
> I would have no choice where I landed.

Choosing a reasonably large flat meadow, Buchholz turned toward it. He decided he would land the fighter in a hard sideslip to port, hoping the side forces would wipe off the undercarriage legs and allow the aircraft to slide to a halt on its belly. It was a reasonable plan, but it failed to take into account the sturdiness of the plane's undercarriage:

The undercarriage proved stronger than I had expected. It held. The port wing took the main force of the impact and buckled. The aircraft then swung round, the motor struck the ground so violently that it broke away, the fuselage then rolled over and finally came to rest upside-down. Bruised all over and covered in blood, I managed to fight my way out of the cockpit.

Some farmers took pity on the pilot's miserable condition and helped him to their village, where a German army vehicle later picked him up.

Fritz Buchholz spent the next six weeks in hospital recovering from his various wounds. Then he rejoined *II./JG 6*, which by then had pulled back to Uedenbach near Bonn. He arrived to find only three or four survivors from the forty or so pilots that had set for France in August. The rest were dead, recovering from wounds or in enemy prison camps. Shortly afterwards Buchholz was sent to instruct at a training unit assigned to convert ex-bomber pilots to fly the Fw 190.

Fritz Buchholz's combat career as a single-engined fighter pilot had lasted just two missions: during the first, he had a hard fight merely to stay alive, during the second he never saw his assailant before he was shot down and wounded. So far as he is aware, his presence over the battle zone failed to cause the slightest inconvenience to Germany's enemies. In the summer of 1944, the skies over France were no place for a beginner.

CHAPTER FOURTEEN

Act of Desperation

When a nation's existence is under threat, desperate times will lead brave men to take desperate measures. This was the position in which the Luftwaffe *home-defence fighter force found itself during the autumn of 1944, as it suffered debilitating losses week after week.*

BY THE AUTUMN of 1944, the *Luftwaffe* day fighter units defending the homeland had been reduced to a pitiful state. The US strategic air forces in Europe possessed technical superiority, as well as superiority in numbers and in training. Forced to fight three or four major air battles each week, the German air defence fighter units had suffered heavily during the first six months of the year. Its losses had totalled 2,010 fighters and 1,291 aircrew killed or missing – the great majority of them pilots. The bustling German aircraft industry would make good the losses in aircraft relatively easily. Replacing the lost pilots was a quite different matter, however. Among those lost were several *Geschwader*, *Gruppe* and *Staffel* commanders, experienced leaders who could not be replaced. Although it had sacrificed quality for quantity, the *Luftwaffe* pilot-training organization was quite unable to fill the gaps in the ranks.

Had the *Luftwaffe* been able to inflict serious losses on the US heavy bomber formations during the big air battles, there would have been something to show for those terrible losses. But this was no longer the case. During nearly every major attack after mid-1944, the US long-range escort fighters had been able to impose their superiority in the skies over Germany to protect the bombers.

From the summer of 1944 the Allied heavy bombers had focused part of their attack on the German oil industry and were wrecking the various production centres in turn. A systematic pattern of re-attacks prevented the repair teams from bringing these plants back into full production. The outcome was a steadily worsening shortage of all types of motor fuel, which imposed progressively more severe constraints on each aspect of military operations.

In the summer of 1944, as an attempt to defeat the destructive daylight raids, the *Luftwaffe* had introduced the so-called *Sturmgruppe* units. The latter flew the heavily armed and armoured *Sturmbock* version of the Focke-Wulf 190, intended to move in close behind US heavy bomber formations and knock down individual bombers with their heavy 30mm cannon. As a tactic of last resort, if he failed to destroy the bomber, a *Sturmgruppe* pilot was expected to knock it down by ramming it.

The extra weight of the armour and heavy cannon made the *Sturmbock* fighters unwieldy in action, however. So each *Sturmgruppe* was accompanied by two *Gruppen* of normal fighters whose duty was to fend off the US fighters while the *Sturmgruppe* moved into an attacking position behind the bombers' formation. In the event the ramming tactic was used only rarely; if an Fw 190 could get that close to a heavy bomber, its heavy cannon were usually able to inflict lethal damage.

While the *Sturmgruppe* tactics occasionally achieved heavy losses against individual US bomb group formations, as 1944 wore on that happened less and less. The US planners sent formations of fighters to sweep the skies in front of and alongside each stream of bombers. If they could break up the 90-strong formation of a *Sturmgruppe* with its escorts before it reached the bombers, the German fighters still suffered heavy losses. Clearly, these tactics did not provide an adequate answer to the grave problem facing the *Luftwaffe*.

In essence, the problem facing the Reich air defence units can be summed up as follows. If its fighters carried an armament heavy enough to knock down the heavy bombers, those fighters were so unwieldy that they fell as easy prey to the US escorts. If, on the other hand, the defending fighters were lightly armed, although they could engage the US escorts effectively they lacked the firepower necessary to engage the heavy bombers with any chance of success.

Against this background of near-despair, *Oberst* Hans-Joachim Herrmann submitted a revolutionary proposal for the defence of the Reich. 'Hajo' Herrmann, a talented and highly decorated bomber ace, had moved to the air defence role in 1943. In the following year, he was appointed commander of the 1st Fighter Division responsible for the air defence of central Germany including the area around Berlin. He told me:

> I did not have a *Sturmgruppe* in my Division, but I knew about them of course. I knew they were not effective in the long run, on account of the losses they suffered from the escort fighters. It was clear to me that no system of destroying the enemy bombers would work unless some way could be found of avoiding the escorts. The long-term answer was to use the Me 262 jet fighter [which carried a heavy armament of four 30mm cannon]. But its introduction into service would take time, and we desperately needed some means of inflicting an unacceptably high loss on one or two American raiding formations, so the attacks would cease and we would gain a breathing space to get the jet fighters into service in large numbers.

Hermann proposed the formation of special units manned by volunteer pilots, to destroy American heavy bombers in large numbers by *ramming*. With ramming as their tactic of first resort, these fighters would not need to carry heavy cannon. The ideal vehicle would be a high-altitude fighter version of the Messerschmitt Bf 109 G or K, carrying a self-defence armament of either a 13mm or a 15mm machine gun with just half its normal complement of ammunition. Thus lightened, these fighters would be able to outclimb and outrun the US escorts and would not require fighter protection to help them to reach the enemy bombers.

The scenario Herrmann envisaged was as follows. When an enemy bomber formation was tracked approaching central Germany, the lightweight fighters were to take off individually and climb rapidly to altitudes around 33,000ft. There they would be safely out of reach of the enemy escorts. The Messerschmitts would then be directed by radio into an attacking position over a formation of bombers. Each German pilot was then to select a bomber and dive on it from almost vertically above, aiming to hit his victim at its weakest part immediately in front of the tail unit.

Herrmann proposed the formation of several ramming *Gruppen*, which he wanted to employ in a single large-scale operation with up to 800 aircraft. If half of the ramming attempts succeeded, as many as 400 American heavy bombers might be destroyed in a single day. Herrmann argued that it would take the US Army Air Force several weeks to recover from a successful operation of this type. If such an attack halted the US heavy bomber offensive for even a few weeks, that would give the breathing space to allow the oil industry and perhaps also the fighter force to stage a recovery.

Herrmann did not minimize the personal risks to those taking part in the ramming operation. Having examined the available reports detailing ramming incidents so far, he thought maybe half of the pilots who rammed enemy bombers might bail out successfully. The other half – about 200 German pilots – were likely to be killed or suffer serious injury. This would be a high price to pay and at first sight might appear to be a callous way to use men, even though they had volunteered for the operation. But war by its nature is a callous business. If implemented in full, Herrmann's scheme stood a good chance of halting the destructive daylight attacks that were tearing the guts out of German industry and out of the *Luftwaffe*.

In time of war, the correct tactics are those that secure the aim for the lowest cost in men and materials. During its attempts to stop the

American attacks by use of conventional tactics, the *Luftwaffe* fighter force was losing pilots at a rate of over 300 per month. And it had failed to halt the bombardment. Herrmann's tactical scheme promised to secure a more tangible result, for the loss of fewer pilots than would fall during a month of normal air defence operations. He wrote:

> Regardless of the scale on which the [ramming] operation is carried out, it is the most effective course open to us under present conditions. It is in no way more expensive in personnel than are ordinary operations. It will consume only one-third as many aircraft, and one-fifth to one-tenth as much fuel, as would normal operations . . .

Herrmann submitted his proposals early in 1945 and they sparked a lively debate within the *Luftwaffe* High Command. Initially *Reichsmarschall* Goering was lukewarm to the idea, but after discussions he accepted it. The revolutionary proposal then had to go to Adolf Hitler himself for final approval. The Führer said he would not *demand* that any German should make such a sacrifice. However, if sufficient volunteers could be found who were willing to ram the enemy heavy bombers, the scheme had his blessing.

The various discussions took time, and time was running out for the Third Reich. It was early in March 1945 before the secret appeal for volunteers was posted at operational and flying training units throughout the *Luftwaffe*, over the signature of *Reichsmarschall* Goering. The appeal did not go into detail, it merely asked for pilots to volunteer for a decisive operation from which there was 'only a small chance of returning' but which would help rescue the nation in its hour of peril.

There was no coercion for individuals to volunteer; there was no need. The appeal produced an immediate and overwhelming response, with more than 2,000 pilots offering themselves for the forthcoming operation. That was many more than Herrmann's plan required, and it allowed the *Luftwaffe* to reject those pilots it could least afford to lose. In particular, it needed its most experienced pilots to fly the new jet fighters that would soon become available in quantity. It will be remembered that one reason for the operation was to allow a breathing space so more jet fighter units could form. The *Reichsmarschall* ruled that the bulk of the ramming force should comprise student pilots from the fighter training schools, with a sprinkling of more experienced pilots to lead them into action.

On 24 March, the selected volunteers began arriving at the fighter airfield at Stendahl near Berlin, which was the main base for the operation. On the following day, the pilots learned the nature of the hazardous task for which they had volunteered. Even at that stage, anyone who wished to recant was allowed to do so. Those that wished to could leave the operation without recrimination.

The preparation of the pilots for the special operation lasted just two weeks, and it fell well short of what was needed. It would have been desirable for the pilots to gain experience in handling the specially lightened Messerschmitts at high altitude and in high-speed dives, but there was insufficient fuel available for such training. Much of the time was taken up with ground instruction in flying and the required tactics. The pilots also underwent political and battle indoctrination, with lecturers stressing how much Germany's military position would improve if the planned operation succeeded.

MESSERSCHMITT Bf 109K-4

(Figures for lightened ramming variant in parentheses)

ROLE Single-seat interceptor and air superiority fighter.

POWER One Daimler Benz DB 605 12-cylinder, liquid-cooled engine developing 2,000hp at take-off.

ARMAMENT One 30mm MK 108 cannon, two 15mm MG 151 cannon (one 15mm cannon).

PERFORMANCE Maximum speed 452mph at 20,000ft (about 460mph at 20,000ft); climb to 32,800ft, 6min 42sec (about 30sec less).

NORMAL OPERATIONAL TAKE-OFF WEIGHT 7,475lb (about 7,020lb).

DIMENSIONS Span 32ft 8½in; length 29ft ½in; wing area 173 sq ft.

DATE OF FIRST PRODUCTION MESSERSCHMITT Bf 109K-4 October 1944.

Oberst Herrmann felt it imperative that the ramming operation, code-named Operation *Wehrwolf*, should not be mounted until sufficient forces were available. At the end of March, he stressed that point in a letter to Goering:

> With only 150 or 250 pilots ready for 'Wehrwolf' only limited objectives can be achieved. This will not serve our purpose and it is important that we aim higher. The operation should be carried through with a minimum of 650 pilots. The time until the Me 262 can be brought into large-scale service must be bridged, before the fighter arm is wiped out in normal operations and on the ground. We have to achieve such a massive success that the enemy will be forced to alter his methods and the frequency of his attack.

But the time had passed when such fine arguments could carry the day. At the beginning of April British and American troops had crossed the Rhine in strength and were thrusting deep into Germany. In the east, Soviet forces were within 50 miles of Berlin and were massing for their final assault on the capital. Operation *Wehrwolf* had to be launched as soon as possible with the resources in hand.

Early in April those volunteers judged ready for the ramming action moved to the airfields from which the operation was to be mounted: in addition to Stendahl these were Delitzsh, Moertitz, Gardelegen and Sachau in the Berlin area. Other pilots moved to airfields near Prague in Czechoslovakia, for a coordinated operation to be mounted from there. The modified fighters were to be delivered shortly before the operation was launched, so as not to attract air attacks on those airfields.

On 6 April the pilots assigned to '*Wehrwolf*' learned they were to go into action against US heavy bombers on the following day. About 250 pilots were chosen for the operation and the fighters assigned to the mission began arriving at the various airfields.

On 7 April the US Eighth Air Force sent more than 1,300 B-17s and B-24s, with more than 800 escort fighters, to attack airfields, railway marshalling yards and fuel storage areas in central Germany. For the

Germans, there were several last-minute glitches, due in large part to the late delivery or non-arrival of fighters. Thus, when the operation was launched late on the morning of 7 April, it did so with only about 200 Bf 109s. Supporting them were about a hundred conventional fighters and Messerschmitt 262 jet fighters.

Mounted with far fewer aircraft than Herrmann had proposed, the ramming operation soon ran into difficulties. Several fighters suffered technical failures that forced them to return to base. Some of the inexperienced pilots also failed to maintain formation with their leaders, became lost and never reached their rendezvous point. In another blow to the operation, soon after take-off it became clear that the 60-strong contingent of ramming fighters at airfields near Prague were too far to the south-east to engage the bombers. After taking off, these pilots were ordered to return to base.

After those reductions to its strength, the ramming force that actually went into action was down to about a hundred fighters. The main weight of its attack fell on B-17 Flying Fortresses of the 3rd Air Division as they were passing north of Hanover. The US escorting fighters, P-47 Thunderbolts and P-51 Mustangs, fought a fast and furious action to defend their charges. With far fewer ramming fighters available than had been planned, the attackers failed to achieve the overwhelming concentration that Herrmann had hoped for. Several Bf 109s were shot down, others suffered damage, which forced them to break off the action. Others found their path blocked by enemy fighters. Ten of the fighters succeeded in penetrating the escorts and rammed Flying Fortresses. Seven of the bombers went down immediately but remarkably, despite heavy damage, the remaining three reached airfields in friendly territory and made normal landings.

The 2nd Air Division also came under attack, though there the escorts were able to ward off most of the attempts to reach the bombers. One Messerschmitt dived into the B-24 Liberator leading the 389th Bomb Group. Badly damaged and out of control, the wounded bomber swerved into the next bomber in the formation and all three planes fell out of the sky. Another Liberator was rammed but was able to regain friendly territory.

The total losses suffered by the US Eighth Air Force that day amounted to 17 bombers (1.3 per cent of those attacking) and five fighters (0.6 per cent). 'The Mighty Eighth' could shrug off such losses and, to underline the point, on each of the next four days it delivered similarly powerful attacks on a spread of targets in Germany.

As for the ramming force, it has been estimated that it lost about 40 pilots killed in the course of the first action. The *Luftwaffe* was accustomed to losing that number of pilots in a single day's fighting, to secure a far smaller result. Herrmann attempted to assemble forces for a second ramming operation, but in the final chaos of defeat it proved impossible to bring together the necessary planes and fuel.

THERE IS LITTLE doubt that had Operation *Wehrwolf* been mounted at the time and in the strength originally proposed, it might have secured its specified aim. Whether it could have done more than provide a breathing space is another matter, however. In fact, the execution of '*Wehrwolf*' was a classic case of 'too little, too late'. In the timing of a drastic operation of this type, a sort of 'catch-22 situation' comes into play. Such operations do not receive serious consideration until the military position is truly desperate, but once that point has been reached it is probably too late for such an operation to have any decisive effect anyway.

CHAPTER FIFTEEN

Defeating the SAMs

July 1965 was the start of a difficult period for US Air Force planes operating over North Vietnam, after a Soviet-built SA-2 surface-to-air missile system knocked down a tactical fighter plane near Hanoi. In the year that followed this type of missile was responsible, either directly or indirectly, for serious losses in aircraft. After some unsuccessful attempts, an effective counter to the missiles was perfected and applied.

FOLLOWING THE loss of a Phantom fighter to an SA-2 battery on 24 July 1965, the USAF immediately retaliated. Its first target was the most obvious: the two launch sites, one of which was thought to have been responsible. The attack, three days after the Phantom shoot-down, involved 54 F-105 Thunderchief attack fighters.

Captain Chuck Horner (who later, as a general, commanded the Coalition air forces during the war to evict the Iraqis from Kuwait) piloted one of the F-105s that day. He later wrote:

> The first indication of trouble came as we headed north toward the target. 'Buick Lead in the river' informed all that the Lead Takhli Thud [F-105] was down. To my left I saw Bob Purcell's F-105 rise up out of a cloud of dust with its entire underside on fire, roll over and go

straight in. We were doing 650 knots ... I looked out to the left and saw anti-aircraft artillery lined up in rows with their barrels depressed, fire belching forth from their ends. Looking up, I saw the familiar black, greasy clouds with orange centres as the shells burst over our jets, which were now scraping banana and palm trees. Emergency beepers began to fill our radio as we scanned the ground for the target. Seeing something, we let go of our ordnance and broke left to safety, west of the Red River. Ahead of us, Capt. Bill Barthelmus asked Maj. Jack Farr to look over his jet as they crossed the Mekong River, but Bill's flight controls failed just as Jack positioned himself over the stricken F-105. The jets collided, killing both.

The disastrous action cost the USAF six F-105s and an RF-101 reconnaissance plane. Significantly, none of these planes had fallen to an SA-2. The returning pilots reported having inflicted considerable damage at both missile sites. Later, however, photographic reconnaissance established that the 'radars' and 'missile launchers' they attacked had been wooden dummies set out conspicuously to bait the traps. Expecting just such an attack, the North Vietnamese Army had moved its precious new hardware clear of the sites and placed it under camouflage. Clearly, the first round in the unfolding prizefight had gone to the defenders.

Other early attempts by attack fighters to hit missile sites proved no more successful, and incurred further losses from anti-aircraft artillery (AAA) fire. Soon the idea of delivering frontal attacks on the sites was dropped. It was ruled that only high-priority targets in missile-defended areas were to be attacked. Moreover, aircraft were to be routed to spend as short a time as possible in those areas, and while there they were to keep below 4,000ft where the SA-2 system was relatively ineffective. As they neared their target the raiders commenced rapid climbs to around 7,000ft to identify the target before entering their attack dives. The new tactics held down losses from missiles, but flying below 4,000ft put the aircraft within the engagement envelope of the medium-calibre 37mm and 57mm anti-aircraft guns deployed in large numbers in North Vietnam. The losses to AAA rose sharply.

Following some experimenting, US fighter pilots discovered an evasive manoeuvre that was effective against the SA-2's Guideline missile, provided the pilot saw it in good time. If a pilot saw a missile coming in his direction, he turned to position it in the 10 o'clock or the 2 o'clock position from his cockpit. That meant he was flying obliquely towards the missile but had a good view of it. He then selected maximum power and pushed forward on the stick, so the plane entered zero gravity and achieved maximum acceleration. The pilot entered a dive, aiming to gain as much energy as possible to sustain the manoeuvres that might follow. He then waited until the missile was about 1 mile away. Pilots were told, 'Don't worry about judging the distance. When it is 1 mile away, you'll know!' At that point, the pilot looked to see if the side of the missile was visible. If it was, the missile was not after him and he need not worry about it further. If he could not see the side, the pilot turned the plane and waited to see whether the missile readjusted its trajectory to follow him. If it did, the time had come for drastic measures. The pilot hauled on the stick to make a 6-G pull-up. By now the missile was close to the plane, and the sudden change in the relative position of the target gave the missile a difficult intercept problem. If

---

SA-2B SURFACE-TO-AIR GUIDED MISSILE SYSTEM

ROLE Semi-mobile target defence system to counter aircraft flying at medium or high altitude.

CONTROL RADAR Fan Song E band track-while-scan radar, range of 75 miles in search, 38 miles in track.

MISSILE Guideline two-stage commanded guided missile, produced in several versions. Typical parameters were length at launch 35ft, weight at launch approximately 5,000lb; high explosive warhead weight 280lb; the maximum range of missile was 13 miles against a high-altitude non-manoeuvring target; maximum speed of missile 1,980mph (Mach 3) at high altitude.

the manoeuvre was carried out properly, the missile could not readjust its trajectory quickly enough and it flashed harmlessly past the plane. If other missiles were now heading for the aircraft, its pilot would attempt to avoid these by repeating the process but pushing forward on the stick.

Late in 1965 the F-105 force abandoned the policy of transiting through missile-defended areas at low altitude. From then on, attack fighters were to fly through these areas at around 18,000ft, safely out of reach of most AAA. If a missile was seen approaching, the threatened F-105 flight would split up and the planes would react individually.

Although the missile evasive manoeuvre was usually effective if carried out in good time, it had several disadvantages. To achieve the required agility and acceleration, the pilot of the attack fighter usually had to jettison the bombs as he entered the initial dive. The manoeuvre also caused raiding flights to scatter, leaving the individual planes vulnerable to attack from enemy fighters. Worst of all, if there was more than one missile to avoid, the manoeuvres rapidly depleted a plane's energy level. By the end of the process aircraft often found themselves at low energy states and within the lethal zone of AAA. That was not a healthy place to be.

Certainly the missile evasive manoeuvres saved many pilots and aircraft, but it was not a complete answer to the problem. If US aircraft were to continue their strikes on targets in North Vietnam, it was clear that a more effective countermeasure to SA-2 was needed.

EARLY IN THE 1960s the General Electric Company had designed and built 150 examples of a radar-jamming pod suitable for carriage on a fighter's underwing weapons pylon. Produced under a Quick Reaction Capability contract, the pod was designated the QRC-160 in order to circumvent the normal procurement process. It was 8ft 4in long, had a diameter of 10in and weighed just under 100lb. The pod contained four separate noise-jamming transmitters, which were tuned on the ground to counter individual Soviet gun and missile control radars. Or all four transmitters could be tuned to jam the same spread of frequencies. A simple on/off switch in the cockpit controlled the transmitters.

For a time during the spring of 1965, a few QRC-160 jamming pods underwent operational testing over North Vietnam. Carried by reconnaissance fighters, the pods were intended to jam enemy AAA fire control radars while the planes made their photographic runs. The pods appeared to have no effect on the volume or the accuracy of AAA fire, however, and after a brief period the experiment was discontinued.

AFTER THE INITIAL SA-2 shoot-down in North Vietnam, anyone with ideas on how to counter the weapon found a ready ear. Lieutenant Colonel Ingwald 'Inky' Haugen had retired from the USAF in 1961 after nearly 20 years' experience in electronic warfare. He now worked as a civilian project officer at the Electronic Warfare Test Division at Eglin Air Force Base, Florida.

Several years earlier, while serving as a staff officer at the Pentagon, Haugen had addressed a nearly similar problem. He had studied the initial intelligence reports on the first Soviet surface-to-air missile system to be fielded, the SA-1. That system's missile control radar, like that with the SA-2, was a track-while-scan system which radiated two fan-shaped beams. One beam measured the target's position in azimuth, the other beam measured its position in elevation.

It was clear that this type of radar could not be defeated by the low-powered noise jammers then carried by Strategic Air Command (SAC) bombers. The enemy radar operators could command their missile to fly up the jamming strobe towards the aircraft and, when the weapon was sufficiently close to the target aircraft, its radar proximity fuse would detonate the warhead.

With this in mind, Haugen conceived the idea of using a four-plane unit of bombers, B-47s or B-52s, all radiating jamming. Each plane was to occupy an adjacent radar resolution cell (see Glossary), flying just far enough apart so the radar would see all four bombers if there was no jamming. That required a lateral spacing of 1,000 to

1,500ft between adjacent planes, which also flew at different altitudes.

If all the planes radiated noise jamming on the radar's frequency, Haugen thought the operators at the separate azimuth and elevation scopes would each see four closely spaced jamming strobes that merged into each other. Although a single aircraft radiating noise jamming could not defeat the track-while-scan radar and the missiles, Haugen believed four such planes flying in a carefully spaced formation might do so.

The SA-2's Guideline missile did not home on the target aircraft. The weapon was command-guided from the ground to fly to the desired impact point, in much the same way as a radio-controlled model airplane is steered in flight. Thus, if the planes flew in the special formation and they all jammed, Haugen believed the missile operators could not determine the position of any plane accurately enough to guide a missile on to it.

It was accepted that Haugen's idea would probably work but it was not practical for a nuclear war, and in the 1950s that was the only type of war SAC was preparing to fight. If a ground-to-air missile fitted with a nuclear warhead engaged the force, its single burst would knock down all four aircraft in the formation.

By 1965, the air fighting over North Vietnam was quite different from that which had determined SAC's tactics for nuclear war a decade earlier. Haugen thought that four F-105s, each carrying a couple of QRC-160 noise-jamming pods and correctly spaced in azimuth and elevation, could seriously degrade the SA-2 system. He discussed his ideas with his boss, and the latter passed them up the chain of command.

The Tactical Air Warfare Center at Eglin, Florida, was ordered to carry out a top-priority test of Haugen's proposal. As the jamming pods arrived at the airbase, each one was carefully checked and adjusted to ensure that it performed to specification. Then four F-105s were each fitted with two of the jamming pods.

The programme required the F-105 formation to fly a series of runs against a US-built copy of the SA-2 missile control radar. The aircraft were to fly in the 15,000 to 20,000ft altitude band, which put them

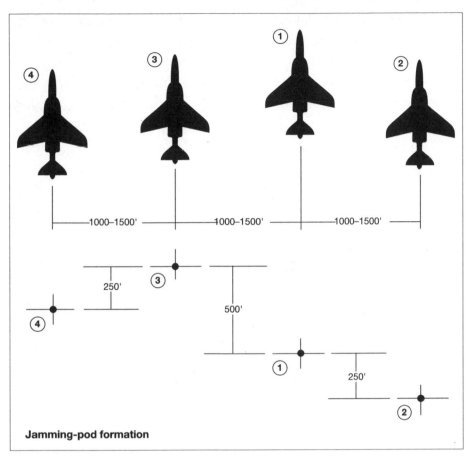

Jamming-pod formation

above the effective engagement range of most AAA weapons but well
inside the optimum engagement bracket of SA-2.

The tests quickly revealed that Haugen's idea was a winner. With
the planes in their special formation, the jamming pods screened all
four aircraft from all aspects and at most ranges. When the aircraft
came broadside on to the radar site, the aircraft could be seen through
the jamming for a short time. But that glance through the jamming did
not last long enough for enemy operators to guide a missile in for the
kill. To achieve full degradation of the missile system it was necessary
to have all four aircraft present, in the correct position, each with at
least one jamming pod working properly. With three jamming aircraft
there was a reduction in effectiveness, and an even greater reduction if

there were only two. If just one plane was jamming its chances of surviving missile attack were slim.

BASED AT TAKHLI, Thailand, the 355th Tactical Fighter Wing suffered fearful losses during July and August 1966. In that two-month period the wing, with a nominal establishment of 54 F-105 Thunderchiefs, lost exactly half that number during operations over North Vietnam. Eighteen of its pilots had been killed or taken prisoner.

In September Lieutenant General William Momeyer, Seventh Air Force Commander, directed the Takhli Wing to carry out an evaluation of the jamming pod formation under operational conditions. A batch of 25 carefully prepared pods was flown to Thailand for installation on F-105s.

Before pilots went into action with the jamming pods, they needed a period of training to fly the special formation. The pattern of jamming emitted by the pods resembled a huge inverted saucer (a rather chunky saucer) rigidly attached to the underside of the plane. So, if the pilot applied too much bank, the jamming 'footprint' on the ground shifted to the outside of the turn and it might miss the enemy radar altogether. In order to achieve the required 'footprint' of jamming, while flying through missile-defended areas, the F-105s were not to perform any manoeuvre that led them to exceed a banking angle of 15 degrees. As one fighter pilot remarked:

> The jamming pod formation was wide, it was stacked and it was awkward to fly. It you were in the high position and the leader went down or turned into you, you couldn't roll upside down and pull down like you normally would to keep positive G on the airplane. If you did that, your jamming would point way into the sky. You had to push on negative G to hold your place in formation, and that was uncomfortable. If the formation turned, it was either very slow and gentle, or else it was very aggressive and hard. Everything else was done with wings level, cither pull back or push down. Judging distances was not difficult. The big deal was, don't get closer than 500 feet from the next guy, and don't get further away than 2,500 feet.

The operational evaluation began with a two-week period during which a four-plane flight of F-105s, flying in jamming-pod formation with each plane carrying two jamming pods, accompanied raiding forces on 19 occasions. At first, the targets were in the relatively sparsely defended area in the southern part of North Vietnam. The pods were set to radiate jamming on the frequencies used by the SA-2 and gun control radars.

As each flight reached the target area, it climbed rapidly to 10,000ft to identify its target, before commencing its attack dive. The F-105s with jamming pods began their climb a little earlier than the other fighters. Once at altitude, they remained exposed for longer before commencing their attack dives. The jamming F-105s attracted no missiles and no accurate gunfire, though the aircraft in accompanying flights suffered from both.

Gradually the jamming F-105s shifted to the more heavily defended targets. During an attack on fuel storage tanks in a high-threat area at Nguyen Khe on 8 October, there came the clearest proof yet of the value of the jamming-pod formation. Two flights of podded F-105s formed part of an attacking force. The non-podded planes received a

---

REPUBLIC F-105D THUNDERCHIEF

ROLE Single-seat attack fighter.

POWER One Pratt & Whitney J75-P-19W turbojet engine developing 26,500lb thrust with afterburner.

ARMAMENT (Internal) one 20mm M61 cannon; (external) typical loads of free-fall bombs carried during attacks on North Vietnam were two 3,000lb or two 2,000lb, or six 750lb or six 500lb; a QRC-160 jamming pod was carried on the outer weapons station.

PERFORMANCE Maximum speed carrying external war load 650 knots (747mph).

NORMAL OPERATIONAL TAKE-OFF WEIGHT 52,546lb.

DIMENSIONS Span 34ft 11¼in; length 64ft 3 in; wing area 385 sq ft.

DATE OF FIRST PRODUCTION F-105D Summer 1959.

hot reception from the North Vietnamese SAM batteries, but in contrast the jamming aircraft drew very little attention.

People at Takhli now became very enthusiastic about the QRC-160. In response to their demands for more pods, another batch was rushed to the airbase together with a contingent of engineers from General Electric to maintain them. When the other Thailand-based F-105 Wing, the 388th at Korat, heard about the development it too demanded jamming pods. That posed a problem, however, because there were insufficient jamming pods in the Air Force to fit two to each plane.

In October 'Inky' Haugen flew out to Takhli to brief pilots on the new tactics. When he arrived he was greeted with the sight of a line of F-105s on the ramp, each with a jamming pod under either wing. He recalled:

> When I reached Takhli one of the first questions Colonel Scott [commander of the 355th Tactical Fighter Wing] asked me was 'Will it work as well if there is only one pod on each aircraft?' I could only answer 'I don't know.' With hindsight, it might seem strange that we had never tested this ... But I had always assumed that with the deep belly of the F-105 protruding so far beneath the wing, there was bound to be considerable screening of the jamming on the opposite side.

For the small-scale tests carried out at Eglin, there had been plenty of pods. Haugen's aim had been to show that the technique worked and to get it accepted by the front-line units, rather than try to work out refinements. He continued:

> I immediately called Eglin on the 'hot line' and asked our people to fly a mission using only one QRC-160 on each F-105, to see how that worked. Back came the answer two days later 'Its great! There's no observable difference on the radar if only a single pod is carried!'

On receipt of that news, the Takhli Wing passed half of its jamming pods to Korat. From the end of November 1966, all F-105s flying into missile-defended areas carried jamming pods. Paradoxically, that provided a further test of nerve for the attack fighter pilots. Now the North Vietnamese missile batteries could no longer ignore the jamming aircraft and concentrate on the F-105s without jammers, for there were none of the latter. For the first time, the jamming-pod formations had to face determined attacks from the missile batteries.

Pilots quickly learned that salvation lay in maintaining formation integrity and avoiding banked manoeuvres. When a Guideline missile headed towards their formation, each man had to grit his teeth and hold a straight and level flight path. That called for a high degree of self-discipline, for every basic instinct of survival told the pilots to break formation and pull into a missile-evasive manoeuvre to avoid the danger. If it seemed that the missile was heading for one aircraft in the formation, the leader took all four down in a shallow descent. Usually that was sufficient to avert the threat, and the missile-passed harmlessly over the formation.

Crews reported seeing missiles guide toward their formation. Then, instead of singling out an individual aircraft, they usually flew erratic paths and sped past the formation before exploding harmlessly when well clear. Due to the wide spacing of the planes, there was ample room between adjacent machines for the missiles to pass through the formation without getting close enough to trigger the warhead's proximity fuse. Now, when an F-105 was lost to missile attack, it was usually because it had broken out of the pod formation to begin its attack dive or for some other reason. Or it was because one or more planes in the formation had malfunctioning jamming pods.

Once attack fighter pilots had became accustomed to using the jamming pods and the new formation, the improvement in survivability was clear beyond possible doubt. In the six months up to October 1966, the USAF had lost 72 F-105s to SAMs and AA guns over North Vietnam. In the six months following the introduction of the new tactics the F-105 losses fell sharply, with 23 aircraft lost to SAMs and anti-aircraft guns.

Colonel William Chairsell, commanding the 388th Tactical Fighter

Wing at Korat, informed the Director of Operations at Seventh Air Force Headquarters:

> The introduction of the QRC-160A-1 pod to the F-105 weapon
> system represents one of the most effective operational innovations I
> have ever encountered. Seldom has a technological advance of this
> nature so degraded an enemy's defensive posture. It has literally
> transformed the hostile air defence environment we once faced, to
> one in which we can now operate with a latitude of permissibility.

Often, when a new countermeasure is introduced, it enjoys only a limited period of success before the enemy develops a counter-counter-measure. That did not happen with the jamming pod-formation, which remained an effective tactic against the SA-2 missile system until the air war against North Vietnam ended in January 1973. New and improved types of noise-jamming pod were introduced later in the war, giving greater jamming powers and improved reliability, but the special spaced-out formation remained a key element in keeping down losses.

CHAPTER SIXTEEN

Reconnaissance to Hanoi

Following an air attack on an important target, it was essential to

determine the extent of the damage so the planning staff at headquarters

could decide whether a repeat strike was necessary. To run past the

target in order to take photographs, so soon after the main strike force

had left the area having alerted the defences, was no job for the faint-

hearted. Moreover, even when the photographic aircraft had safely

negotiated the enemy defences, its crew still faced the more mundane

but equally dangerous 'normal' hazards of flying.

ON 10 MAY 1972 US Air Force attack forces struck at the Paul
Doumer Bridge immediately to the east of Hanoi, and the nearby rail
yard at Yen Vien. As the bomb-carriers sped away from their targets,
two RF-4C Phantoms from the 14th Tactical Reconnaissance Squadron based at Udorn, Thailand, prepared to run through the target area
to take photographs. The two planes positioned themselves north of
the enemy capital, then prepared to accelerate to high speed to penetrate the defences. Major Sid Rogers, in the leading aircraft, gave the
order to jettison the underwing tanks and both of his fell away cleanly.
But when Captain Don Pickard in the No 2 aircraft pressed the button

to release his, the Phantom suddenly yawed violently to the left. It was as if the pilot had stomped on one of the rudder pedals. The tank under the right wing had gone, but that under the left wing had failed to release and the Phantom started to roll on to its back. Pickard regained control of the plane and the tank separated.

The reason for the Phantom's antics became clear when Pickard checked his fuel gauges. Instead of the 12,400lb of fuel he expected to have, only 9,500lb remained. He had one quarter less fuel than he had thought. The left drop tank had not been feeding fuel properly, and probably it was still full when it fell away. Full, the tank weighed about 3,000lb, and that asymmetric load on the left outer-wing pylon had made the plane lurch so violently before the tank fell clear. Pickard did some quick calculations to see if he had sufficient fuel to continue with the mission. He calculated that if he husbanded his remaining fuel he should have sufficient to get home with a small reserve.

At the start line some 25 miles north of Hanoi, the Phantoms accelerated to 750mph (650 knots). Then, varying altitude between 4,000 and 6,000ft, they described a huge elongated 'S' in the sky as they charged past the MiG base at Phuc Yen, the rail yard at Yen Vien and the Paul Doumer Bridge. Shutters clicking at regular intervals, the fan of automatic cameras fitted in the nose of each plane captured on film the scene ahead and on either side. As he swept past the Yen Vien rail yard Pickard saw plenty of signs that it had been hit, though the smoke from numerous fires made it impossible to make any detailed assessment of the damage.

During their photo runs the Phantom pilots had to make conscious efforts not to let their planes go supersonic – that would have deprived them of the manoeuvrability they needed to align the cameras on their target. Flying in loose pair, the Phantoms lined up on the Paul Doumer Bridge with Pickard slightly behind and about 1,000ft to the right of his leader.

By then the defending gunners were beginning to zero in on the two Phantoms and they laid on an awe-inspiring firework display. Pickard recalled:

After we passed the rail yard we got everything in the world shot at us. We started jinking and as we approached Hanoi, there was a trail of black puffs from bursting shells behind Sid. I said to my back seater, Chuck Irwin, 'Good God, look at that stuff behind lead!' Chuck replied 'It's a good thing you can't see the stuff behind us!'

As the pair swept past the Paul Doumer Bridge, about half a mile to the west of him, Pickard glanced at the structure and saw that all its spans seemed to be in place. Near Gia Lam airfield Pickard suddenly noticed a MiG-17 about 500yd behind him and to the left, seemingly trying to get into a firing position. The two RF-4Cs dropped their noses and easily outdistanced the somewhat slower MiG.

As the Phantoms continued their photographic runs heading south from Hanoi, a SAM battery joined the unequal contest and loosed off a missile. Although his cameras photographed the SAM approaching from below, Pickard saw nothing of it before the warhead detonated. The first he knew of the missile's presence was when the Phantom bucked under its blast:

> I didn't see the SAM but I saw a whole bunch of red things, like tracer rounds but fanning out, come past my nose. I ducked, it looked like we were going to hit them.

Miraculously, all the missile fragments missed the plane. Then, Pickard recalled, there was another MiG scare.

> As we headed away from Hanoi, Red Crown [the US radar surveillance ship off the coast] called to say we had a bandit behind us. At that time I was trying to conserve fuel, I was down to 5,300 pounds. But we started accelerating to the southwest in [after] burner. We were at low altitude and really using gas, it was beginning to hurt.

As soon as they were clear of the MiG, the Phantoms again slowed down. But even at that reduced rate of consumption Pickard now had insufficient fuel to get home. He needed to go high, to the rarefied air above 40,000ft, where the plane's aerodynamic drag was only

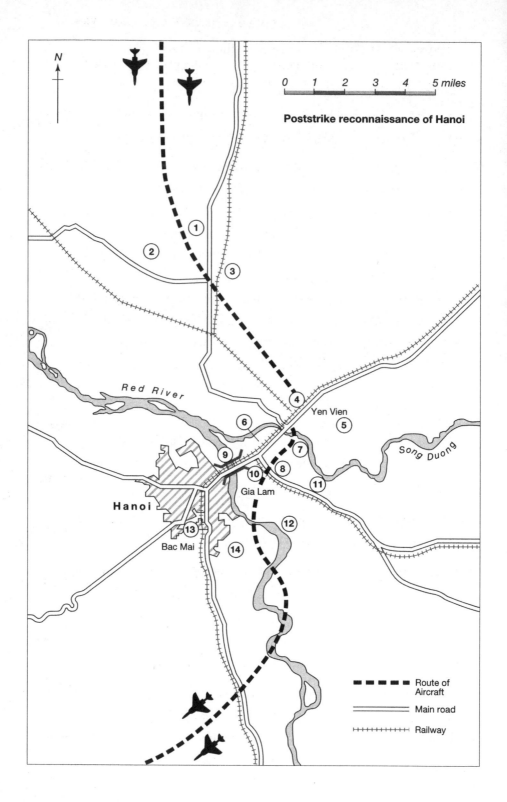

Poststrike reconnaissance of Hanoi

N

0 1 2 3 4 5 miles

Red River

Yen Vien

Song Duong

Hanoi

Gia Lam

Bac Mai

Route of Aircraft

Main road

Railway

ANALYSIS OF PHOTOS TAKEN DURING THE POST-STRIKE RECONNAISSANCE
BY MAJOR SID ROGERS AND CAPTAIN DON PICKARD, 14TH TACTICAL
RECONNAISSANCE SQUADRON

1 Three field guns and seven howitzers parked off the road with trails in travelling position.

2 Phuc Yen airfield, partial coverage: two MiG-21s, one MiG-17 and three Il-28 bombers, all parked.

3 AAA site: eight guns, probably 37mm, part of the airfield defences.

4 Yen Vien railroad yard, smoke-limited interpretation: cratering of through lines, nine of twelve tracks in classification yard appeared cut; several craters and secondary fires noted in immediate area; about 100 assorted items of rolling stock remained, apparently undamaged, in the classification yard.

5 SAM site VN 347: three SA-2 missiles on launchers, three empty launchers, one Fan Song radar; two SA-2 missiles on transporters and four possible SA-2 missiles on transporters nearby; numerous support vans.

6 AAA site: four guns, probably 85mm, firing at aircraft.

7 AAA site: six 85mm guns in revetments, one Firecan (gun-control) radar.

8 AAA site: six 57mm guns, possible Firecan radar.

9 Paul Doumer railroad and highway bridge: all spans in place, but the impact point of the bombs could not be determined. There were 27 vehicles on the bridge. On the photographs the bridge appeared operational, though a break at the eastern end prevented wheeled traffic.

10 Gia Lam airfield: two Il-12 and two Il-14 (twin-engined transports), three Li-2s (Soviet-built Douglas DC-3s), six An-2 (single-engined biplane transports), two Mi-1 (helicopters).

11 AAA site: eight guns, probably 85mm, in revetments.

12 SAM site VN 009: site unoccupied, no missiles or radar observed; Mi-4 helicopter observed.

13 Bac Mai airfield: no aircraft observed (airfield out of use).

14 SAM site VN 243: five SA-2 missiles on launchers, one empty launcher, one Fan Song radar.

one-third that at sea level. Up there, each pound of fuel consumed would carry the plane more than twice as far as at low altitude. Although the plane would burn more fuel during the climb to high altitude, the much-improved consumption once it got there would outweigh that disadvantage. Swiftly the two Phantoms rose to 43,000ft, then throttled back and levelled out.

The unexpected appearance of that final MiG had forced the Phantoms to divert well to the east of their planned egress route. That took them well clear of the KC-135 airborne tanker rendezvous area, where the Phantoms might have replenished their tanks. Pickard did a quick recalculation of his remaining fuel and saw that if he took the direct route to Udorn, and provided there were no further problems, he could reach the airfield. Don Rogers, still with plenty of fuel, flew behind and to one side of Pickard in a covering position ready to give whatever help he could.

Pickard called to the control tower at Udorn, declaring that he had an emergency and asking permission for a priority straight-in approach and landing. Back came the reply with the worst possible news: a few minutes earlier a plane had run into the airfield's crash barrier. Until it could be towed clear, the runway at the base was blocked.

McDONNELL RF-4C PHANTOM

ROLE   Two-seat reconnaissance aircraft.

POWER   Two General Electric J.79-GE-15 turbojets with afterburners, each developing 17,000lb of thrust.

ARMAMENT   None carried during the mission to Hanoi on 10 May 1972.

PERFORMANCE   Maximum speed during low-altitude (between 4,000 and 6,000ft) photographic runs 748mph (650 knots).

NORMAL OPERATIONAL TAKE-OFF WEIGHT   58,000lb.

DIMENSIONS   Span: 38ft 4in; length 62ft 11in; wing area 530 sq ft.

DATE OF FIRST PRODUCTION RF-4C   May 1964.

Yet again, Packard recalculated his remaining fuel. If he throttled back and descended slowly for the next 100 miles, he had just enough fuel to reach the airfield at Nam Phong about 45 miles south of Udorn. That was the fallback position, however. If he could, he still wanted to land at Udorn. Pickard asked the controller to tell him immediately when the runway became clear.

I had passed Udorn, heading for Nam Phong, when the controller called: 'The runway is clear. You're cleared to land right now, we can hold the runway for you.' I was high, over 20,000 feet, Udorn was closer than Nam Phong so I turned back. I pulled one engine back [to idling power] and at 12,000 feet I threw the [landing] gear and flaps out and started a steep turning descent to the runway.

Now Pickard had a good chance of getting his Phantom down in one piece, but there was no margin for error. As he lined up on the runway centreline but still high, his fuel gauges indicated less than 300lb remaining. At low altitude, the Phantom needed 500lb of fuel to fly a closed circuit pattern and land. Pickard told his crewman to prepare for the worst:

I told Chuck Irwin to rotate the handle so that if he ejected, we would both go. I told him that if we did not land first time I was going to climb and head south. As soon as the first engine quit, he was to pull the handle and eject us both. There was no way we could make it back to the runway.

The steep visual approach to the runway went off perfectly until, just short of touchdown, Pickard eased on power to halt his plane's fierce rate of descent. With so much on his mind he had overlooked one vital switch setting, and the omission was about to jeopardize both the plane and those aboard it. During the return flight through the stratosphere the outside air temperature had been around minus 56° C, colder than the coldest deep freeze. The inside of the plane's perspex canopy was chilled below freezing point. As the Phantom's engines wound up to give the selected power, the plane's air conditioning system gulped in warm moist air from outside the plane and blew it over the inside of the cockpit canopy and windscreen. In no time at all, a layer of opaque white frost had formed across both surfaces.

Pickard shut off the air conditioning system to prevent things getting worse. Then, his right hand holding the control stick, he tore off his oxygen mask with his left hand and used his teeth to pull off his left flying glove. Using his fingernails, he desperately scratched the frost away from a small area at the side of the canopy. Through that small clear patch Pickard could just make out the runway coming up to meet him; fortunately, in a previous appointment as a flying instructor, he had experience of landing a plane with little forward visibility:

> As an instructor I had spent a lot of time landing or teaching landings from the back seat. I banged the Phantom down on the runway, we rolled to the end and turned off. We had less than 200 pounds of fuel left . . .

Lacking sufficient fuel even to reach his squadron's dispersal area, Pickard taxied off the runway and moved to a point where he would not get in the way of other planes, then shut down his engines. Within a couple of minutes a jeep arrived to remove the all-important film magazines from the RF-4C, and rush them to the analysis centre. As the jeep sped clear, a truck arrived to tow the Phantom to its assigned parking spot.

AT THE PHOTOGRAPHIC analysis centre at Udorn, photo interpreters pored over the still wet film negatives to extract every possible crumb of information from the sortie. During their hectic dash past Hanoi, the planes' automatic cameras had run continuously. The photos showed that all the spans of the Paul Doumer Bridge appeared to be in place, though there were signs of damage on the eastern edge. Other photos gave proof that the Yen Vien rail yard had suffered considerable damage. The films also provided cover of three airfields, three SAM sites and five operational anti-aircraft gun sites – one of which was shooting at the planes at the time it was photographed – as well as other items of military equipment.

On the following day, the raiders returned to Hanoi for another attack on the Paul Doumer Bridge. On that occasion the planes concentrated their attack on a damaged span at the eastern end, and dropped it into the Red River to render the bridge unusable. A few minutes later, a pair of reconnaissance Phantoms sped through the area to take photographs to confirm that result.

CHAPTER SEVENTEEN

Combat Rescue

When a plane is shot down over enemy-held territory, those aboard it will do everything possible to avoid capture. One of the most tenacious efforts ever made in this respect was by Captain Roger Locher of the 555th Tactical Fighter Squadron, whose F-4 Phantom fighter was shot down over North Vietnam on 10 May 1972.

THE FIGHT WITH MiG-21s was going well for Oyster Flight of the 555th Tactical Fighter Squadron. At least one North Vietnamese fighter had already gone down, as Major Robert Lodge racked his Phantom behind another. Captain Roger Locker, weapon systems officer in the fighter, recalled:

> We were in his jet wash. There he was, [after] burner plume sticking out, the shiniest airplane you've ever seen. He was going up in a chandelle to the right, we were right behind him.

The MiG was too close to the Phantom for the latter to attack with missiles, so Lodge eased off his turn and the range of the enemy fighter opened rapidly.

Then, suddenly, the tables were turned. Zooming up from below to gatecrash the fight came a pair of MiG-19s. In a sweeping left turn, one of them passed behind Lodge; then closed on him from his right.

Lieutenant John Markle, to the left of Lodge and in no position to engage the MiG, shouted warnings:

'You got a Bandit in your 10 o'clock Bob, level!'

'Bob reverse right, reverse right Bob. Reverse right! The Bandit's behind you!' Seconds later, 30mm explosive shells thudded into the Phantom. The right engine exploded and the fighter yawed hard to the right. A fire in the rear fuselage blazed hotter and began to eat its way forwards. Roasted by the heat, the transparent plastic of the canopy over Locher's head turned an opaque orange and smoke started to seep into the cockpit. The back-seater selected full oxygen to keep the fumes out of his mask.

> I looked at the altimeter, we were passing 8,000 feet. I said 'Hey Bob, we're passing 8,000 feet. It's getting awful hot back here, I'm going to have to get out.' He looked over his right shoulder and said 'Why don't you eject then?'

At the time Roger Locher pulled his ejection seat handle the fighter was upside down, well ablaze and falling fast. He saw his canopy go, then he felt the force of the wind blast as his body was hurled into the airflow. There was a loud 'Thwack!' as the parachute opened, then a roar as a pair of MiG-19s swept past.

The other members of Oyster Flight watched in dread fascination as the Phantom went down, silently praying for the sight of parachutes. Nobody saw Locher's parachute. His seat had fired downwards, and probably the smoke from the burning aircraft had screened him. It appears that the pilot, Major Robert Lodge, was still in his cockpit when the fighter plunged into the ground.

Locher's parachute deposited him among 40ft-high trees on a wooded ridge line, and he took some knocks as he crashed through the upper branches. He undid the quick-release and stepped out of his harness, then tried to pull the parachute down. But the canopy was draped over several branches and resisted all attempts to jerk it clear. Next, the airman tried to disconnect the survival pack from the parachute harness. Still in shock after the ejection, his fingers refused to obey his brain's commands. There was no alternative, he had to abandon the parachute and the precious survival pack as they would betray his point of arrival.

Next, Locher took out a beeper radio. He did not think rescue would be possible so deep in enemy territory, but he needed to tell his colleagues that he had reached the ground safely. He switched on the radio and made a brief call. Then, fearful the transmission might give away his position, he switched it off. He discarded his flying helmet and set out at a brisk trot to distance himself from the parachute.

Locher had covered about half a mile when he heard a babble of voices. It was the posse sent to bring him in. The airman scrambled into a small depression and covered himself with leaves and brush:

It was wet and uncomfortable – but better than the alternative!
They took about two hours to get from the crash site to where I was.
When I first heard them I thought they were tracking me, it sounded
like they were coming straight for me. Of course, you imagine that.
They had a good search party of adult men, starting at about noon
they searched fairly thoroughly. People yelled and screamed to
get me to move, and once every 15 minutes somebody fired three
rounds from an automatic rifle into the ground.

Locher thought it was only a matter of time before he was found, but he resolved to remain still. He explained his line of thinking:

If they wanted me, they would have to stand on me. I grew up in
Kansas and spent a lot of time hunting pheasants. A lot got killed
because they got nervous. They would sit among cover on the ground
and you could walk past without seeing them. But if you stopped
for a cigarette one might flush out from just behind you, three feet
away, and you would get it. Had it sat tight it would have lived.

At dusk, the searchers went home. Stepping quietly in case someone had stayed behind, the fugitive moved a few hundred yards before dark. Then he picked out a relatively soft piece of ground and sat down to make an inventory of his possessions. He had a stout pair of boots, underwear, flight suit, G-suit and life jacket. He had two beeper radios and four batteries, a survival knife, a .38 calibre Browning pistol and ammunition, a mosquito net, a small medical kit and various sig-nalling devices – flares, smoke markers, signal mirror and whistle. Fol-lowing the loss of the survival pack his only sustenance was two pints of water and a couple of chocolate snacks, none of which survived his first meal in North Vietnam.

Locher knew he was somewhere near Yen Bai, to the north of Hanoi. He thought it unlikely that US helicopters would venture so far into enemy territory to pick him up. If he could reach the sparsely inhabited mountainous area to the west he thought his chance of rescue would be much better. The straight-line distance was 90 miles. A Phantom in a hurry could cover that in about five minutes. If he averaged 2 miles a day through the difficult country, moving mainly at dusk and shortly after dawn, the journey would take about six weeks. On the way he would need to cross the Red River, so he decided to take his life jacket. For food he would 'live off Mother Nature'. Whatever else it lacked, Roger Locher's escape plan certainly had the merit of simplicity.

Any attempt to move across North Vietnam would have been doomed had the airman suffered any serious injury, but in that respect Roger Locher had been lucky. Apart from the shock, which had soon worn off, he had suffered only minor burns ('no worse than a bad case of sunburn') to unprotected skin on his neck and wrists.

After dawn the next day the airman covered only a few hundred yards before the search party returned. Again he hid in a patch of rot-ting foliage, and again the searchers looked for him elsewhere. At dusk on the second day the search ended and again Locher moved a few hundred yards before nightfall. On the morning of the third day it was raining when the search resumed, though again the fugitive was able to move short distances in the morning before sunrise and in the evening after sunset. Rain was falling at dawn on the fourth day, as Locher resumed his trek to the west. But this time the area remained quiet; the hunt had been called off. Locher decided to hide for the rest of the day and start moving at dusk.

Initially, Locher had been too busy evading capture to worry about the lack of food. But now, having shed his pursuers, his rumbling stomach dominated all thoughts. When he could find them he ate wild fruit and shoots, but it was early spring and there was not much new growth.

> My stomach was growling, I was always thinking about eating. I found a few dariens, small pods about the size of an apricot which contained edible kernels. Another fruit looked like a pithy cherry, it too had an edible inside. And there were weed shoots. They had no taste, they were just a bland blah. I avoided meat. There were plenty of grey squirrels about, I could have shot them but I figured somebody might come to investigate. And I had no way to cook the meat; I didn't want to catch parasites I couldn't handle.

Several streams ran through the area, providing Locher with a plentiful supply of fresh water.

The airman's days now followed one by one in a regular pattern: get up at first light and walk a mile or so away from the rising sun, then hide. At dusk walk a few hundred yards towards the setting sun, then find a place to bed down for the night. By day, the mosquitoes were bothersome and Locher found it necessary to wear a mosquito net over his head. The hilly terrain varied between relatively lightly wooded areas, and thick primary jungle with trees 80ft high, forming a dense canopy beneath which was perpetual twilight. In places, the hills were steep and sometimes he took circuitous routes to avoid them. He saw few trails, and he kept clear of those he did find.

At irregular intervals Locher switched on a radio and listened for calls from US aircraft. Sometimes he transmitted a brief voice call, keeping the transmission short so as not to betray his position to North Vietnamese listeners. Nobody replied.

Thirteen days after his shoot-down, Roger Locher's desire to make progress nearly cost him his freedom. He was trudging west, locked in his thoughts, when suddenly he realized he had walked into a village. If he went out the way he had come, he thought he would be seen. So he crawled into a patch of foliage, covered himself with brushwood and leaves, and resolved to stay put until dark. Everything went well until late in the afternoon:

> The kids were bringing in the cattle and this water buffalo must have smelled me. He stopped, standing on one of the saplings covering me, and refused to go on. The kids shouted and hit him, but he wouldn't budge. Then one of the kids went running off to the village. I thought they'd seen me, and were going to get dad with his gun. A little while later the kid came back with his bigger brother who hit the animal hard enough to make it go. As they went off I looked up and there was the butt of the water buffalo, first kid, second kid, and a little kid who ran after them, tripped and fell down, got up and ran on. The animal had knocked the camouflage off my right leg; if they had been looking for me they would certainly have found me. It's a good thing water buffaloes can't speak!

The airman replaced the camouflage, waited until dark, and then silently left the village.

By the final week in May, food no longer dominated Locher's thoughts. It was as though his body had given up caring. He knew he was getting weaker, for even to stand up required inordinate effort. On the 31st, he reached the end of the high ground. Ahead lay the flat plain of the Red River Valley, and beyond that was the high ground he was making for.

The airman now faced a miserable choice. If he went forward into the populated area, he knew there was an increased risk of capture. But if he stayed put he might starve to death and perhaps nobody would ever know. He decided to start out at first light the next day and get as far across the valley as he could before the peasants came to work the fields. Then he would hide.

That night, rain kept the fugitive awake. The following morning, 1 June, he overslept. By the time he awoke, the sun was high in the sky and peasants were working the fields. There was no point in starting out so he decided to delay his departure until dusk. He did not realize it at the time, but Lady Luck was smiling.

Midway through the morning a thunderous 'Whoooosh!' rent the air: the SAM battery near Yen Bai had launched a missile. The significance of the commotion did not escape Locher:

> If they were firing, there had to be American aircraft nearby. I monitored Guard frequency on my radio but heard nothing. So I waited about 5 minutes then I came up 'Any US aircraft, if you read Oyster 1 Bravo come up on Guard.'

To the south of Yen Bai, Phantoms of the 8th Tactical Fighter Wing were on the way home after attacking a target near Hanoi. One of the pilots heard the call and informed his flight leader, but by then the jets were beyond range of Locher's transmitter. A following flight was asked to reply to the call.

At this stage the downed airman's aim was simple; he merely wanted to get word back that he was still alive. The flight leader made contact and Locher repeated the earlier call and gave more detail.

> About five minutes later Fletch Leader came back and said 'We passed the word, and the Jollies and Sandies [Jolly Green Giant rescue helicopters and A-1 Sandy escorts] are on their way.' That put a big weight on my shoulders. I thought there was no way a rescue force would come in so far for me – but I didn't tell them not to come!

THAT MORNING CAPTAIN Dale Stovall of the 40th Rescue and Recovery Squadron was on airborne standby, cruising over Laos in his Jolly Green Giant helicopter. When he learned of the radio call he knew there was a risk it was a North Vietnamese trap. But it was decided to investigate the transmission further. Cautiously the rescue force, comprising two Jolly Green Giant helicopters and four A-1 Sandy attack planes, advanced into North Vietnam. Four Phantom fighters provided top cover.

It took the leading pair of A-1s about 20 minutes to reach the Yen Bai area and re-establish radio contact with Locher. Then the A-1s had an important task. The rescue crews were brave but they were not foolhardy.

Before the vulnerable helicopters could enter the area, an A-1 pilot had to ascertain that the caller was indeed Locher. Each US aviator flying on operations in the theatre left at base four questions and answers that were personal to himself. A question and answer from Locher's list went by secure radio link from Headquarters Seventh Air Force near Saigon to the Rescue Co-ordination Centre at Nakhon Phanom, thence to the HC-130 Hercules airborne command post over northern Laos, thence to the A-1 leader. Locher was asked his mother's maiden name, and he answered correctly. The operation could proceed.

Two big helicopters clattered low over the ground towards Yen Bai. As the aircraft passed over villages, people stood in the open and waved, thinking the unfamiliar machines that deep in North Vietnam had to be friendly. It seemed the rescuers might have a clear run. Then things started to go wrong.

A SAM battery launched a missile at an A-1, without success. Then it engaged the escorting Phantoms and caused serious damage to one of them, forcing it and its flight to break away. Worse followed, in the shape of a MiG-21 which closed on the rescue force. Clearly the element of surprise was lost, and without fighter cover the helicopters had to abandon the rescue attempt. The Jolly Green Giants turned around and went home.

Waiting in his hideout, Roger Locher was disappointed the rescue attempt had come to nothing. But throughout it he had fought not to

---

SIKORSKY HH-53B 'SUPER JOLLY GREEN GIANT'

ROLE Long-range combat rescue helicopter, with operating crew of five.

POWER Two General Electric T64-GE-3 turboshaft engines, each developing 3,080hp at take-off.

ARMAMENT Three 7.62mm GAU-2A miniguns.

PERFORMANCE Maximum speed 196mph at sea level.

NORMAL OPERATIONAL TAKE-OFF WEIGHT 73,500lb.

DIMENSIONS Main rotor diameter 79ft; length (rotors turning) 88ft ½in.

DATE OF FIRST PRODUCTION HH-53B: 1966.

let his hopes run too high. At least people now knew he was still alive. He also realized how lucky it was that he had overslept. If he had set out at dawn, as he had planned, he would have found only sparse cover on the river plain.

AT ROGER LOCHER'S base at Udorn, Thailand, intelligence officers and friends played and replayed the tape of the conversation between the F-4 crew and the downed airman. Their unanimous view was that it was Locher, and it seemed he was not speaking under duress.

It was one thing for a bunch of relatively junior officers at Udorn to establish the identity of a flyer down in North Vietnam and conclude that he was not speaking under duress. It was quite a different matter to secure authority for a major operation to extricate him.

That particular buck stopped on the desk of General John Vogt, the Seventh Air Force commander. He saw it would require a substantial effort to rescue Locher, and it would involve risk to a large number of planes and crews. On the other hand, he knew that a major motivating factor for his crews was the thought that if they came down in enemy territory, senior commanders would spare no effort to get them out. If that were ever in doubt, morale would tumble. General Vogt ordered the rescue operation to be repeated. To ensure that he would have the necessary resources, he postponed all offensive air operations for the following day.

SOON AFTER DAWN on 2 June the two helicopters and four A-1s took off from Nakhon Phanom for the 3½-hour flight to Yen Bai, accompanied as far as northern Laos by the HC-130 Hercules command plane. A huge supporting operation then took shape around the rescue force. Sixteen Phantoms were to attack Yen Bai airfield, to crater the runway to prevent MiGs based there from interfering with the rescue. A further sixteen Phantoms were to hit anti-aircraft gun positions in the area. The rescue force and the bombers, plus their attendant F-4 escorts, radar-jamming EB-66s, F-105 defence suppression aircraft and KC-135 refuellers totalled 119 aircraft.

ROGER LOCHER ROSE at first light and turned on the bleeper radio that was his lifeline to the outside world. Still he fought to keep down his hopes of rescue, as he could not believe helicopters would again go so far into enemy territory for him.

The flyer had answered correctly the authenticating question the day before, but there still remained an outside possibility this was a trap – the airman might have had a gun pointed at his head. So this time there was a new question, devised by an officer who had studied at the same university as Locher. Locher described what happened after he made radio contact with the Captain Ron Smith piloting the lead A-1:

> Ron Smith said 'Hey Oyster, I got a question for you and you'd better answer it right.' I'd been studying my other three questions all night, I knew the answers to those. But it wasn't one of them. He said 'What's Kite's?' Kite's? Everybody at Kansas State University knew the drinking haunt frequented by students. I said 'It's a place to drink beer.' He said 'Drink what?' 'Beer!' He said 'You sound like the one I want.' I said 'You're damn right I'm the one you want!'

Locher's snap reply and indignant quip established beyond doubt that there was nobody with him telling him what to say.

Then the downed aviator heard the whistle of distant jets, followed

---

DOUGLAS A-1E 'SANDY'

ROLE   Single-seat attack aircraft used to escort combat rescue helicopters.

POWER   One Wright R-3350-26WA air-cooled, 18-cylinder, radial engine developing 2,700hp at take-off.

ARMAMENT   Four 20mm cannon, up to 8,000lb of ordnance or fuel on the underwing pylons.

PERFORMANCE   Maximum speed 311mph at 26,000ft.

NORMAL OPERATIONAL TAKE-OFF WEIGHT: 17,000lb.

DIMENSIONS   Span 50ft; length 40ft; wing area 400 sq feet.

DATE OF FIRST PRODUCTION A-1E (ORIGINALLY DESIGNATED AD-5)   1951.

by the wail of air raid sirens at Yen Bai. Four F-4s rolled in and attacked the south end of the airfield, while another four went for the north end. Simultaneously, more F-4s dive-bombed anti-aircraft batteries in the area, causing secondary explosions that sent columns of smoke high into the sky.

The rescue force advanced towards the survivor with Dale Stovall again flying the lead helicopter. As the planes crossed the Red River, they came under machine-gun fire from the ground. The helicopters' gunners replied in kind. A few minutes later Locher heard an A-1 roar past. By the time No 2 came in he had his signal mirror up and ready to point at the approaching aircraft. The A-1 pilot saw the bright flash of the sun off the mirror, called 'Tally Ho!' on the radio to indicate he had visual contact, and began circling the survivor. Then the A-1s laid a smokescreen between the downed pilot and the Red River Valley.

The rescue helicopter swept in behind the A-1s, clattered over the survivor, pulled into a tight semicircle and nosed towards him in a slow hover. The pick-up went exactly according to the book but, as Stovall later explained, the same could not be said for the first part of the withdrawal:

It took less than two minutes to get Roger on board the helicopter, and we were all on our way over the ridge line. Jerry [Captain Jerry Shipman, pilot of the backup helicopter] was waiting for us, and we started back in formation. Every village had been alerted and we started taking small arms fire on the way back.

As we came over a ridge line before we dropped into the Red River [Valley] we had the surprise of our lives. A train coming down that railroad from China had seen the smoke at Yen Bai and had stopped exactly at our crossing point. We came over the ridge line in formation, and sitting in front of us was a 14-car train. Two cars had sandbagged gun positions, similar to what you see in the World War II movies. Their gunners were looking down the Red River Valley. They tried to get their guns cranked around to fire at us, our gunners were trying to get a shot at them.

While the A-1s kept the enemy gunners busy, the helicopters made their escape heading south-west.

During all of this, Roger Locher was sitting in the fuselage of the helicopter, oblivious to what was happening outside. Someone had passed him a box of rations and, like an orphan who had found the key to the treats cupboard, he gobbled cookies as fast as he could. When he could get no more in his mouth, he stuffed them into his pockets. He still did not think he was going to get out of North Vietnam, and he was determined that if he went down a second time he would have something to eat. After the cookies he worked his way through a can of apricots and some other items before his stomach, unaccustomed to such gluttony, issued a stab of protest.

After a three-hour flight, the rescue formation reached Udorn. A large crowd was waiting at the airfield to greet the airman's return, and the reception committee included General Vogt in person who had flown in from Saigon especially. Dale Stovall described the rescuers' arrival.

> The A-1s broke out and got ahead of us a little ways. Then all made a low pass on the field, pitched out and landed. We came in behind them, made a low pass down the flight line, popped our red smokes [smoke markers] and came back in, landed and taxied in. We had been in the aircraft about eight hours and we were hot and sweaty and extremely excited.

As Locher stepped from the helicopter, he was greeted with loud cheers and yells from those standing on the ramp. Weak from lack of food, he walked like an old man; he had left the base weighing 180lb, now he was down to 150lb. Willing hands helped him into the waiting ambulance. He was home at last.

ROGER LOCHER'S FEAT, to remain at liberty for 23 days in the enemy homeland before a successful rescue, established a record for the Vietnam War. It also ranks among the most successful combat evasion episodes in history. The rescue also set a record for those who retrieved him, for the operation took the Jolly Green Giant helicopters deeper into North Vietnam than on any other such mission.

Ironically, Locher's determined attempt to ease the task of his rescuers achieved virtually nothing. During the three-week trudge he moved only about 12 miles to the west. Had he stayed put after the Vietnamese gave up the search for him, his eventual rescue would have been no more difficult than it was.

CHAPTER EIGHTEEN

Ground Attack Harriers over the Falklands

In April 1982 Tony Harper was one of the Royal Air Force Harrier

GR 3 pilots of No 1 Squadron chosen to go to the Falklands. In this

account he describes his preparation for that conflict and some of his

combat missions.

IN THE SPRING of 1982 Flight Lieutenant Tony Harper was serving with No 1 Squadron at Wittering in Cambridgeshire. It was his third flying tour, having completed one on Harriers in Germany and another serving as an instructor on Hunters. During the week following the Argentine invasion of the Falklands, it became clear that No 1 Squadron was likely to become involved.

As the unit's pilots learned what was in store for them, it was clear this would be no picnic. Staging through St Mawgan in Cornwall, they were to fly direct to Ascension Island, which would involve more than nine hours airborne with several air-to-air refuellings. From the airfield at Ascension, they would make a brief hop to land their Harriers on the deck of the container ship *Atlantic Conveyor*, which would carry the squadron to the South Atlantic. Once in the operational theatre they were to take off from the container ship and fly to the aircraft carrier HMS *Hermes*, which would serve as their base for subsequent combat missions.

During operations over the Falklands the Harrier pilots' survival would depend on their ability to fly fast and low when they penetrated the enemy defences. During the couple of weeks before they departed to join the British Task Force, the Harrier pilots honed their skills at low flying. Over selected areas they were now allowed to go as low as 100ft, somewhat lower than was permissible for normal training. Tony Harper described the concept of this type of operation:

> If somebody is pointing a radar, a missile or a gun at you, you need to put something physical between you and him. In nine cases out of ten, the best thing is going to be a hill. So, you look for the blind spot on the other side of the hill from the weapon or the radar. If the hill is 1,000 feet high, you need to fly only 900 feet above the ground on the other side of that hill. But if the hill is only 50 feet high, you have to be at 30 feet on the other side of the hill. In normal training we are allowed down to 250 feet. Exceptionally we are allowed to train down to 100 feet, but no lower because of the risk to the aircraft. Anti-aircraft weapons, missiles and guns, are sited on hills to give good coverage, but the lookdown performance of most weapons is very limited. So the lower you can fly the better your chances of survival.
>
> The problem of flying at 600 knots [690 mph] at 100 feet is that it feels as if you are flying through a 'tunnel'. There is a segment of about 15 degrees either side of the nose of the aircraft where you can see clearly; on either side, the ground is just a blur. Because you are looking through that 'tunnel', and you are so close to the ground, you dare not look anywhere else but where you are going. There is no time to look at a map. You certainly cannot look over your shoulder for possible enemy aircraft which may drop in behind you, or cover the rear of your wingman.
>
> The first time I flew that low at high speed, it really did put the wind up me. For the first 10 hours flying at low altitude, you are able to do nothing but look straight in front of you and fly. However, with practice, you get more comfortable at it. And when you are used to it, you can devote more attention to doing the other things that need to be done.

In RAF parlance, being cleared to fly at 100ft in training meant not going below that altitude, it did not mean flying at 100ft longer than necessary. Tony Harper explained how this worked in practice:

> Basically, you fly as low as you need to fly. So you plan the route taking into account the terrain over which you are flying, and tune in your mind to those parts of it where you will need to go that low. Maybe the approach for the first 30 miles of the route to the target is over friendly territory and you are shielded from the enemy by a line of hills. Then you can fly at 500 feet. But where you might be exposed to enemy radars or defences, you have to come down.

At the beginning of May the squadron's period of intensive training came to an end, and on 2 May the initial wave of six Harriers flew from Wittering for St Mawgan. On the following morning the first three Harriers took off for Ascension Island, accompanied by two Victor tankers which supplied them with fuel. So far as Tony Harper was concerned, the biggest problem was the boredom of being cooped up in a Harrier cockpit for 9 hours 15 minutes.

The RAF Harrier pilots arrived to find a hive of activity at Ascension Island. Everybody was working flat out.

> The second part of the Task Force, with the amphibious forces, was just arriving. Everybody was busy rushing around, helicopters were moving stores, loading ships. Aeroplanes were coming in full of people, and going off all through the day and night. The Vulcans were setting up their raids on Port Stanley. We had a short wait for the rest of the Squadron.

On 4 May the second wave of three Harriers arrived on Ascension, and on the 5th three more reached the island. On 6 May a succession of Harrier GR3s took off from Ascension and landed on the container ship *Atlantic Conveyor* lying at anchor off the coast. The container ship set sail that evening. On her open deck, sitting in specially made protective plastic bags, were the six Harrier GR 3s of No 1 Squadron, in addition to eight Royal Navy Sea Harriers and seven Wessex, a Lynx and four Chinook helicopters. On 18 May *Atlantic Conveyor* made its rendezvous with the British Task Force and began to transfer her Harriers and Sea Harriers to the aircraft carriers.

The Harrier GR3s flew their first mission on 20 May, when Wing Commander Squire led his two flight commanders, Squadron Leaders Jerry Pook and Bob Iveson, in a three-aircraft attack on an Argentine fuel dump at Fox Bay on West Falkland. Tony Harper's first mission was on the following day, 21 May, after British troops began landing on East Falkland. He and Squadron Leader Jerry Pook flew an armed reconnaissance mission to the airfield at Dunnose Head each carrying two BL755 cluster bombs. The airfield was devoid of planes and the pilots found no target worth attacking, so they returned to the carrier with their bombs.

Elsewhere that day, two of the Harriers took hits. As he was strafing Argentine helicopters on the ground near Mount Kent, Flight Lieutenant Mark Hare's aircraft took hits but he was able to return to the carrier. Later, Flight Lieutenant Jeff Glover was shot down by ground fire over West Falkland and taken prisoner.

During their early missions the Harrier pilots were concerned that

---

BRITISH AEROSPACE HARRIER GR3

ROLE Single-seat short/vertical take-off and landing ground attack and reconnaissance fighter.

POWER One Rolls-Royce Pegasus 103, vectored-thrust, turbofan engine developing 21,500lb thrust.

ARMAMENT CARRIED DURING THE FALKLANDS CONFLICT One or two Aden 30mm cannon mounted under the fuselage as well as two BL755 cluster bomb containers, or two parachute-retarded 1,000lb bombs, or two pods each containing thirty-six 2in air-to-ground rockets.

PERFORMANCE Maximum speed 690mph (600 knots) at low altitude.

NORMAL OPERATIONAL TAKE-OFF WEIGHT 25,000lb.

DIMENSIONS Span 25ft 3in; length 45ft 7¾in; wing area 201 sq ft.

DATE OF FIRST PRODUCTION HARRIER GR3 1976.

they might be engaged by the higher-performance Mirage III and Dagger fighters operated by the Argentine Air Force. To their surprise, however, that never happened. Tony Harper described how he and his colleagues came to view that threat:

We never got blasé about the threat from enemy fighters. Every morning we were told: their guys are bound to twig some time, and come and have a fight. So, we briefed very carefully what we were going to do if we met enemy fighters at high altitude. Basically, we were going to stand our aircraft on their noses, and go straight down to about 500 feet and fight them on our terms down there. If you roll the Harrier on its back and pull back on the nozzles, you will put it into the vertical and go down very quickly indeed. But in the event their fighters never came near us.

Tony Harper flew on armed reconnaissance missions on the next two days. Then, on the 24th, came his first 'big one'– an attack on Port Stanley airfield. For this mission two Sea Harriers approached the target from the north-east and tossed their radar airburst fused bombs to explode over the anti-aircraft gun positions. While the defenders were thus distracted, a pair of Harriers ran in from the north-west and another pair from the west to attack the runway with parachute retarded 1,000lb bombs.

As we came in we saw mushrooms of smoke in the sky, from the Sea Harriers' VT [radar airburst] fused bombs. We did not go through the target particularly fast on that raid because we were trying to bomb as accurately as possible; we flew at about 480–500 knots [550–575 mph], almost 'tunnel vision' speed. My pair ran in to attack from the northwest, going across the runway towards the control tower. I followed Bob [Squadron Leader Bob Iveson] in, he was offset to one side, about half a mile in front and 45 degrees out of my left. He was to straddle the runway about half way up, I was briefed to try to straddle the runway about a quarter of the way up. In fact I got my nearest bomb on the western edge, just off the end.

It just missed the runway and caused no real damage. During my attack run I saw somebody standing on the control tower 'at the end of the tunnel' pointing something at me with flashes coming out of it. But I was not seriously fired at, it was exciting without being dangerous.

In the days to follow the squadron made several attacks on Argentine troop positions. Then, on 28 May, Tony Harper took part in what was to be the most significant mission flown by Harrier GR 3s during the conflict. The target was Argentine artillery positions at Goose Green, which were causing difficulties for the advancing British paratroops.

Major Chris Keeble, commanding the paratroops, later outlined the difficulties facing him:

The first problem was that as we closed on Goose Green from three directions, we had insufficient ammunition left to clear the settlement that evening. I didn't want to fight amongst houses at night. The second problem was that they had at least three 35-mm anti-aircraft guns shooting at us in the direct fire role, from the tip of the peninsula. The third problem was that they had an artillery battery somewhere and we had been unable to locate it during the battle. We couldn't be accurate enough with our own artillery in the counter-battery role, because we couldn't actually see their guns and we were worried about hitting civilians in the settlement.

As Keeble saw it, the answer was an immediate air strike and he sent an urgent request to the carrier.

Aboard HMS *Hermes*, Tony Harper was one of the pilots at readiness and he prepared to respond to Keeble's call.

I was No 2 to Squadron Leader Peter Harris. We had been briefed to go to Goose Green, where we knew the Paras were having a push and there was a fight on. We expected a lot of opposition when we went in so we were not looking forward to it. But we planned a good attack route, well shielded by the terrain.

When he heard of the urgency of the mission, Squadron Leader Jerry Pook volunteered to add weight to the attack.

Peter Harris led the force towards the islands at 25,000ft in standard defensive battle formation, with Squadron Leader Jerry Pook behind and to the left and Tony Harper behind and to the right. The pilots maintained station about a mile apart, scanning the sky for possible enemy fighters. After making radio contact with the forward air controller at Goose Green, the small force descended to low altitude over Falkland Sound. The Harriers accelerated to attack speed and closed on their target rapidly from the north-west.

> At high altitude on the way in we made radio contact with the forward air controller and had time to look at our target maps. So we had everything squared away as we ran in at low altitude across the sea at about 50 feet. In the distance we could see the thin columns of smoke rising above the battlefield, it looked like the aftermath of a battle. It all looked so very peaceful, the water was nice and smooth. Everything seemed more relaxed than during previous attacks; we had planned the route carefully, it was all on the rails and we were going for the target. We left the initial point at Terra Motas Point knowing exactly what we were going to do.
>
> There was hardly any wind, I remember seeing the smoke from the burning gorse on the battlefield rising almost vertically. Conditions were absolutely ideal. The target was easy to find, the buildings led us to it. We went to the left of them, we were particularly conscious that the Falkland Islanders were in the buildings and we did not want to hit them. About a mile before we passed the houses we started the pull up to release our cluster bombs. Still everything was going as planned, nobody seemed to be firing at us.
>
> Peter Harris was to my right and ahead, he was going to get there first and hopefully would give me some sort of correction. He dropped his weapons, I saw the cluster bomblets going off. Then he called up and said 'Drop yours to the right!'

Harper released his weapons as he had been asked. Meanwhile the third aircraft, Jerry Pook's, swung away to the left and then reversed its turn to attack the target from the north. That Harrier carried two pods each containing 36 high-velocity rockets. If Pook delivered his attack from behind the other two planes there was a risk, albeit a small one, that a rocket might ricochet off the ground and strike one of the planes in front. Pook ripple-fired his rockets into the target, to complete the 'pincer attack' which put down a dense pattern of bomblets and rockets across the Argentine position.

From a hill to the north of the target, Major Chris Keeble watched the aircraft sweep in low to release their bombs and fire the rockets. Later he commented:

> The attack gave a great boost to the morale of our troops. I think some of them thought the Harriers had come in a bit too close for comfort, but that is war. After that there was a marked slackening in the fighting, which had gone on very fiercely the whole day. Afterwards I sat down and thought, 'Where have we got to now? What is the enemy thinking?' I tried to assess the situation from his point of view. Now he was encircled and we had demonstrated that we could bring in the Harriers and attack his positions surgically. It was then I began to get the notion that their will had broken and maybe we could go for a surrender.

Chris Keeble's analysis proved correct. On the following morning the Argentine troops at Goose Green surrendered, and only then did the paratroops discover that the defeated enemy force had greatly outnumbered their own.

The Harrier attack on Goose Green was a textbook example of a successful close air support operation: a hard-hitting surprise attack against a target of great importance to the enemy, with results that could clearly be seen by both sides' ground troops. Launched at a crucial juncture in the land battle, it strengthened the resolve of the paratroops and demoralized their opponents.

Tony Harper flew further missions on 30 and 31 May, followed by four days of poor weather which halted attack operations. Tony Harper's next memorable mission was on 12 June, when he and Flight Lieutenant Nick Gilchrist flew an armed reconnaissance mission to the Port Stanley area.

> Just south of Sapper Hill we found a force of Argentine troops in the open, moving along the road towards Port Stanley. As I ran in to attack them with cluster bombs, I saw blokes hurling themselves flat and diving into ditches. Nick was following me in, and he said my bombs went in the right area and it looked a pretty good attack. He put down his bombs in the same place. Afterwards I discovered I had collected three hits from small arms fire during the attack, though none was serious. One went through the leading edge of the wing, one through the left of the fuselage and one through the rear fuselage.

That mission proved to be Tony Harper's last, and two days later the Argentine forces on the Falklands surrendered.

In the course of the Falklands conflict three Harrier GR 3s from No 1 Squadron were destroyed in action. All three pilots ejected safely, two were rescued soon afterwards and one was taken prisoner. No RAF Harrier pilot was killed or seriously wounded.

CHAPTER NINETEEN

The Vulcan's Impromptu Visit to Rio

Several factors can make an air operation go wrong, quite apart from actions taken by an enemy. As we saw in Chapter Sixteen, the prospect of running out of fuel will lead a pilot to take desperate measures. This was the case during the Falklands conflict, when an RAF Vulcan bomber had to make an unscheduled deviation from its flight plan.

BY THE BEGINNING of June 1982 the Falklands conflict was entering its final phase. British troops had begun their advance on Port Stanley, the capital, but Argentine ground forces still held the ring of defensive hill positions protecting it from attack.

On the afternoon of 3 June, the RAF dispatched another Vulcan attack against Port Stanley. By this stage of the war it was important to knock out parts of the Argentine air defence system around the capital, to reduce the danger to Harriers flying close air support missions when the ground forces closed in for the final battle. For its role the Vulcan was loaded with four Shrike radar-homing missiles, mounted on pylons under the wings.

The one-way journey from Ascension Island to Port Stanley involved an eight-hour flight covering almost 3,900 miles, or about as far as from London to Karachi in Pakistan. At the time these were the longest-distance air strikes ever mounted. Eleven Victor tanker aircraft supported each operation, passing fuel between themselves and to the single Vulcan bomber. They aimed to get the bomber to the target with sufficient fuel to deliver its attack and get about halfway back to Ascension Island. Then it would rendezvous with another Victor tanker and take on sufficient fuel to complete the return flight.

For this mission, Squadron Leader Neil McDougall was flying his second attack with Shrike missiles against Port Stanley. Few pilots knew more about handling the big delta-winged bomber than he did, for he had spent 16 years flying Vulcans first as a co-pilot and then as a captain. Yet, as he headed south, he had no inkling that his flying skills would be severely tested in the hours to follow.

The long and complex support operation by the tankers went off reasonably smoothly, and around midnight the Vulcan approached its target from the north-east at low altitude. McDougall pushed open his throttles to begin a rapid climb to 16,000ft, hoping to entice Argentine radars to lock on to his plane and so render themselves vulnerable to attack. By now the enemy radar operators knew what to expect when an aircraft behaved in this way, however. The RAF pilot recalled:

> As we got to about 9 miles from Port Stanley the radars started to switch off. As we went past and flew out to sea, they came on. We went round and round repeating that process for about 40 minutes. Then, on the final run before we had to go home, I decided to go into a descent towards the airfield to tempt them into switching on the radars to have a go at us.

McDougall eased off the power and the bomber went down. When he reached 10,000ft, a gun-control radar took the bait and locked on to the bomber. Then a gun battery opened fire at the plane and shells burst below it.

In the rear of the Vulcan Flight Lieutenant Rod Trevaskus, the Air Electronics Officer, locked two Shrikes on to the offending radar and launched the weapons. As the missiles detonated, McDougall saw the flashes of explosions light up the mist covering the ground. Later it would be learned that one missile had impacted close to a Skyguard fire control radar, causing severe damage and killing four of the operating crew. Its mission completed to the extent that its remaining fuel allowed, the Vulcan turned away from the target and headed north, climbing to begin the high-altitude cruise for its base.

The crew's adventures were far from over, however. Some four hours after leaving Port Stanley they made their rendezvous with a Victor tanker, and prepared to take fuel to complete the return flight. Shortly after the bomber plugged into the hose, however, its windscreen was suddenly drenched in kerosene. McDougall eased back the throttles to break contact with the tanker and assess what had gone wrong.

The supply of fuel ceased, and in seconds the airflow cleared the liquid from the bomber's windscreen. Then McDougall saw the cause of the problem: his refuelling probe had broken off. Breaking a probe during refuelling is an occupational hazard, but in this instance it happened at the worst possible time for the Vulcan crew. Unable to take on further fuel, they had no chance of reaching Ascension Island 2,000 miles away. The nearest usable airfield was the civil airport at Rio de

---

AVRO VULCAN B.2

ROLE Five-seat, medium bomber (a sixth crew member, an additional pilot experienced in air-to-air refuelling, was carried during the attack missions to the Falklands).

POWER Four Rolls-Royce (Bristol) Olympus 301 turbojet engines, each developing 20,000lb thrust.

ARMAMENT During this operation, Vulcan XM 597 carried four Shrike anti-radar missiles mounted on underwing pylons.

PERFORMANCE Cruising speed Mach 0.93 (707mph) at 45,000ft; combat radius of action without refuelling 1,725 miles; ceiling 58,000ft.

NORMAL OPERATIONAL TAKE-OFF WEIGHT 200,000lb.

DIMENSIONS Span 111ft 6in; length (including refuelling probe) 105ft 6in; wing area 3,964 sq ft.

DATE OF FIRST PRODUCTION VULCAN B.2 Spring 1960.

Janeiro some 400 miles to the west. Heading to an uncertain reception in that country was not an ideal solution, but short of bailing out of the bomber it was the only one available to McDougall.

McDougall informed the tanker that he was diverting to Rio, and swung the nose of the Vulcan round to the west. In the minutes that followed there was frenetic activity in the bomber's cabin. The Vulcan still carried a couple of Shrike missiles and McDougall had no wish to have them aboard when he landed at Rio. He told Trevaskus to fire the weapons into the sea, and to limit the missiles' range he lowered the bomber's nose. The first missile fired properly, but the second resisted everything to get it to launch.

During the attempts to launch the Shrike the Vulcan had lost a lot of altitude and was now at 20,000ft. Flying Officer Chris Lackman, the co-pilot, made a rapid check of the remaining fuel and how far it would take them. Grimly, he announced that at the rate the bomber was burning fuel it would never reach Rio at that altitude. McDougall abandoned the idea of getting rid of the missile, and began a climb to 40,000ft where the remaining fuel would take the bomber much further.

The other thing McDougall wanted to be rid of before he reached Rio was the secret documents and target information folders carried in the plane. The crew gathered these in the navigator's canvas holdall, and added a couple of hefty ground locks to ensure the bag would sink when it hit the sea. By the time that process was complete the Vulcan had reached 40,000ft. The cabin was depressurized, the door on the underside of the aircraft was opened, and the bag with the secret documents sailed out into space.

When the crew tried to close the door, however, it refused to lock shut. So long as that remained the case, the cabin could not be repressurized. By now McDougall was in radio contact with the air traffic control centre at Rio de Janeiro and had declared a full Mayday emergency. Now at high altitude in the unpressurized cabin, the crew were breathing pure oxygen under pressure. This produced an effect on their voices similar to that experienced by saturation divers breathing oxygen and helium. McDougall recalled:

We tried to discuss our emergency with a Brazilian but he could not understand us – which is hardly surprising, since his English was not all that good and we all sounded like Donald Duck!

Fortunately another controller came on the air who spoke better English, and details of the bomber's difficulties were passed. Eventually the door was closed and locked shut, the cabin was repressurized and the voices returned to normal.

There followed an anxious half-hour as the Vulcan closed on its new destination, with the needles of the fuel gauges edging relentlessly towards the zero mark. As the bomber neared the coast McDougall eased back the throttles to bring it down to 20,000ft. With the limited fuel remaining, that was as low as he dared go until he committed himself to a landing. The pilot continued:

An American-speaking controller came up and said, 'Can you see the runway ahead of you?' I said 'Yes'. He said, 'If you're critically short of fuel you can land on that.' By that time we certainly were critically short of fuel: the gauges showed about 3,000 pounds, and a Vulcan needs 2,500 pounds to do a circuit. In other words, if we missed our first approach we were going to crash, there was no doubt about it.

The runway was about 6 miles ahead, and the bomber was flying nearly 4 miles high. Neil McDougall now had to draw on every ounce of skill and experience he had amassed during his long career as a pilot to bring the Vulcan down safely. He shut the four throttles, set the air-brakes to the high-drag position, lowered the undercarriage and wound the bomber into an 80-degree bank to the right. At the same time he pushed down the Vulcan's nose, forcing the bomber into a very steep descending turn.

It was a virtuoso performance with the plane under control, but to the watching Brazilians it looked anything but that. People on the ground thought a disaster was about to happen with the unannounced visitor crashing into their city. Afterwards McDougall commented:

It [the Vulcan] fell out of the sky. It was not the sort of manoeuvre I would recommend anyone to use unless the situation is desperate, because if you make a mistake you are going to crash ... There was no great thinking process to consider the pros and cons. There weren't any pros and cons, I really did not have any other option.

At the end of the manoeuvre, the Vulcan was exactly where its pilot wanted to be: about 800ft above the ground and 1½ miles from the end of the runway. But the bomber was flying at 300mph, far too fast to make a landing. So, exploiting the barn-door effect of the bomber's huge delta wing, McDougall raised the plane's nose to get maximum drag to 'mush off' the excess speed.

When the pilot next lowered the nose of the Vulcan, it was ready to land: the bomber was three-quarters of a mile from the touchdown point, at its usual approach speed and height of 155mph at 250ft. The subsequent landing was normal in every respect. The Vulcan taxied off the runway and shut down the engines. Later examination would reveal that it had only 2,000lb of fuel left, not enough to make another approach if the first one had been unsuccessful.

The Brazilian police immediately threw a cordon around the bomber, which was soon surrounded by a curious crowd. The Shrike missile still in position on its launcher drew considerable interest. McDougall was taken to meet the colonel commanding the military side of the airfield. The RAF pilot recalled:

We exchanged names, then he asked about the type of mission I had been flying. I said, 'Sorry, Sir, I cannot tell you that until I have spoken to the British Air Attaché.' He replied, 'Sorry, I cannot let you speak to your Air Attaché until you tell me what you have been doing.' 'But I have my orders ...' 'Sorry, Squadron Leader McDougall, but I have my orders too.' He said he would have to speak to higher authority, but in the meantime perhaps I would like something to drink?

The colonel poured a couple of stiff brandies and passed one to McDougall. The encounter was friendly enough, but both men knew this matter would be resolved by people far above their respective pay grades.

The men were exchanging pleasantries when the telephone rang. The colonel spoke briefly in Portuguese, then handed the receiver to McDougall with a brisk 'It's for you!' The caller was the British Air Attaché in Rio, Wing Commander Jerry Brown, who said he would get to the airport as soon as possible to assist.

Before he arrived, however, the scene degenerated into low farce. McDougall continued:

> As I put the phone down there was a knock on the door. The adjutant came in and spoke very quickly in Portuguese from which, even with my limited command of the language, I recognised the word 'Press'. Outside I could hear a commotion; the Press had arrived to interview me, en masse.
>
> The Colonel wanted to play the whole thing in a low key and I certainly did. He ushered me to the other door of his office and quietly we sneaked out and left the building. It was the only thing gentlemen could do in the circumstances!

Rapid negotiations between the British Embassy and Brazilian government officials established the visitors' immediate status. The Brazilian officials said the RAF officers were free to leave the country any time, but until matters were settled the bomber was impounded and had to remain at the airport. The British position was that it was preferable for the crew to stay where they were until the bomber was released. McDougall continued:

> It was all very friendly. But if we were to stay we could not go off base because we had no passports, and we could not wander around the base because we had no uniforms. He therefore asked that we restrict our movements to the Officers' Club, the cantina and the swimming pool.

If one had to sit out a war, there were many worse ways of doing it. That night, at the Officers' Club, Neil McDougall sneaked down to the telephone box and made a reverse-charge call to his wife Elizabeth at their home near Lincoln. He told her that everyone was well and they were being well treated. He asked her to pass that message to the wives of the other crew members and also to the station commander at their base at Waddington.

FOR SOME WEEKS PAST, the Brazilian people had enthusiastically been preparing for a visit from the Pope. The Pontiff was on his way to Argentina, but his aircraft was to make a brief stopover at Rio de Janeiro airport on 11 June. The plan was for the airliner to halt beside the VIP lounge where the Pope would descend the steps and ceremonially drop to his knees to kiss the ground of Brazil. About 300,000 people were expected at the airport to receive the Pope's blessing. The only potential hitch to this emotional occasion was the grim-looking camouflaged Vulcan bomber that threatened to block the view of part of the crowd.

There was much discussion on how and where to move the Vulcan so it would not interfere with the proceedings. No doubt that requirement was one factor that influenced the Brazilian government's decision on 9 June to allow the bomber and its crew to leave the country the next day.

On 10 June, the day before the Pope was due, the Vulcan was refuelled and took off to complete its interrupted flight to Ascension Island. The impromptu visit to Brazil had lasted for exactly seven days, almost to the hour.

For the determination and exemplary flying skill he displayed during the mission to safeguard his aircraft and crew, Neil McDougall was later awarded the Distinguished Flying Cross.

CHAPTER TWENTY

Desert Storm Warthogs

In time of war, combat planes are often used in ways markedly different from those for which they were designed. That was certainly true in the case of the Fairchild A-10, unofficially nicknamed the 'Warthog', when it first went into action. Although it had been designed specifically for the close air support role, most of its operations were of a quite different type.

LATE IN 1990, during the run-up to Operation Desert Storm, intended to evict Iraqi forces from Kuwait, the USAF deployed 144 of A-10 Warthog tank-busting aircraft to King Fahd International Airport in Saudi Arabia. The various units came under the overall control of the 354th Tactical Fighter Wing (Provisional).

The A-10 had been designed specifically for the close air support role, that is to say operations near to the line of battle and in close proximity to friendly forces. The specification called for a plane that could survive hits from small-calibre rounds and lightweight anti-aircraft missiles, the sort of weapons it might encounter when engaging enemy front-line troops. Those parts of the aircraft that were vulnerable to battle damage were protected or duplicated. The pilot sat under a canopy of thick toughened glass while beneath him was an armoured 'bathtub' of titanium thick enough to withstand hits from 23mm rounds. The plane's two engines were mounted in separate pods with separate fuel systems, so if that on the one side was shot out the other would continue working. The fuel tanks were self-sealing and filled with fire-retardant foam. The hydraulically operated flying controls had a secondary manual back-up system. If enemy rounds caused a rudder, an aileron or an elevator to jam, the control surface on the opposite side would provide sufficient control authority to bring the plane home. If the undercarriage hydraulic system was damaged, the pilot could unlock the wheels to let them drop from their housings under gravity. The airflow then pushed the legs back and down until they locked into place. With a maximum speed at low altitude of only 375mph (325 knots), the A-10 was not particularly fast. But it was not intended to go more than a few miles into enemy-held territory, and it needed to keep clear of highly defended areas.

Part of the definition of the close air support mission is that it is 'air action against hostile targets *which are in close proximity* to friendly [ground] forces'. Usually the close air support mission is appropriate only when one side is attacking or about to launch an attack. Then close support aircraft can support the attack or buttress the defence. Otherwise, when troops are in static positions, dug in and camou-flaged, there are few worthwhile targets for close air support planes. For most of the war against Iraq the opposing ground forces were not in contact, so the A-10 could not perform the mission for which it had been designed. These planes flew most of their missions in the battle-field air interdiction role, hitting targets in the enemy rear area. That did not mean these were not worthwhile targets, however.

CAPTAIN TODD SHEEHY of the 511th Tactical Fighter Squadron flew 40 combat missions in A-10s during the Gulf War. His experi-ences provide an insight into the ways the aircraft was employed.

It was still dark on the second day of the war, 18 January, when Todd Sheehy and wingman Captain Scott Johnson walked out to their planes to fly their first combat missions. Each A-10 carried the stan-dard armament load for the type; six 500lb bombs with radar airburst fuses, one IR-guided Maverick missile and another with TV guidance, two AIM-9M Sidewinder air-to-air missiles for self-protection and 1,200 rounds of depleted uranium ammunition for the internally mounted 30-mm cannon.

After completing their initial checks, the pilots started engines and Sheehy called the squadron operations centre to learn his task. He was told to head for a position off the coast of Kuwait where the Marine air support controller would assign him a target. Sheehy had just received taxi clearance, and the crew chief had pulled the chocks from the wheels, when the pilots' deliberate air of calm was rudely shattered. Over the Guard radio channel an urgent voice announced, 'Alarm Red, Alarm Red, Alarm Red'.

An enemy attack on the base was imminent, but the broadcast gave no indication of the nature of the threat. Everybody's greatest fear was a gas attack. Sheehy turned off the plane's environmental control system to prevent outside air getting into the cockpit. He then glanced forward to confirm that his gas mask was wedged between the glare shield and the canopy, within easy reach if needed. Outside, he saw the crew chief unplug his intercom lead, close the ladder door on the side of the plane and run for cover, pulling on his gas mask as he did so.

As Sheehy eased on power to edge the Warthog out of its revetment, he found he had a problem. When he pushed the rudder pedal to turn the plane it continued straight ahead; the nosewheel steering had failed. He was able to steer the A-10 using differential braking, but it was a difficulty he could have done without. Later he commented:

> There I was on my first combat sortie, with a thousand thoughts running through my mind. The base was under attack. Were planes about to drop bombs or was it a Scud missile? Would we be able to repel the attack? Would the Patriot missiles protecting our base work as advertised? There was all of that to think about, as well as the normal cockpit tasks of getting the aircraft off the airfield. To add to that it was dark, and as a day fighter unit we did not practise a lot of night operations ... With an attack imminent all of the lights had

been turned off and I had to use my taxi light to find my way. And my nosewheel steering didn't work. So my first combat mission was definitely not going very well!

When he reached the holding point beside the end of the runway, Sheehy brought the plane to a halt and waited for the weapon-arming crew to remove the safety pins from the bombs and missiles.

It was an eerie sight when the arming guys came running out in full chemical warfare gear, gas masks, suits, gloves, boots, flak vests and helmets. They probably set a World record for arming of an A-10! Then, as quickly as they had arrived, they were back in the bunker.

I attempted to contact the control tower who, in the confusion of the impending attack, were not answering my calls. I visually checked the sky around the runway and, since it didn't look as if anybody was landing, we rolled on to the runway and took off.

By then the alert F-15s based at the nearby Al Kharj airfield were also scrambling into the air and there seemed to be strobe lights all over the sky. Todd Sheehy saw his wingman move into position behind him then:

Suddenly there was a large flash over my right shoulder. Wow, did my heart start pumping then! I thought it was either a Scud impact, or a Patriot intercepting a Scud [in fact it was the latter]. I began to worry about what my squadron mates and what my airbase would look like when I get back. Had the missile landed there? Did it have a chemical warhead?

Sheehy forced himself to calm down and concentrate on the mission ahead. The A-10s flew parallel to the coast at 22,000ft, keeping over the sea as they headed for the target area. By then the sun was rising in the east, to reveal a fine day with clear skies below the aircraft and a thin layer of cirrus above them at about 27,000ft. Sheehy called the control centre and learned that his target was an artillery site just inland from the pier at Mina Sa'ad in Kuwait.

The Warthog pilots found the pier, armed their weapons and turned inland to begin their attack. The plan was to drop the 500lb free-fall bombs in a steep dive, then use the Maverick missiles and heavy cannon as appropriate in follow-up attacks. Unfortunately for the A-10 pilots, just as they located their target the Iraqi anti-aircraft gunners located them. As the planes headed inland a string of big white smoke balls suddenly appeared below them with more puffs being added – almost certainly these were 57mm rounds. Sheehy commented:

> We could see the muzzle flashes, and the guns were on the coast between us and our target. We tried to come in from different directions, but the flak followed us. Although the bombs were the most effective ordnance we had against an artillery site, putting our noses down that chute with those gunners definitely watching us just didn't seem like the smart thing to do.

Sheehy retreated over the sea and, with his wingman covering him, tried several times to lock on one of his Maverick missiles. There was insufficient image contrast to use the weapon, however. Things took a turn for the worse when Johnson suddenly called 'Break right!' to avoid an upcoming missile. Sheehy did as he was bid, punching out Chaff and decoy flares.

FAIRCHILD A-10 THUNDERBOLT II ('WARTHOG")

ROLE Single-seat, close air support aircraft.

POWER Two General Electric TF34-GE-100 turbofans, each developing 9,065lb thrust.

ARMAMENT One built-in GAU-8 30mm high-velocity cannon with 1,200 rounds of ammunition; the typical external load carried was six 500lb Mark 82 bombs, two Maverick missiles with IR or TV guidance and two AIM-9M Sidewinder air-to-air missiles for self-protection.

PERFORMANCE Maximum at low altitude 375mph (325 knots).

NORMAL OPERATIONAL TAKE-OFF WEIGHT 35,980lb.

DIMENSIONS: Span 57ft 6in; length 54ft 4 in; wing area 506 sq ft.

DATE OF FIRST PRODUCTION A-10 1976.

As I looked out the side of the canopy I saw a glowing orange ball with a long white smoke trail streaking toward me from the pier. I rolled out to put the missile off my right wing and kept the flares coming. I was greatly relieved to see the missile moving aft across my canopy, which meant that it was not guiding on me any longer. The smoke trail abruptly stopped and I watched the missile fall into the Gulf.

Sheehy pondered what to do next, and recalled a briefing to his unit from Lieutenant General 'Buster' Glossen shortly before the outbreak of hostilities:

He said 'Right now there's nothing in Kuwait or Iraq worth dying for. When we get ground troops up there, there will be something worth dying for.' I thought, no allied ground troops are in trouble, this is just an interdiction campaign. Whether we attacked the target then or a few hours later, did not matter. It would be irresponsible and stupid to risk myself, my wingman and our aircraft to try to win the war all by ourselves. We could go back later, there was no shame in that. Had our forces been in contact with the enemy then, certainly, I would have pressed our attack. But that was not the case.

By then, the A-10s were starting to run low on fuel. Sheehy informed the controller that he had been unable to hit the assigned target due to the strength of the defences. He said he was returning to base to refuel, and would be back later.

When the pair reached King Fahd International Airport, Sheehy was delighted to see that his worries about an attack on the base were unfounded. The missile had fallen some distance away. Later that morning Sheehy took off in another A-10. He and Johnson returned to their original target and delivered an accurate attack, and on that occasion the defences had ignored them. The lesson was obvious: in war, the only thing that is really easy is to get killed. Unless friendly ground forces were directly threatened, and they were not, discretion was the better part of valour.

Todd Sheehy's next 23 sorties were against similar targets, Iraqi artillery positions and vehicles situated well back from the border. Then, on his 27th combat sortie on 15 February, he led a pair of A-10s to Mudaysis in the south of Iraq. His assigned target was Suhkoi 7 'Fitter' fighter-bombers hidden in revetments in the desert a few miles from the airfield. Each Warthog carried four CBU-57 cluster bombs in addition to its usual complement of Maverick and Sidewinder missiles.

> We found four revetments, three of the planes had been destroyed previously so we attacked the fourth. We dropped to 15,000 feet to set up the attack, commenced the dive and released the cluster bombs at 10,000 feet. They scored what looked like good patterns on the target, but there was no explosion or fire. Then I made a pass with my gun, I rolled in at a 45-degree dive angle and started shooting at 10,000 feet. I fired a two-second burst, using about 150 API [armour-piercing/incendiary] and HEI [high explosive/incendiary] rounds. The Fitter exploded and burned. As we headed out of the area it was very satisfying to look back and see the black smoke cloud rising from the wrecked aircraft.

The A-10s still had fuel for another 30 minutes in the area, and they still had their missiles and nearly full magazines for their cannon. Sheehy returned to 20,000ft and told the AWACS controller that he and his wingman were available to attack other targets if required. Sheehy continued:

> He said 'I got a low and slow contact bearing 027 [degrees] for 30 miles, can you check it out?' I said yes, I had 20 minutes of gas, I would check it out. I started in that direction and I told my wingman to start cooling down the [Sidewinder] missiles because I knew it was an air-to-air contact, probably a helicopter. I started a shallow descent on the heading of 027, with my wingman about 6,000 feet behind and 45 degrees to one side and slightly above.

Sheehy asked for an update on the contacts and was informed that they had faded from the radar screen.

As he said that, I saw dust flying up and some movement on the east side of the road. I rolled into a 45-degree dive and opened fired from about 10,000 feet. I loosed off about 300 rounds at a medium-sized helicopter, either an Mi 8 Hip or a Puma, moving fairly quickly and very low across the desert floor. I recovered at 8,000 feet, circled and looked back. It appeared that the helicopter had stopped moving. Either it had been downed or it was in the hover, smoking slightly . . . I dived at about 55 degrees, fired 200 more rounds, and pulled out at about 5,500 feet. I bottomed out of the attack at about 4,500 feet, which was the lowest I went over enemy territory the whole war.

Sheehy glanced back and saw a cloud of black smoke rising from a fire on the ground, obviously marking the point where the helicopter had gone in. The pilot informed the AWACS controller that they had attacked a medium-sized helicopter and destroyed it.

The ground war opened on 24 February, but Todd Sheehy did not fly his first close air support mission until two days later. He and Johnson were sent to assist an advancing US Marine unit south of Kuwait City, which had come under artillery fire. As the Warthogs arrived in the area, they had to descend to 5,000ft to get below the thick banks of black smoke from the burning oil wells. The A-10 pilot would never forget the sight that greeted him:

Visibility decreased to about three miles and, even though it was midday, under the clouds it was more like dusk. The scene below us was amazing: thousands of Coalition vehicles in columns moving north. We could even see the corridors that had been cut through the barbed wire barriers and minefields as the columns bottled up at these choke points before moving northward again. Our guys were definitely on the offensive.

Sheehy contacted the F/A-18 Hornet pilot acting as forward air controller in that area, who briefed him on the locations of Iraqi artillery and air defence units. Then the A-10s were handed over to the ground controller for final clearance to deliver their attacks. It took several minutes to transmit the exact positions of friendly and hostile forces in the area, but that was an essential part of the operation. The fundamental tenet of the close air support mission is that it is far better to attack no target at all, than to risk hitting friendly forces. Once briefed, the A-10 pilots were directed on to the offending artillery positions. Sheehy could see the muzzle flashes from the self-propelled guns that were causing the trouble. He directed Johnson to move into the trail position and both pilots prepared the switches for an attack with IR-homing Maverick missiles.

On Sheehy's infrared monitor in the cockpit, the enemy guns appeared white-hot – obviously, they had already fired several rounds. The weapons were perfect targets for IR missiles and as he rolled into a shallow dive he locked a Maverick on to one of the revetted artillery pieces. Sheehy launched his IR Maverick from a range of 3 miles, then turned away. As the weapon impacted the target, the A-10 pilot saw several secondary explosions around the revetment. Meanwhile Johnson had delivered his attack on another Iraqi gun.

The A-10s pulled clear of the target and orbited, while the F/A-18 forward air control pilot moved in to reassess the situation on the ground. The latter reported that the planes had scored good hits and the shelling had ceased. He then directed the A-10s to attack Iraqi tanks moving south down the coastal highway; the pilots dispatched the leading pair using TV-homing Mavericks. Then, starting to run short of fuel, they headed for home.

That was Todd Sheehy's first and only close air support mission of the war. For him and most A-10 pilots, the ground war was a time of considerable frustration:

> As a fighter pilot I really wanted to deliver close air support for the guys on the ground. That is the primary job of the A-10. The reality was that they just did not need us. Except for a few cases the majority of us flew up there, orbited, and brought all of our ordnance home. It was frustrating and we saw it all day long, planes coming back with their full ordnance. We wanted to contribute, but I guess had already

done our job. Things were going so well that they didn't need us. And that was a greater satisfaction, I guess, than a long ground war slugging it out with the enemy.

THE SLOW-FLYING A-10 was never intended to go deep into enemy territory to hit targets. But, because its primary close air support mission was not possible or not required for most of the conflict, interdiction missions well beyond the front line made up the bulk of its sorties. During these missions the Warthog proved more versatile, and better able to survive, than people had expected.

During the six weeks of the conflict, five A-10s were lost in the course of over 8,000 combat sorties (a loss rate of .062 per cent). Twenty A-10s returned with significant battle damage and 45 more returned with light damage that could be repaired between sorties.

With its long loiter time and heavy armament load the A-10 has the ability, rare in a ground attack aircraft, to deliver several separate attacks during a single sortie. This, and the plane's proven ability to survive battle damage, makes it the best fixed-wing close air support aircraft in the world.

The Warthog is not a handsome aircraft. But to a team of infantrymen cut off, under fire and taking losses, one of the most beautiful sights in the world is a pair of these planes with full ordnance and fuel for 45 minutes.The most beautiful sight is eight such pairs.

Multiple MiG Shoot-down

With the opposing forces likely to close on each other at a rate of more than 20 miles per minute, air-to-air combat in the late 1990s combined high-technology equipment with split-second decision-making.

DURING OPERATION Allied Force and the Kosovo conflict in the spring of 1999, the NATO air forces opened the action with attacks on air defence targets in Serbia. There were fears that the Yugoslav Air Force might try to retaliate against NATO forces, particularly against its troops in Bosnia or NATO aircraft flying over that state. To guard against that danger, NATO maintained round-the-clock fighter patrols over Bosnia throughout the conflict.

On the afternoon of 26 March, three days into Operation Allied Force, a pair of F-15Cs and two pairs of F-16s left their bases in Italy to fly defensive air patrols over Bosnia. Over the Adriatic Sea the six USAF fighters topped off their tanks at the tanker, then headed for their patrol lines over the cities of Tusla and Sarajevo.

Their mission plan laid down that, at any time throughout the period between 1600 hours and 2000 hours (local), there would be a pair of fighters patrolling over each city, with the third pair either refuelling or in transit to or from the tanker.

Two hours into the patrol, dusk fell. By then Captain Jeff Hwang, leading Dirk Flight with two F-15Cs of the 493rd Tactical Fighter

Squadron, was at the eastern edge of the Tusla orbit pattern. The two fighters were flying at 28,000ft at Mach .85 [685mph]. Suddenly, on his radar screen, Hwang saw what looked like a single aircraft some 40 miles to the east and well inside Serbia, heading towards him. Hwang's wingman, Captain Joey McMurry, saw the contact at about the same time.

Hwang immediately reported the radar contact to Boeing E-3 AWACS (airborne warning and control system) aircraft covering the area, but the latter had not seen it. Hwang commented:

> The contact was doing over 600 knots [690 mph] at about 6,000 feet, which was much faster than I would expect any non-fighter type aircraft to be going. At the time we were close to the Bosnia/ Serbia border and it didn't make sense to continue heading east. For one thing, it would have taken us over enemy territory and too far from our supporting assets. For another thing, our Intel [intelligence] people had briefed us on the possibility that the enemy might send up aircraft to try to lure us into one of their missile engagement zones.

To build spacing between the F-15Cs and the radar contact, whatever it was, Hwang and McMurry turned through a semicircle and accelerated to supersonic speed. If there was to be an engagement Hwang wanted to fight it on his terms and over friendly territory. Once the US fighters had the separation they needed, they turned around and headed towards the threatening radar contact. By then the AWACS aircraft had also seen the radar contact. Jeff Hwang continued:

> When we had turned back, both my wingman and I had the contact on radar. It was heading west, directly towards us. We were running at way above supersonic speed, and the indications [on the F-15C's classified air-to-air identification system] were that the contact was a MiG 29 and it was flying supersonic too. We were closing at more than 20 miles per minute.
>
> The sun was setting in the west. I had not planned it that way, but

I could see the sun was on our backs and I knew the MiG pilot would have the sun in his eyes. I think maybe his ground control had told him where we were, or perhaps he was going after one of the tankers.

Each F-15C carried the standard air-to-air armament load for that conflict: four AIM-120C advanced medium-range air-to air-missiles (AMRAAM) active radar weapons, two AIM-7M Sparrow radar semi-active missiles, two AIM-9M Sidewinder infrared missiles and a 20mm cannon with 940 rounds. It also carried three external fuel tanks, one under each wing and one under the fuselage.

The US rules of engagement stated that before a fighter could engage a target beyond visual range, the pilot had to get clearance from the AWACS aircraft to confirm that no friendly aircraft was in that area. The AWACS had still not issued that clearance when events overtook the need for it. Hwang and his wingman had no doubt that the contact was hostile, a MiG-29, and at that rate of closure it would soon be in a position to engage the F-15Cs. With the F-15Cs themselves under threat, the AWACS clearance was not necessary before initiating the engagement. Again, Jeff Hwang takes up the story:

> I directed our formation to combat jettison, to punch off the wing tanks and arm up the weapon systems. I told my wingman he was to be the primary shooter, and cleared him to shoot.
>
> Our basic tactical employment with radar is that if there is only one hostile group or contact, both pilots should not lock our radars on the same group. I put my radar back into search to look for additional contacts; you have to assume there is more than one enemy plane present.

To his left, Hwang saw the bright flash of the rocket motor as the AIM-120 missile streaked out in front of his wingman. The weapon left a grey smoke trail as it accelerated rapidly to its maximum speed. Almost immediately afterwards the AWACS called to say that the radar contact had split into two: there were at least two planes. Looking into his cockpit, Hwang also noticed that on his radar the contact had split into two. He remembered:

> I locked up on the leader, then went to narrow scan. That enabled me to engage multiple targets with AIM-120s. I was able to target both contacts, but I could not tell which one my wingman had fired at. At that time both planes were in the mid teens altitude. They turned toward the northeast, then turned back towards us.

By now the F-15Cs were just below 30,000ft and within 16 miles of the MiGs. Hwang pressed the button to launch his first AIM-120, but the programmed two-second delay before the missile left the rail was like an eternity. Then with a 'Whoosh' the missile roared ahead of the fighter. Once the first missile was away, Hwang moved the marker on his screen to the other radar contact and pressed the firing button again. Yet again there was the seeming eternal wait, then a second AIM-120 surged out in front of the fighter. Despite the frustrating wait, both weapons were on their way within ten seconds of Hwang's first press of the firing button. As the missiles exhausted their fuel the glows of the two rocket motors disappeared, the smoke trails ceased

---

McDONNELL DOUGLAS (BOEING) F-15C EAGLE

ROLE Single-seat, air superiority fighter.

POWER Two Pratt & Whitney F100-PW-100 turbofan engines, each developing 23,800lb thrust with afterburning.

ARMAMENT Four AIM-120C advanced medium-range air-to-air missiles (AMRAAM) active radar missiles, two AIM-7M Sparrow radar semi-active missiles, two AIM-9M Sidewinder infrared missiles and one multibarrelled 20mm cannon.

PERFORMANCE Maximum speed 1,650mph (Mach 2.5) above 36,000ft; 915mph (Mach 1.21) at low altitude.

NORMAL OPERATIONAL TAKE-OFF WEIGHT 56,000lb.

DIMENSIONS Span 47ft 10in; length 63ft 9in; wing area 608 sq ft.

DATE OF FIRST PRODUCTION F-15C 1979.

and the weapons coasted unseen towards their targets. There were three AIM-120 missiles in flight, but nothing seemed to be happening.

The high rate of closure soon brought the F-15Cs within 10 miles of the radar contacts, and Hwang was worried that the approaching fighters might be preparing to attack his flight. He gave a brief radio call with the code word 'Naked!', to say his radar warning receiver did not indicate a radar locked on to his plane. McMurry replied with a similar 'Naked!' call. Thus assured, the F-15C pilots continued to press their attack, descending as their pilots sought to make visual contact with the MiGs. Jeff Hwang continued:

> Against broken cloud, just below the horizon, I picked up a black dot ahead but a fair way off my nose, about 8 miles away. It was the MiG which I assess to have been the trailer. Still there had not been any explosions, the missiles launched earlier had still not 'timed out'.
>
> I was starting to think about engaging with Sidewinders when, just outside my head-up display, I saw an explosion. It looked just like a torch being swung through the air at a Hawaiian Luau party. That was not the plane I had seen, but another that I assessed was the

---

MIKOYAN-GUREVICH MiG-29 'FULCRUM'

ROLE Single-seat, air superiority fighter.

POWER Two Tumanskii R-33D turbofan engines, each developing 18,300lb thrust with afterburning.

ARMAMENT (AIR-TO-AIR ROLE) One AA-7 Apex semi-active radar-guided missile, one AA-7 Apex infrared homing missile, two AA-8 Aphid infrared homing short-range dogfight missiles and one multibarrelled 30mm cannon.

PERFORMANCE Maximum speed 1,540mph (Mach 2.3) at high altitude, 913mph (Mach 1.2) at low altitude.

NORMAL OPERATIONAL TAKE-OFF WEIGHT 36,000lb.

DIMENSIONS Span 37ft 8in; length 56ft 5in; wing area 358 sq ft.

DATE OF FIRST PRODUCTION MIG 29 1984.

leader. I turned my attention back to the trailer and a couple of seconds later he too exploded into flame in the same way as the first.

Hwang called the controlling AWACS plane to report the shoot-downs: 'Dirk 1, Splash two MiG-29s!' The F-15Cs maintained their easterly heading, their pilots searching on radar and visually to see if other MiGs were following the initial pair. The F-15C pilots observed no other planes, and then the AWACS confirmed that the sky in front of them was clear.

From the initial radar pick-up, until the second MiG went down, about four minutes had elapsed, which included the turn-away to open the range. In jettisoning their wing tanks before the engagement, each F-15C had lost about 8,000lb of fuel. Now their first priority was to return to the tanker to top off their depleted tanks. Despite the excitements of the past few minutes, the two pilots were scheduled to remain on CAP for a further 2½ hours before they were to be relieved. Between them the two F-15Cs still had 15 missiles remaining, sufficient to fight more significant air battles.

Shortly after the F-15Cs resumed their patrol after refuelling, the AWACS aircraft called: 'Multiple contacts across the border.' Once more the adrenalin level in the fighters' cockpits rose, as the F-15Cs and a pair of F-16s moved forward to investigate the threat. Their pilots saw no sign of enemy planes on radar, however, and then the AWACS informed them that the contacts had turned around and were heading back into Serbia. The US fighters returned to their patrol lines. After one further refuelling, Dirk Flight returned to its base at Aviano. Even before the F-15Cs landed, news of their shoot-downs had been broadcast on CNN.

Later analysis of the data recordings from the F-15Cs revealed that Hwang's missiles had accounted for both MiGs. The flight leader commented:

At the time we did not care whose missile hit which jet, we had worked together as a team and each supported the other. All that mattered was that there had been two of them, that we had shot both down, and my wing man and I had emerged from the encounter intact.

The two MiG-29s had belonged to the Yugoslav Air Force's 127th Fighter Squadron. Both wrecks fell on open ground near Bijeljina in Bosnia, close to the border with Serbia. Lieutenant Colonel Slobodan Peric, the flight leader, ejected and reached the ground safely. He then escaped into Serbia. His wingman, Captain Zoran Radosavljevic, was killed.

The action demonstrated the formidable effectiveness of modern, active radar air-to-air weapons like the AIM-120. With the advent of missiles of this type, air combat has entered a new and more lethal era. And the world has become a dangerous place for pilots sent into action against such advanced weapons, if they lack similar systems of their own.

CHAPTER TWENTY-TWO

The Unmanned Air Vehicle: A Pointer
to the Future

During the 1980s a new type of aircraft made its appearance in the

combat arena, the unmanned air vehicle (UAV). This differs from a guided

missile in that it is not a one-shot expendable system. At the end of its

sortie the UAV is programmed to land in friendly territory, where it is

prepared for reuse. In this chapter I examine the operations by one type of

UAV during the conflict in Kosovo in 1999.

THE UNMANNED AIR vehicle (UAV) had its origins in the radio controlled target drones used during live-firing exercises with anti-aircraft
gun and missile systems. If the drone survived the encounter, it made
a controlled landing at its base and was prepared for reuse. From there
it was a relatively small step to build an unmanned reconnaissance
vehicle which, controlled from the ground, operated over enemy territory to secure the required intelligence and return to its base after the
mission. Soon, instead of merely replicating the capabilities of manned
aircraft, reconnaissance UAVs began demonstrating useful new war-
fighting capabilities of their own.

During the conflict in Kosovo in 1999, the US armed forces
employed three types of unmanned air vehicle: the Air Force used the

Predator, the Navy used the Pioneer and the Army used the Hunter. The missions assigned to UAVs during this action were general surveillance, real-time targeting and bomb-damage assessment, and providing cueing for other reconnaissance and surveillance systems. This account describes the operations flown by the US Army's Hunter UAV, illustrating some of the unique capabilities these vehicles have brought to military operations.

For a modern combat aircraft, the Hunter's performance is less than sparkling. Power comes from two Moto Guzzi flat twin-piston engines, each developing 64hp. These give the vehicle a top speed of 122mph and a normal loitering speed of 75mph. The Hunter has a ceiling of 15,000ft and, as operated over Kosovo, its endurance is about 8 hours. The UAV has a maximum take-off weight of just under 1,600lb, or about the same as the Sopwith Camel scout of the First World War (described in Chapter Three).

As used over Kosovo, the Hunter carried an optical TV camera and a forward-looking infrared (FLIR) camera permitting reconnaissance by day or night. A data-link system relayed the selected image from the TV camera or the FLIR to the ground station in real time. The optical and infrared sensors were fitted with zoom lenses, enabling them to observe objects on the ground in great detail. With mission equipment the Hunter costs about £1.5 million; while that was too costly for the vehicle to be treated as expendable, the occasional loss was acceptable.

The Hunter has a fixed-wheel undercarriage and it takes off from a runway in the conventional manner. When it returns at the end of the sortie it lands conventionally, then its arrester hook picks up a cable and brings it smoothly to a halt in a manner similar to a carrier deck landing. During the take-off and landing phases of the flight, an external pilot stands beside the runway and controls the UAV in the same way as a radio-controlled model aircraft.

For the main part of its mission, the Hunter is controlled from a separate ground station which, during the Kosovo missions, was situated off the airfield. Once the Hunter is airborne and clearing the airfield, the Internal Pilot (IP) in the ground station takes control. The UAV's

global positioning system receiver keeps track of its position throughout its flight. The IP views a map display showing the position of the
UAV, and positions the vehicle so that its optical TV or IR sensor secures
the required imagery.

At the ground station the mission payload operator (MPO) sits
beside the internal pilot. The MPO's screen shows the imagery relayed
from the UAV via the data link. His task is to select the optimum sensor
for the lighting conditions at the target, train it on the objective and
adjust the zoom lens to produce the required amount of detail. All the
imagery is recorded on the ground for later analysis.

In order to maintain a reliable two-way flow of instructions and
imagery via the data-link system, the Hunter has to remain within
line-of-sight range of its ground station. Thus, if the UAV operates at a
distance of 100 miles from its base station, it needs to be flying at
10,000ft or higher.

SHORTLY AFTER THE start of Operation Allied Force, in April 1999,
Alpha Company of the 15th Military Intelligence Battalion, US Army,
deployed to Petrovic airfield near Skopje in Macedonia. From there, the

---

TRW HUNTER

ROLE Short-range, reconnaissance, unmanned air vehicle.

POWER Two Moto Guzzi four-cylinder, air-cooled engines, each developing
64hp.

PAYLOAD Up to 93lb. During operations over Kosovo, this vehicle carried an
optical TV camera and a forward-looking infrared (FLIR) sensor. A data-
link system relayed the images from these sensors in real time to the
controlling ground station.

PERFORMANCE Maximum speed 120mph; normal loitering speed 75mph;
ceiling 15,000ft.

NORMAL OPERATIONAL TAKE-OFF WEIGHT 1,583lb.

DIMENSIONS Span 29ft 2½in; length 22ft 9½in.

DATE OF FIRST PRODUCTION HUNTER 1990.

company flew between four and six UAV sorties each day, each sortie lasting up to eight hours. Despite its low performance, the small, relatively simple UAV demonstrated a formidable reconnaissance capability. In the course of a single sortie, a Hunter might spend up to seven hours over hostile territory. During that time it could overfly a succession of areas of interest, or it could loiter for a time to maintain a sustained watch on one of them, or it could combine both in the same mission.

Army Sergeant Antonio Mitchell served as a Hunter Internal Pilot with Alpha Company during the conflict. Discussing the UAV's value in providing real-time targeting air strikes, and real-time bomb-damage assessment, he cited a night mission that he controlled almost at the end of the conflict:

> We were told to check a factory building in Kosovo for activity, and get accurate target co-ordinates for an attack. When the UAV arrived in the area, I flew it around the building so we could look it over. We could see there was a security fence around the building, and it was guarded. On the FLIR, we could even see which guards were smoking. Over the course of the next few minutes we saw several trucks pull up to the building, and later drive away. Obviously, it was some sort of supply depot.
>
> Then I was told to move the UAV to a stand-off position about five miles away, but to keep the building under observation. I was told that a B-52 was coming in. After a wait we suddenly saw little fires dotted all over the building, cluster munitions going off. The fires quickly took hold and we saw people running out of the building. The UAV left the area, but the next day I sent one back to look at the building. It was just a burned-out shell, with the roof collapsed.

That ability to loiter over a single point of interest in enemy territory for hours on end and observe what transpired is virtually unique to the UAV. Although manned reconnaissance aircraft have the theoretical capability to perform this task, unless there are exceptional circumstances the tactic would be considered too dangerous for a human operator.

The UAV's loitering capability was also useful to scan areas suspected to contain enemy troops, so that it could wait for somebody to make the mistake that would betray their presence. During one night mission, Antonio Mitchell was ordered to keep watch on a large wooded area. The Yugoslav troops were skilled at camouflage and there was no sign that any were in the area. Then, soon after midnight, something unusual occurred:

> We saw a truck driving along the road by itself, at about 3 miles per hour. It looked like it might be a military vehicle, so we followed it to see where it went. From time to time the truck stopped, the driver and passenger got out and walked into the woods. About ten minutes later they came back, got into the truck and drove on. But after about half a mile, it stopped again. That process was repeated several times; we followed that truck for over an hour.

This was not the sort of behaviour to be expected from a civilian vehicle at such an hour, and afterwards the area came under intense scrutiny from other sensors. Probably the truck was delivering orders, mail or hot food to troops in the field. The point of the story, however, is that no other type of reconnaissance vehicle could have followed the movements of a single vehicle deep inside enemy territory in that way.

Even by day, the Hunter's small size and light grey colour made it difficult to see from the ground above 10,000ft; also, the sound of its small engines was barely discernible on the ground if there was any wind or background noise. If the Hunter was engaged with optically laid guns, its low 75mph loitering speed was an asset. When engaging fixed-wing aircraft, AAA gunners are taught to aim well in front of the target. Most of the enemy rounds fired at Hunters passed safely clear in front of them.

Nevertheless, some UAVs were lost in action. Near the end of May 1999, Antonio Mitchell suffered an 'out-of-body experience' when his Hunter was shot down. He recalled:

> The first sign I had of anything amiss was when one engine suddenly

stopped. That was unexpected – usually we had some warning if an engine was about to fail. Then I lost the downlink signal and the video picture. I repositioned the antenna to re-align it on the UAV, and the downlink came back for three or four seconds. During that time, the instruments showed about fifty failures aboard the UAV. Then I lost the downlink again and never regained it.

During UAV operations, a level of attrition has to be accepted. In the Hunters' two-month spell of operations over Kosovo, Alpha Company lost seven UAVs. Four were either definitely or probably lost to enemy action, two crashed following technical failures and one flew into the side of a mountain.

Throughout the operations over Kosovo, those planning the UAV sorties had to be particularly careful to keep these machines clear of normal air traffic. Because the UAV could not 'see' other planes, it could not turn to avoid them. For that reason the Hunters were confined to operating in a narrow band of altitudes. Manned aircraft were advised to keep out of that band unless operational circumstances dictated otherwise, in which case pilots were to exercise caution.

The Hunters' base at Petrovic was a busy international airport. As well as military transports and helicopters from the NATO air forces, civil airliners were arriving and taking off on scheduled services. Integrating the UAV operations into the normal pattern of flight traffic presented difficulties, as Antonio Mitchell explained:

The airliners were carrying passengers, so our operations were not allowed to impose any delays to their flights. A lot of times we would be ready to launch, but the airport was not ready for us. So, we had to wait before we could set up our equipment. We needed the runway to ourselves for about 5 minutes before the UAV took off, to position the arresting gear across the runway – if a UAV had to abort the take-off, it dropped its hook and picked up the arrester cable. Because it was sometimes hard to get a launch slot, we usually sent off a pair of UAVs each time, one behind the other.

At the end of a Hunter sortie, recovery presented other problems. If manned aircraft were operating in the vicinity of the airport, the returning UAVs had to orbit over a point well clear, sometimes for more than half an hour. That meant the UAVs needed to arrive at the holding area with fuel for at least one hour's flight at loitering speed.

THE SUCCESS OF the Hunter and other UAV types over Kosovo has highlighted the value of these systems. Up to the time of writing, the only operational task the UAVs have performed on a regular basis is reconnaissance. In the near-term future we are likely to see them taking on other roles considered too dangerous, or too mind-numbingly boring, for human aircrew. Two such roles being considered are those of airborne communications relay and airborne signals intelligence collection, both of which might involve loitering for long periods close to or over enemy territory.

Looking ahead further, we are likely to see more lethal types of UAV joining the fray. A likely initial role for this is the suppression or destruction of enemy air defence systems, a task that the latest surface-to-air missile systems have made increasingly hazardous for manned aircraft. For that role, a specialized reconnaissance UAV might locate and laser-mark the target and then armed UAVs would deliver lethal ordnance against it.

Finale

IN ASSEMBLING THE material for this book I have chosen 22 air actions which, in my opinion, exemplify the roles of combat aircraft during the past nine decades. The accounts demonstrate the ways in which aircraft have brought their influence to bear in a spread of conflicts. Since the first faltering attempts to employ aircraft in combat, in 1911, the technology of air power has advanced out of all recognition.

Despite all the technical advances it is those who fly the planes, often at risk to their lives, who have fashioned the air weapon into the potent force it is today. In the long and rapidly changing history of military aviation the one constant factor has been the bravery, the determination and the ingenuity of those who fly in action. As the accounts in this book have shown, these qualities have never been in short supply.

Yet, notwithstanding that essential truth, there are clear pointers that future historians may come to regard manned combat flight as no more than a transitory phase in the long evolution of warfare. October 2011 will mark the centenary of the beginnings of manned combat aviation. By then, it is likely that plans will be well advanced to build a family of unmanned air vehicles that will replace manned aircraft in many of their combat roles.

Glossary

AAA Anti-aircraft artillery.

AI Airborne interception (radar).

AMRAAM Advanced medium-range air-to-air missile. The title given to the AIM-120 active radar-guided weapon.

ASV Air-to-surface vessel (radar).

AWACS Airborne warning and control system. The name given to the E-3 aircraft which provides interception control and other assistance for fighters in combat.

Chaff US term, now in general use, for electrically conducting strips released from aircraft to create false targets on enemy radar.

Elint Electronic intelligence.

Fan Song NATO code name for control radar used with the SA-2 missile system.

Firecan NATO code name for Soviet AAA fire-control radar.

FLIR Forward-looking infrared system.

GCI Ground-controlled interception (radar).

Geschwader Second World War *Luftwaffe* flying unit with an established strength of about 96 aircraft.

Gruppe *Luftwaffe* flying unit with an established strength of about 30 aircraft.

H2S Generic term for microwave ground-mapping radar fitted to RAF bombers, produced in several versions between 1942 and the early 1960s.

HARM High-speed anti-radiation missile. A US missile designed to home on the emission from enemy fire-control radars, the modern successor to Shrike.

LGB Laser-guided bomb.

Mandrel Radar-jamming equipment to counter the German Second World War *Freya*, *Mammut* and *Wassermann* early warning equipment.

Maverick US air-to-ground missile that homes on image contrast produced by the target. There are two main types: a TV-guided version that homes on optical contrast and an infrared-guided version that homes on IR contrast.

PI Photographic interpreter.

PR Photographic reconnaissance.

QRC-160 Type of jamming pod fitted to US tactical fighters during the Vietnam War, built under a quick-reaction capability contract to shorten the procurement process.

Radar resolution cell A rectangle in space, within which a radar indicates only one object present, though there might be more than one. If there are objects producing radar echoes in two or more adjacent resolution cells, these appear as a single large object. Similarly, if noise jamming originates from two or more adjacent resolution cells, on the radar the jamming appears to have come from a single enlarged source. The size of the resolution cell varies between the different radar types. In range it is proportional to the pulse width of the radar, in azimuth it is proportional to the beam width of the radar.

RHWR Radar homing and warning receiver.

Rope Code name given to long lengths of metal foil dropped to confuse radar.

Rotary engine. Type of aero-engine commonly used up to the end of the First World War , at a time when planes were not fast enough to provide efficient cooling for fixed air-cooled engines. The crankshaft was fixed to the engine bulkhead, so that the radially arranged cylinders revolved around it. The propeller was bolted to the crankcase and rotated with it. Thus the rotational speed of the cylinders provided a high-speed flow of air past them to assist cooling, resulting in an engine that produced high power for low installed weight.

SAC Strategic Air Command.

SAM Surface-to-air missile.

SCUD Soviet-built surface-to-surface missile employed by the Iraqis in the long-range bombardment role during Operation Desert Storm.

Seetakt German surface search and gun-ranging radar.

Shrike US anti-radiation missile designed to home on the emissions from enemy fire-control radars.

Sidewinder US air-to-air missile, using infrared homing.

Sparrow US air-to-air missile using semi-active radar homing.

TFR Terrain-following radar.

UAV   Unmanned air vehicle.

'Window'   British wartime code name for chaff, metal foil dropped to confuse enemy radar.

'Window spoof'   Feint operation in which a few aircraft dropping large amounts of chaff give an appearance on enemy radar similar to that from a large force of attacking bombers.

WSO   Weapon Systems Officer (crew member in F-4 and other US Air Force multi-seat combat planes).

INDEX